D1631285

MORE Tell Me Why

Why do flies rub
their legs together?

How can glass be blown?

What's the difference
between rabbits and hares?

What is a genius?

MORE
Tell Me Why

By ARKADY LEOKUM

Illustrations by
CYNTHIA ILIFF KOEHLER
and ALVIN KOEHLER

Answers
to over
300 questions
children ask
most often

HAMLYN

First published 1967
Shortened version 1973
Shortened version, eighteenth impression 1990
Published by
The Octopus Publishing Group Limited,
Michelin House, 81 Fulham Road,
London SW3 6RB
Text © 1967 by Arkady Leokum
Illustrations © 1967 by Grosset & Dunlap Inc.
Published pursuant to agreement with Grosset & Dunlap Inc.,
New York, N.Y., U.S.A.

ISBN 0 600 36080 6
Printed in Czechoslovakia
51085/21

INTRODUCTION

The success that attended the publication of *Tell Me Why* has encouraged the preparation of this second volume, which follows the general plan of the previous book and has been similarly devised to appeal to a young, international readership.

The 300 and more questions have been drawn from many diverse branches of knowledge, from geography, and history, from the world of living things, of invention and discovery, from physiology and technology, from the immediate present and distant past, and the intervening ages.

The purpose of the book is not merely to present information in an entertaining form but to stimulate the quest for knowledge, to broaden young people's interests and to contribute towards developing the habits of intellectual curiosity that bring adventure to everyday life.

CONTENTS

Chapter II

Living Creatures Around Us

Chapter III

All About Human Beings

Chapter IV

How It Began

Chapter 1

OUR WORLD

The moon doesn't look as if it's very far away, but its distance from the earth averages 239,000 miles. The diameter of the moon is 2,160 miles, or less than the distance across the United States. But when the moon is observed with a very large telescope, it looks as if it were only about 200 miles away.

WHY DOES THE MOON FOLLOW US WHEN WE DRIVE?

Because the moon seems so close and big to us, we sometimes forget that 239,000 miles is quite a distance away. It is this great distance that explains why the moon seems to follow us when we drive in a vehicle and look up at it.

To begin with, our feeling that this is happening is just that—only a feeling, a psychological reaction. When we speed along a road, we notice that everything moves past us. Trees, houses, fences, the road—all fly past us in the opposite direction.

Now there's the moon, part of what we see as we look out, and we naturally expect it also to be flying past us, or at least to be moving backward as we speed ahead. When this doesn't happen, we have the sensation that it is "following" us.

But why doesn't it happen? Because the distance of the moon from the earth is quite great. Compared to the distance our vehicle travels in a few minutes, that distance is enormous. So as we move along, the angle at which we see the moon hardly changes.

In fact, we could go along a straight path for miles and the angle at which we would see the moon would still be basically the same. And as we notice everything else flying past, we get that feeling of the moon "following" us.

While we can't fully explain light, we can measure it quite accurately. We have a pretty good idea of how fast light travels. Since a light-year is merely the distance that a beam of light will travel in a year, the real discovery had to do with measuring the speed of light.

HOW WAS THE LIGHT-YEAR DISCOVERED?

This was done by a Danish astronomer named Olaus Roemer in 1676. He noticed that the eclipses of one of the moons of Jupiter kept coming later and later as the earth moved in its orbit to the opposite side of the sun from that occupied by Jupiter. Then, as the earth moved back into its former position, the eclipses came on schedule again.

The difference in time added up to nearly 17 minutes. This could mean only that it takes that length of time for light to travel the diameter of the earth's orbit. This distance was known to be very nearly 186,000,000 miles. Since it took light about 1,000 seconds (nearly 17 minutes) to go this distance, it meant that the speed of light is about 186,000 miles per second.

In our own time, Professor Albert Michelson spent years trying to determine the exact speed of light. Using another method, he arrived at a speed of 186,284 miles per second, and this is now considered quite accurate.

If we multiply this speed by the seconds in a year, we find that light travels 5,880,000,000,000 miles in a year — and this is called a light-year.

Thousands of years ago, astronomers probably used the pyramids in Egypt and the towers and temples in Babylonia to help them study the sun, moon, and stars. There were no telescopes then. In time, astronomical instruments were developed, and as they became larger and more numerous, observatories were built to house them. Some observatories were built more than a thousand years ago.

WHAT IS AN OBSERVATORY?

An observatory has to be built in the right place, a place with favorable weather conditions, moderate temperatures, many days of sunshine and nights without clouds, and as little haze, rain, and snow as possible. It must also be away from city lights and neon signs, which make the sky too light for good observation.

There are buildings which include living quarters in addition to telescopes. The instruments are housed in structures of steel and concrete. The building for the telescope is constructed in two parts. The lower part is stationary, and the upper part, or roof, is in the shape of a dome which can be rotated.

The dome has a "slit" which opens to permit the telescope to look out toward the sky. By rotating the dome on a track, the slit can be opened to any part of the sky. Both the dome and the telescope are moved by electric motors. In a modern observatory the astronomer only has to punch a number of buttons to move the equipment.

Of course, in order to see, the astronomer must always be near the eyepiece of the telescope or the camera attached to it. So, in some observatories the floor can be raised or lowered, or there is an adjustable platform.

Astronomers don't depend on their eyes alone to observe the skies. They have many complicated instruments and attachments to the telescope, such as cameras, spectroscopes, spectrographs, and spectroheliographs, all of which provide them with important information.

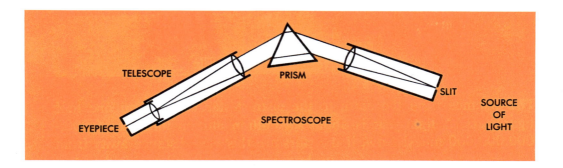

We know that just by studying the spectrum an astronomer can tell you what a star billions of miles away is made of and the elements present, take the star's temperature, figure out how fast it is moving, and whether that motion is toward earth or away from it!

HOW DOES THE SPECTRUM INFORM US ABOUT THE UNIVERSE?

The spectrum consists of the lines into which white light is broken up when it is bent, as when it goes through a prism. All across the spectrum, in addition to the shadings of color, there are hundreds of parallel lines. They are known as Fraunhofer lines, in honor of their discoverer.

Each chemical element in a gaseous or vapor state has its own pattern of lines occupying its own place in the spectrum. The lines stand for the colors taken up from the light by the element when it is heated so that it glows. This means that a scientist can find out what materials are present in any substance, no matter how far removed. Each element makes its own "dark line" or absorption spectrum, different from those of any other element. By simply comparing the spectrum of a material being studied with the spectra of elements known in the laboratory, the physicist can tell what it is. In other words, each element leaves its fingerprint in light patterns.

Since the temperature causes an element's line positions to change in the spectrum, astronomers can tell a great deal about the temperature of stars billions of miles away. When a star is moving toward us, lines in the spectrum are shifted toward the violet end of the spectrum. When a star is moving away, the lines are shifted toward the red end of the band. From the amount of shift or displacement, scientists calculate that some stars are hurtling through space at the rate of 150 miles per second!

15

The distance from the earth to the nearest star is four and one half light-years. A light-year is about six million million miles—or 6,000,-000,000,000 miles! Now, if the stars are this vast distance away from

HOW CAN WE MEASURE THINGS ABOUT THE STARS?

us, how can we measure how big they are, what they're made of, and so on?

At one time, the only instrument the astronomers had was the telescope. To-day, a whole group of special instruments exists to help astronomers study the motions, brightness, color, temperatures, and composition of the stars.

First of these is the camera, which is used to make permanent records of the stars observed. Another instrument is the spectrograph. This is used to photograph the spectra of the stars, or the rays of light coming from them. With the help of the spectrograph, astronomers have learned most of what they know about what the stars are made of, their temperatures, and the speeds at which they are moving.

One star may have a spectrum that is like that of other stars. The stars in each spectral class are found to have the same color. The colors range from blue to red. Our sun is a yellow star, in the middle of the range. The temperature of a star can also be found by measuring colors in the spectrum. The blue stars are large, hot, and brilliant, with temperatures of 25,000 degrees or more. Red stars are rather cool and have surface temperatures of 1,600 degrees or less.

To find what chemical elements are in the stars, the astronomer compares their spectra with spectra made in the laboratory. All the elements found in the stars are also present in the earth, but the stars are basically balls of very hot gas, mainly hydrogen and helium.

The astronomers also use special types of telescopes which can photograph large areas of sky. Still another type of instrument is the radio telescope. This has a very large antenna, a receiver, and a registering meter. This instrument records the strength of radio waves from the stars and planets. So, you see, we are able to overcome the great distance and find out quite a bit about the stars with a variety of instruments.

When you look up at the stars, does it sometimes seem to you that you can trace out squares, letters, and other familiar figures? In nearly all parts of the world, people of long ago did this, too. As they observed groups of stars, they gave them names.

HOW MANY CONSTELLATIONS ARE THERE?

It is not always easy to make out in the sky the figures that suggested the names. So don't expect the constellations to actually have the outlines that the names suggest.

The Greek astronomers listed 48 constellations, and 40 more have been named since their time, so that we have 88 constellations in the sky.

Of course, not all of the constellations can be seen from any one place on earth. Some are in the skies of the Southern Hemisphere; some can be seen only south of the equator.

As the earth travels around the sun, new star groups appear above the horizon. The circumpolar constellations, which seem to wheel around the North Star, stay in sight all year. In addition, there are constellations that appear only in the winter, spring, summer, or autumn.

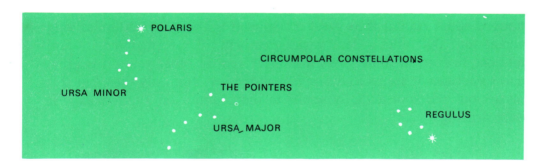

Now that we are all reading about satellites and travel to outer space, a great deal of curiosity has been aroused about the other planets in our solar system. With the possible exception of Mars, the most interesting one to us is probably Jupiter.

HOW MANY MOONS HAS JUPITER?

To begin with, Jupiter is really like a miniature solar system in itself! At present, no less than sixteen satellites, or moons, have been discovered revolving around Jupiter. Four of these are approximately the size of our own moon. Two of them are only about 30 miles in diameter, and some of them are real midgets. They are 15 miles in diameter or less!

Jupiter is the largest of all the planets with a volume more than 1,300 times that of the earth. When you look at it with the naked eye, it appears as a brilliant and beautiful spectacle. Yet it is 367,000,000 miles from the earth at its nearest approach!

Astronomers find a constantly changing "show" when they look at Jupiter through a telescope. It has dark streaks, or belts, separated by bright spaces called zones. The belts don't keep their shape, but often break up into irregular markings of all kinds. The zones change, too, from time to time, with dark spots and bright white areas suddenly appearing. Sometimes a belt, or part of a belt, will disappear for a few weeks altogether. Astronomers believe that what we see as belts, or zones, are a shell of clouds or vapors which are often in a disturbed condition.

One of the strange things about Jupiter is that it often displays striking colors on its surface. Two of the belts change from very red to brown, grey, or even a bluish color. It is thought that this has something to do with Jupiter's revolution about the sun. This takes 12 years, and the changes in color seem to follow a cycle that repeats itself every 12 years.

Probably the most interesting and curious thing that has been noticed about Jupiter is its great red spot. It is about 30,000 miles long and about 8,000 miles wide. It varies greatly in color, form, intensity, and motion. In fact, in some years it is brick red, in other years it is grey, and sometimes it seems to disappear altogether. Not only that, but this mysterious red spot actually seems to move about on Jupiter, as if it were drifting.

The discovery of things in the heavens often comes about much like the solving of a mystery. This is the way the asteroids were discovered.

Two men, Titius and Bode, had at different times figured out that

WHAT IS AN ASTEROID?

there must be a planet between Mars and Jupiter; there was such a large gap in the distance between them. So several astronomers set about searching for this planet.

In 1801, a planet was actually found there. It was named Ceres, but it was a very tiny planet indeed, with a diameter of only 600 miles. So it was believed that it could be only one of a group of small planets and the search went on.

In time, three more tiny planets were found, the brightest of which was only half the size of Ceres. Astronomers decided that a larger planet must have exploded and left these four tiny pieces. But after 15 years of searching, another astronomer found still another tiny planet and this started the hunt again.

By 1890, 300 small planets had been found, and between 1890 and 1927, 2,000 had been discovered! These tiny planets, mostly orbiting around the sun in the area between Mars and Jupiter, are called asteroids.

It is estimated that there are at least 100,000, although many are too small to be easily detected. Some are probably no more than a few hundred yards across, and all together their mass is only a small proportion of that of the earth.

As to how the asteroids were formed, the theory is that a satellite of Jupiter exploded and created these fragments.

HOW WAS THE PLANET PLUTO DISCOVERED?

If you think it's hard to find a needle in a haystack, just consider the problem of "finding" the planet Pluto. It is the outermost planet of our solar system, almost forty times as far from the sun as the earth! It is so faint that a good-sized telescope is necessary to even see it. Yet, somehow it was discovered. How was it done?

There are two sets of laws that help man obtain knowledge of the sizes of planets and their distances. Kepler's laws of planetary motion made it clear that the orbits of the planets around the sun were not quite circles. Newton's law of gravitation helped astronomers estimate the weights, sizes, and masses of the planets. This law states that two objects attract each other with a force that depends on how much material there is in each body (its mass) and how far apart they are. The greater their mass, the stronger is the pull; the closer they are together, the stronger the pull.

Now, with these two laws in mind, two men figured out, in 1846,

19

that there was something peculiar about the planet Uranus, which was then the outermost planet known. It was not moving in its orbit as it should when allowances were made for all the known planets. From the way it behaved, it was possible to figure out that another planet must be affecting it and just where the unknown planet would be. One of these men asked the Berlin Observatory to look for the new planet in a certain part of the sky and it was found there. This new planet was called Neptune.

An American astronomer, Percival Lowell, believed that the motion of Uranus was being affected by still another planet beyond Neptune. This was in 1915. Other astronomers felt that the motion of Neptune itself was being affected by some planet beyond it. So a systematic search began with the telescope and by studying photographs for still another planet.

On February 18, 1930, an astronomer named Tombaugh was studying photographs looking for the new planet and he found it—near the position that had been predicted by Lowell! This is the planet Pluto.

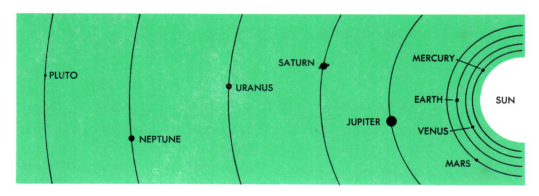

When we look up and see the stars and planets filling the sky, we might wonder if there might not be a collision up there some day. But luckily, this is not likely to happen.

COULD THERE BE A COLLISION OF THE PLANETS?

What we don't realize when we look up is how much farther away certain stars and planets are from the earth than others. To get a better idea of this, let's consider our solar system and its planets. The planets never escape from the pull or attraction of the sun. They keep on moving around it in orbits that are not quite circles. Their speeds depend on their distances from the sun.

So let's start by imagining that your own head is the sun, both in its size and location in the solar system. Your head is then in the center of a number of rings of different sizes. These rings are the orbits which the planets travel around the sun.

With your head as the center, Mercury, revolving in the nearest ring, is 6 metres away from you! It is about as big as the dot at the end of this sentence. (Remember, the size of your head is the size of the sun.) Venus moves around in the second ring 11.9 metres away, and is the size of the letter "o". In the third ring is our own planet, earth, a bit larger than Venus. It is 16 metres from your head (actually 93,000,000 miles or 150,000,000 kilometres away from the sun).

In the fourth ring is Mars, smaller than earth, and 25 metres away. Next we come to Jupiter, the largest of all the planets. In relation to your head (the sun) it looks like a marble, and is as far from your head as the length of a football field! On the sixth ring is Saturn, 12 millimetres in diameter, and nearly twice as far away as Jupiter.

Uranus, 5 millimetres in diameter, is twice as far away as Saturn. Neptune, a little smaller than Uranus, is half as far away again. And Pluto, about half the size of the earth, is eight times as far away as Jupiter. Since each of them goes around you in its orbit without ever changing, you can see why they're not likely to bump into each other!

HOW OLD IS THE EARTH?

This is a question to which we may never have the exact answer. Man has wondered about the age of the earth since ancient times, and there were all kinds of myths and legends that seemed to have the answer. But he couldn't begin to think about the question scientifically until about 400 years ago.

When it was proven at that time that the earth revolved around the sun (in other words, that the earth was part of our solar system), then scientists knew where to begin. To find the age of the earth, it was necessary to explain how the solar system was born. How did the sun and all the planets come into being?

One theory was called the nebular hypothesis. According to this theory, there was once a great mass of white-hot gas whirling about in space and getting smaller and hotter all the time. As the gas cloud grew smaller, it threw off rings of gas. Each of these rings condensed to form a planet, and the rest of the mass shrank into the center to become the sun.

Another explanation is called the planetesimal theory. According to this, millions and millions of years ago, there was a huge mass made up of small, solid bodies called planetesimals, with the sun at the center. A great star came along and pulled on the sun so that parts of it broke away. These parts picked up the tiny planetesimals the way a rolling snowball picks up snow, and they became planets.

Whichever theory is right, astronomers have figured out that it all probably happened about 5,500,000,000 years ago! But other scientists besides astronomers have tackled this question. They tried to find the answer by studying how long it took for the earth to become the way we know it. They studied the length of time it takes to wear down the oldest mountains, or the time needed for the oceans to collect the salt they now contain.

After all their studies, these scientists agree with the astronomers: The earth is about 5,500,000,000 years old!

Erosion is the process whereby the surface of the earth is slowly being worn away. The rain falls on the soft ground and runs off in streams and rivers thick with mud. The wind, scooping earth from the fields, drives sand and dust before it. Swirling currents along the shores of rivers and lakes, and the beating waves, eat away at the clay banks. They grind sand and stones against the rock cliffs, reducing the rock to sand and the sand to finer sand. Then they carry it all out to the sea.

WHAT IS EROSION?

This is erosion. It has produced some of the wonders of the world, such as the Grand Canyon in Arizona. But erosion has its grim side as well. In the late 1930's, it made the fertile plains of Kansas, Oklahoma, and Texas into the Dust Bowl, leaving thousands of people homeless.

Water is responsible for most of the erosion in the world. It seeps into the cracks of the solid rock, and when it freezes, it cracks the rock

apart. After years of this, the rock breaks up into soil. Then the soil is washed away.

Rain is soaked up by the ground until the ground is wet. What is left runs over the surface, down the little gullies into the streams, and down to the rivers. It always carries fine dirt along as mud.

Streams dig the valley they flow in slowly, over many thousands of years. The valleys widen and meet. The land is worn down sometimes almost to sea level by the forces of erosion.

Wind also helps the process of erosion, but it works more slowly than water. In ancient times, much erosion was done by glaciers, which ground away the sides of valleys.

American farming has suffered a great deal from the process of erosion. The farmers didn't realize that their precious topsoil was being carried away. Or they didn't know how to stop it. They plowed the soil deep, and the new surface they turned over was subsoil. It quickly dried to dust and blew away.

Today, new methods of farming help prevent the damage of erosion. For one thing, farmers don't use the plow so much any more. They leave the litter of the wheat and corn crops on the surface, which helps keep the soil there. On rolling land, they cultivate across the slopes, instead of up and down. This is called contour plowing, and there are no furrows running downhill to carry the water away. Today, farmers have learned many ways to protect the precious soil and prevent it from being blown or washed away by erosion!

The Grand Canyon is one of the greatest spectacles on the face of the earth. At some points it appears like a magic city of rock, with temples, towers, and castles of dazzling colors.

HOW WAS THE GRAND CANYON FORMED?

One of the most amazing things about it is that the Grand Canyon was made by a river! The waters of the Colorado River cut out this great gorge in the course of thousands of years. When you consider that it was cut out of solid rock in many places, you begin to appreciate the tremendous force of these waters. Even now, year by year, the rushing Colorado continues to cut deeper into the bottom of the gorge.

In certain places, the gorge of the Grand Canyon is more than a mile deep, and it is from four to 18 miles wide. As the river cut deep into the plateau to form the canyon, it laid bare on the rock walls of the canyon the story of hundreds of millions of years of the earth's history.

Down at the bottom of the gorge beside the river, ancient, crystalline rock is exposed. This is the buried remnant of an ancient mountain range which was folded back on itself and was worn down by weather and water. The rise and fall of this mountain range millions of years ago is revealed only by the erosion of the Grand Canyon.

On the base of this buried mountain range are beds of quartzite, sandstone, and limestone. They were formed as age followed age, as ocean waters from the east and from the west flooded the section, and as whole mountain ranges rose and disappeared. Proof of the fact that great seas once rushed over these rocks is to be found in the fossils that turn up here. There are fossil remains of seaweed, sea shells, and fishes!

The first white man to see the Grand Canyon was a Spanish explorer, Garcia Lopez de Cardenas, who discovered it in 1540. Today, the Government has taken the most beautiful and interesting section, 1,009 square miles in area, and set it aside as Grand Canyon National Park. Thousands of visitors come every year to marvel at it, and it is even possible to go by mule down to the Colorado River at the bottom.

24

Take a look at a map of the world. Now look at the two continents of South America and Africa. Do you notice how South America sticks out to the right where Brazil is, and how Africa is indented on the left

WERE THE CONTINENTS EVER JOINED TOGETHER?

side? Doesn't it seem as if you could fit them together like a puzzle and make them one continent?

Well, 50 years ago a German scientist named Alfred Wegener was doing just that. He wrote: "He who examines the opposite coasts of the South Atlantic Ocean must be somewhat surprised by the similarity of the shapes of the coastlines of Brazil and Africa. Every projection on the Brazilian side corresponds to a similarly shaped indentation on the African side."

Wegener also learned that naturalists had been studying the prehistoric plant and animal life of South America and Africa and had found many similarities. This convinced him that these two continents were once attached and had drifted apart.

He formulated a theory which he called the theory of the displacement of continents. According to this theory, the land masses of the earth were once all joined together in one continuous continent. There were rivers, lakes, and inland seas. Then for some unknown reason, this land mass began to break up. South America split off from Africa and drifted away. North America split off from Western Europe and floated to the west. All of the continents as we now know them were thus formed.

Did this actually happen as Wegener says it did? We don't know. It's only a theory. But as you can see from the map, there is some evidence to support it. And the study of prehistoric plant and animal life makes it seem possible, too. Besides, the earth's crust is still shifting today. So perhaps Wegener was right!

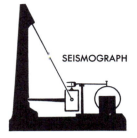

SEISMOGRAPH

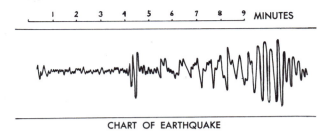

| 1 | 2 | 3 | 4 | 5 | 6 | 7 | 8 | 9 | MINUTES |

CHART OF EARTHQUAKE

When we think of an earthquake, we think of buildings toppling, huge cracks opening up in the earth, and so on. What is there to be "measured?"

HOW DOES A SEISMOGRAPH MEASURE EARTHQUAKES?

Well, an earthquake is a trembling or vibration of the earth's surface. And it is these vibrations that are measured. The cause of an earthquake is usually a "fault" in the rocks of the earth's crust, a break along which one rock mass has rubbed on another with very great force and friction. Much of the vast energy in this rubbing is changed to vibration in the rocks. This vibration may travel thousands of miles, which is why an earthquake in Tokyo can be detected and measured in England.

Earthquake vibrations consist of three or more types of wave motion, which travel at different speeds through the earth's rocky crust. The waves move in different directions. The primary waves vibrate lengthwise; the secondary waves crosswise; and the long waves travel around the earth's surface. The long waves move more slowly, but they have a larger motion and cause all the damage that may be seen by man.

Instruments called seismographs placed in different parts of the world record vibrations every day in the year, for the earth's crust is never still. The record sheets of two or more seismographs help seismologists to see where the quake took place.

A seismograph is a delicately hung weight, which remains still when an earthquake shakes the surrounding parts of the instrument. In other words, this weight, which hangs down from a fixed post, doesn't move during an earthquake. But the post holding it moves, and attached to the post, underneath the weight, is a chart. As the chart moves, a record is made on it by the weight.

Record sheets indicate the time the wave arrives, the force of the motion, and can even indicate the direction from which the wave comes.

26

When we consider a question like this, we should make clear that we mean in *recorded* history—that is, in history of which we have a record. In prehistoric times, and in those days when the earth was forming and taking shape, there must have been incredible eruptions and earthquakes.

WHAT WAS THE GREATEST ERUPTION IN HISTORY?

But as far as we know from records, the greatest eruption took place in 1883 on the volcanic island of Krakatoa in the Dutch East Indies (Republic of Indonesia). The most violent part of the volcanic explosions took place on the morning of August 27 of that year.

Let us see what were some of the effects of this amazing explosion. First of all, the whole northern and lower portions of the island itself were simply blown away! Before the explosion, the island had an area of 18 square miles, and rose from 91 to 4,250 metres above the sea. After the explosion, there was a "hole" in the bottom of the ocean that went down more than 300 metres below sea level!

The columns of stones, dust, and ashes rose 17 miles into the air, and as this material began to spread out it created darkness in the middle of the day in places 150 miles away!

The actual sound of the volcanic explosions were heard over a vast area. In fact, this was the farthest that the sound of an explosion has ever traveled—3,000 miles!

Probably the most serious damage done by this tremendous explosion came as a result of the waves it set up in the oceans. The largest of the waves reached a height of 15 metres, destroyed whole villages, and caused the deaths of 36,000 human beings. These waves also traveled great distances and may even have reached the English Channel, 11,000 miles away.

Incidentally, the volcano on Krakatoa became active again in 1927, but luckily, it was not a major volcanic explosion.

Even if a geyser didn't shoot great streams of water into the air, it would be one of the most interesting marvels of nature. A geyser is really a hot spring, and a hot spring itself is quite amazing. Here is a

WHY IS THE WATER FROM A GEYSER HOT?

hole in the ground filled with hot water. Where does the water come from? Why is it hot? And what makes it shoot up into the air if it's a geyser?

In all geysers, a hole called a tube leads from the surface to underground reservoirs which serve as storage basins for the water. Most of the water comes from rain and snow.

Deeper in the earth, the rock is very hot. This is probably uncooled lava, which is called magma. Gases from these hot rocks, mostly steam, rise through cracks in the rock and reach the underground reservoirs. They heat the water there to boiling and above-boiling temperatures.

This is how a hot spring is created. Now what makes it a geyser? The tube, or passageway from the water to the hot rocks below (where the heat comes from), does not go straight down in a geyser. It is twisted and irregular. This interferes with the natural rise of steam to the surface. If the steam and water can rise freely from below, we have a steadily-boiling hot spring.

The geyser erupts because the water in the irregular, or trapped, section of the underground water system is heated to the boiling point and suddenly turns to steam.

Steam requires more room than the water from which it was formed. So it pushes up the column of water above it. As this steam moves up, it lowers the pressure below, and more water turns into steam. Instead of there just being an overflow at the surface, there is a violent eruption as a result of the steam bursting upward, and we have the spectacle of a geyser!

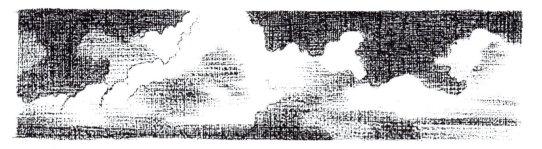

Have you ever flown through clouds in an aircraft, or perhaps been high up on a mountain where the clouds swirled all about you? Then you must have gained a fairly good idea of what a cloud is: just an accumulation of mist.

WHY DON'T ALL CLOUDS PRODUCE RAIN?

As you know, there is always water vapor in the air. During the summer there is more of this vapor in the air because the temperature is higher. When there is so much water vapor in the air that just a small reduction in temperature will make the vapor condense (form tiny droplets of water), we say the air is saturated.

It takes only a slight drop in temperature to make water vapor condense in saturated air. So when saturated warm air rises to an altitude where the temperature is lower, condensation takes place and we have a cloud. The molecules of water have come together to form countless little droplets.

What happens if all these water droplets in a cloud meet a mass of warm air? They evaporate—and the cloud disappears! This is why clouds are constantly changing shape. The water in them is changing back and forth from vapor to liquid.

The droplets of water in a cloud have weight, so gravity gradually pulls them down and they sink lower and lower. As most of them fall, they reach a warmer layer of air, and this warmer air causes them to evaporate. So here we have clouds that don't produce rain. They evaporate before the drops can reach the earth as rain.

But suppose the air beneath a cloud is not warmer air? Suppose it's very moist air? Naturally, the droplets won't evaporate. Instead, the droplets will get bigger and bigger as more and more condensation takes place.

Pretty soon, each tiny droplet has become a drop and it continues falling downward and we have rain!

Rainfall is now being measured in most parts of the world by means of an instrument called a rain gauge. The gauge of the United States Weather Bureau is shaped like a hollow tube closed at the lower end, with a funnel in the top.

HOW DO THEY MEASURE A RAINFALL?

This gauge is placed in an unsheltered place, and a graduated scale shows exactly how much rain has fallen in it. The Weather Bureau says that there has been an inch of rainfall if enough rain has fallen to make a sheet of water an inch deep over a given area.

A place having less than 10 inches (25 centimetres) in a year is called a desert. Ten to 20 inches (25 to 50 centimetres) supports grass for grazing, but more than 20 inches is necessary for agriculture.

If more than 250 centimetres fall in the warm season, vegetation becomes so thick that cultivated plants are choked out. This is the case in the jungles of Brazil, in central Africa, and in India. There is a place in India, Cherrapunji, that gets about 1140 centimetres of rain a year! By way of contrast, Egypt receives about 4 centimetres a year. In the United States, the coasts of Washington and Oregon get the most, about 200 to 250 centimetres. Parts of Arizona get less than 8 centimetres a year. Highest recorded year's rainfall in Britain is 257 inches (653 centimetres) in Cumberland, in 1954.

For as far back as we can go in the history of man, we find records or tales, or legends, about great floods. The reason for this is that there have always been floods. In fact, primitive man deliberately settled in the valleys that were in the paths of floods—because they were so fertile.

WHY DO WE HAVE FLOODS?

What is a flood? It's a condition that exists when a river overflows its banks and the water spreads out elsewhere. What causes a flood?—the accumulation of a great deal of water in a river that comes from heavy rains, or from other streams or reservoirs that feed into the river. A river usually drains a vast area, or "watershed," and it is the heavy flow of water from anywhere in this watershed that makes a river rise and flood over its banks.

Some floods are very helpful. The Nile, ever since man's first written history, has been bringing a life-giving flood every year to farmlands, by carrying down soils from the highlands. On the other hand, the Yellow River in China has brought death and destruction periodically. In 1935, it made 4,000,000 people homeless by flooding over!

Can floods be prevented? This is probably impossible to accomplish, since heavy rains will come whether man wants them or not. But many efforts are being made to control floods, and this will probably be done in time.

There are three ways to control floods. One is to have levees or dikes to protect farm lowlands and other areas where the river waters build up. A second way is to have emergency channels, such as spillways or floodways, to help carry away the excess water. A third way is to develop huge reservoirs to hold back flood waters and feed them more gradually to the larger streams.

WHAT IS AN ARTESIAN WELL?

In an artesian well, the water can leap high into the air like a geyser from its prison far below the surface of the earth. The name comes from the Artois region in northern France where the first European well of this kind was drilled more than 800 years ago. Artesian wells are possible only under certain conditions. There must be a layer of porous rock or sand that is buried between two layers of solid rock impervious to water. Somewhere this porous layer must be exposed to the surface so that water falling as rain or snow will sink downward until it is trapped between the solid, watertight layers above and below.

There the great pressure on all sides holds it prisoner until man releases it. When an opening a few centimetres wide is bored straight down through the solid upper strata to the sandy layer, the freed water gushes to the surface with a mighty force.

The ancient Chinese and Egyptians dug artesian wells. Some of the older European wells required six or eight years to drill. Modern machinery makes drilling today a quick and simple task.

Near Edgemont, South Dakota, two wells drilled nearly 915 metres deep supply some 4,000,000 litres daily. Coming from such a depth, this water registers a temperature of 37 degrees centigrade when it reaches the surface. Another well in this region spouts even hotter water!

Several large cities in the United States, as well as much of the London area, derive part, or all, of their water supply from artesian wells. The world's biggest artesian area is in Australia.

When a stream or river plunges over a wall of rock called a cliff or a precipice, we have a waterfall. If the waterfall is of great size, it is called a cataract. Where the rock wall is steeply slanted rather than

WHAT MAKES A WATERFALL?

vertical, the rushing water is called a cascade. Sometimes in a cascade, the water descends in a whole series of steep slopes.

Niagara Falls is an example of how an overhanging rock ledge can create a waterfall. The upper layers of rock at Niagara are hard beds of dolomite. Below the dolomite is weak shale. The Niagara River plunges over the dolomite cliff into a great pool below, where the swirling water wears away the shale and thus undermines the dolomite above. From time to time, great masses of dolomite fall, keeping the cliff fresh and steep. In other waterfalls of this type, the hard rock may be sandstone, limestone, or lava.

Another type of waterfall is illustrated by Lower Yellowstone Falls. A huge mass of molten rock was squeezed up from below in ancient times. It hardened and later formed a wall in the path of the river's course.

In some cases, ancient glaciers cut deep into mountain valleys, leaving the sides as steep cliffs and precipices from which the waterfalls plunge down. In still other cases, high plateaus have been lifted by movements of the earth's surface and the streams plunge over their edges.

The three most famous cataracts in the world are Niagara Falls, Victoria Falls in the Zambesi River in Africa, and Iguassú Falls between Argentina, Brazil, and Paraguay. Of these three, Niagara Falls has the greatest volume of water.

The world's highest waterfall is Angel Falls in Venezuela, which plunges 1,005 metres down. This waterfall was first seen by Jimmy Angel from a plane in 1935, and was first visited in 1948.

Some waterfalls are very useful to man in providing power. The falls are used to generate the electricity man uses to run factories. About half the world's potential water power is in Africa, but most of it has not yet been developed.

As we read about man's exploration of the moon and the planets, we often come across the question of an atmosphere. Do other planets have an atmosphere, too?

WHAT IS THE ATMOSPHERE OF THE EARTH?

As far as scientists know, there is no other planet or star that has an atmosphere like ours. What is atmosphere? We can think of it as a great ocean of air that surrounds the earth and that extends up for hundreds of miles.

This ocean of air is just about the same the world over. In general, it consists of certain gases which are always found in the same proportions. About 78 percent of it is nitrogen, about 21 percent oxygen, and the remaining one percent consists of what are called rare gases—argon, neon, helium, krypton, and xenon.

The air that blankets the earth has the same chemical composition up to a height of about 18 miles, though it may be that this figure goes as high as 44 miles. When you reach the top layer of this atmosphere, you are at the end of what is called the troposphere. This is the layer nearest the earth.

At 18 to 31 miles above the earth's surface, there is a layer of hot air, probably about 42 degrees centigrade. The warmth is caused by the absorption of heat from the sun by the ozone which is present. Ozone is a special form of oxygen in which a molecule consists of three atoms of oxygen instead of the usual two. The hot ozone layer serves to protect us from the most active of the ultraviolet rays of the sun. Without it, we could not stand the sun's light.

Still higher up is a layer, or series of layers, of the atmosphere called the ionosphere. This extends from about 44 miles to 310 miles above the earth. It consists of particles electrified by the sun.

The molecules in the air are in constant motion. The atmosphere can be maintained only if the molecules keep colliding with others so they can't escape. But as we go higher and higher, the air becomes thinner. The chances become very small that a molecule from below will bounce back from a collision with a molecule above. So the molecules escape to outer space and our atmosphere thins out into nothingness. There is a region called the exosphere where escaped molecules move about freely, which starts at about 400 miles and extends up to about 1,500 miles.

If molecules are in constant motion at terrific speeds, and this is taking place in everything—even a piece of wood—why can't we see things changing shape?

IF MOLECULES MOVE, WHY CAN'T WE SEE THINGS CHANGE?

A molecule is the smallest bit of a substance that can exist and still keep the properties of the whole. For example, a molecule of sugar (sucrose) is the smallest bit of sugar that would still have the taste, color, form, solubility, and other qualities of sugar. If you divided it any more, it would no longer be sugar.

Now molecules of different substances vary greatly. Some are only a few billionths of a millimetre long and some are thousands of times larger. The molecules of the gases of which air is composed are so tiny that in a single cubic centimetre of air there are about 30,675,000,000,000,000,000 molecules!

But even though there are so many molecules in a substance, there is a great deal of empty space between them. Since molecules are always in motion, they move in a perfect vacuum. There is no air between the molecules of air, only a vacuum, and there is no iron between molecules of iron, only a perfect vacuum.

What causes the molecules to dash about is heat. The higher the temperature, the more violent the motion. In a hot gas, this motion is very violent. In a liquid or solid, it is much slower. But there is motion even in a piece of ice!

If the molecules in a substance are continually bumping into each other and pushing each other aside in all directions, why can't we see the effect of this motion? Why can't we see a piece of iron, for example, being changed by the motion? Why does it seem so solid? The reason is that in a solid or liquid the molecules are held in their places by the forces of attraction between the molecules. Otherwise, the substance would be torn apart. The electrical forces which bind the molecules are strong enough to make most solid materials as strong as they are.

But if we apply intense heat, the motion of the molecules becomes greater and the substance becomes a liquid. When still more heat is applied, the molecules overcome the electrical forces, fly apart, and are transformed into a gas!

You look out on the street or road and you see water. An hour later in bright sunshine, it is gone! Or wet clothes are hung out on a line, and by the end of the day, they are dry. Where did the water go?

WHERE DOES WATER GO WHEN IT DRIES UP?

We say the water evaporates. But what does this mean? Evaporation is the process by which a liquid that is exposed to air gradually becomes a gas or vapor. Many liquids evaporate quite quickly, much more quickly than water. This is true of alcohol, gasoline, and ammonia. Some liquids, such as mercury, evaporate very slowly.

What causes evaporation? To understand this, we must know something about the nature of matter. As we know, every substance is made up of molecules. Two forces are at work on these molecules. One is cohesion, which draws them together. The other is the heat motion of the individual molecules, which makes them fly apart.

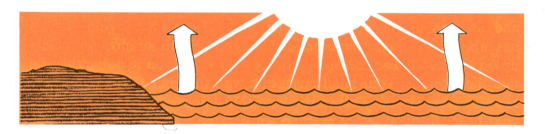

When the force of cohesion is stronger, the substance is a solid. When the heat motion is so strong that it overcomes cohesion, the substance is a gas. When the two forces are balanced fairly evenly, we have a liquid.

Water, of course, is a liquid. But at the surface of the liquid, there are molecules that are moving so rapidly that they fly into space and escape the force of cohesion. This process of escaping molecules is evaporation.

Why does water evaporate more quickly in sunshine or when heat is applied? The greater the heat, the more heat motion there is in the liquid. This means more molecules will have enough speed to escape. When the fastest molecules escape, the average speed of those left behind is lowered. So the remaining liquid is cooled by evaporation.

So when water dries up, what has really happened is that it has become a gas or vapor and part of the air.

Most of us think of air as being "nothing," but air is definitely "something," if it is matter made up of certain gases. A gas does not have a definite size or shape, but it takes up space.

DOES THE AIR HAVE WEIGHT?

The great ocean of air that surrounds the earth and extends for many miles upward is attracted and held to the earth by gravity. Thus air has weight. And since air is everywhere about us, it adds weight to every object it fills. For example, there is a small amount of air in a volley ball. If you were to weigh two such balls, with the air let out of one of them, you would find it's lighter than the other.

The weight of air exerts pressure. The air presses on your whole body from all directions, just as the water would if you were at the bottom of the sea. The great mass of air pushes down on the earth very hard with a pressure of nearly 1 kilogram on each square centimetre.

The kilogram is the weight of a column of air 1 centimetre square and as high as the air extends upward. The palm of your hand has about 77 square centimetres. Imagine 77 kilograms, all held up on one hand! The reason you don't even know you're doing this is that the air under your hand pushes up with the same force as the air above pushes down. There are about 270 kilograms of pressure on your head. But you're not mashed flat because there's air inside your body, too, which pushes out just as the air outside pushes in.

The higher up you go (to a mountain top, for example), the less air there is above you, so the pressure is less. At 6,000 metres the pressure is about 0.4 kilograms per square centimetre. At 3,000 metres it's 0.7 kilograms per square centimetre. If you could get up to 100 kilometres over the earth, there would be almost no pressure.

Would the world really be so much better off if there were no dust? The answer is: in some ways—yes; in some ways—no. What is dust, anyway? It consists of particles of earth, or other solid matter, which

WHAT WOULD HAPPEN IF THERE WERE NO DUST?

are light enough to be raised and carried by the wind. Where do these particles come from? They might come from dead plant and animal matter, from sea salt, from desert or volcanic sand, and from ashes or soot.

For the most part, dust is not a very desirable or beneficial thing. But in one way, it helps make the world more beautiful! The lovely colors of the dawn and of twilight depend to a great extent on the amount of dust that is present in the air.

Particles of dust in the upper air reflect the sun's rays. This makes its light visible on earth an hour or two after sunset. The different colors which make up the sun's light are bent at different angles as they are reflected by the dust and water vapor particles. Sunsets are red because these particles bend the red rays of the sun in such a way that they are the last rays to disappear from view.

Another useful function of dust has to do with rain. The water vapor in the air would not become a liquid very readily if it did not have the dust particles serving as centers for each drop of water. There-fore, clouds, mist, fog, and rain are largely formed of an infinite number of moisture-laden particles of dust.

Fog, dew, and clouds are all related. In fact, just one change in the conditions—such as the presence or absence of air currents—could make the difference as to whether there will be fog, dew, or clouds. Let's see why this is so, and why fogs appear in certain places.

WHY IS THERE FOG OVER LAKES?

Fog particles are small, less than 0.001 millimetres in diameter. When you have a dense fog and can't see in front of you, it's because there may be as many as 1,227 of these particles in one cubic centimetre.

In order for fog to form, the moisture must leave the air and con-dense. This means it must be cooled in some way, because cooler air cannot hold as much moisture as warm air. When the air is cooled below a certain point, called the dew or saturation point, then fog starts to form.

Fog formation also requires that the cool air be mixed into warmer air by an air current. If you have still air, the cooling will take place only near the ground and you will have dew. When there are rapidly rising air currents, the cooling takes place high in the air and you have clouds. So the air currents that mix the cool air into the warmer air must be gentle in order to create fog.

One of the conditions in which this happens is when a mass of warm air passes over a cold land or a cold sea. Or it could be the opposite, with cold air passing over warm water. This last condition is what happens during early morning in the autumn near bodies of water such as lakes and ponds. The cold air and currents of warm air mix gently and you get those familiar fogs which seem to hang in mid-air over a body of water.

If you take practically anything that exists in nature, the chances are that there is also a special science to study it. Oceanography is the study of all the sciences connected with the ocean to help man understand how the ocean was formed and how changes take place in it.

WHAT IS OCEANOGRAPHY?

As you might imagine, this takes quite a bit of studying! Let's see what it includes. Well, we can begin with the shoreline itself. The seacoast, the borderline between land and sea, is always changing due to tides, storms, everyday action of the sea against the shore, and upward and downward movements of the land.

The temperatures and salt content of the oceans are also studied. And strangely enough, man still has no good explanation as to why the ocean is salty. How about the tides? They are regular movements of the waters caused by the pull of the moon and the sun. These are studied constantly by oceanographers.

Then we come to the currents. Ocean currents are like rivers of water flowing through the ocean. They are warmer or colder than the waters through which they pass. Because they are important to man, they are always being studied.

As we all know, there are countless kinds of plants and animals living in the ocean. Oceanographers spend a great deal of time on this subject, too. How deep is the ocean in various places? This also is very important to man, and there are scientists who are concerned only with the question of ocean depth.

Even what is going on at the bottom of the ocean is of interest to man. We know there is a soft, oozy mud covering the floor of the ocean down to a depth of 3,657 metres. It is made up of the limey skeletons of tiny sea animals. The animal and plant life of the ocean bottom can be studied by dredging up portions of the mud from the sea floor.

All in all, the ocean, which looks like just a big body of water to most of us, is really a vast and complicated subject about which man wants to learn everything he can. And oceanographers are increasing our knowledge of the ocean by their constant study of every part of it and everything in it!

Have you ever been at a beach where at low tide you have to walk way out in the water just to get in up to your knees? Yet there are some places where you can hardly tell the difference between high and low tide.

WHY DON'T ALL PLACES HAVE THE SAME TIDES?

The reason for this has nothing to do with the moon. Tides are caused by gravitation. Just as the earth pulls on the moon, so the moon attracts or pulls on the earth, but with much less force. The pull of the moon upon the earth draws the ocean waters nearest to it toward the moon as a broad swell, or wave. This produces high tide.

The water on the opposite side of the earth gets the least pull from the moon since it is farthest away, so it forms a bulge, too. So we have high tide on the side toward the moon and also on the side opposite the moon.

As the moon goes around the earth, these two high "heaps" of water and lower levels of water keep in about the same position on the earth's surface in relation to the moon. In fact, if the earth's surface were entirely covered with water, the rotation of high tides and low tides would be very regular.

But there are many things that interfere with this. One is the great bulk of the continents. They cause tidal currents which follow the shore-lines and pile up in certain places, such as bays.

On coasts that are gently sloping and straight, the incoming tide has room to spread out and may not rise very high. But where the incoming tide enters a narrow bay or channel, it cannot spread out, and the water may pile up to great heights. In the Bay of Fundy, for example, the difference between high and low tide may be more than 21 metres. Yet, in most of the Mediterranean Sea, the water rises no more than 0.5 metres at high tide.

A waterspout and a tornado are very similar. In fact, you might call a waterspout a tornado at sea. So let's first see what a tornado is.

A tornado is really a circular storm. It begins as a black, funnel-shaped cloud in a larger thunderstorm area. The funnel of the cloud is caused by the condensation of moisture through cooling of the air as it expands and is lifted upward.

WHAT IS A WATERSPOUT?

A tornado may rotate either clockwise or counterclockwise. The width of a tornado (the part that touches the ground) averages only about 275 to 365 metres, and its path is usually short, from just a few to about 50 miles (80 kilometres).

Inside the tornado (the vortex) it is believed that the speed of the revolving winds made be 500 miles (800 kilometres) an hour! Where a tornado touches the ground, tremendous damage can result. Buildings can be flattened, or blown into bits, or even moved for hundreds of metres.

Tornadoes (also known as twisters and cyclones) can occur in any season, though they are five times as numerous in spring and summer. They are more likely to occur in the day than at night.

In some cases, a waterspout may simply be a tornado that has formed over land and passed out to sea. But the more common type of waterspout develops over tropical and middle-latitude seas and lakes during the warm season. It starts right over the water, the funnel cloud forming from the base of cumulus clouds or cumulonimbus clouds.

The lower tip of the funnel cloud, as it gets near the surface of the water, first agitates, or stirs up, the sea's surface into a cloud of spray. The funnel cloud dips into the center of this, then draws up a vortex spout of water. But the water that makes up the main part of the spout is always fresh, showing it is made up chiefly of rainwater.

A waterspout usually continues only a few minutes, and the effect is local. Most waterspouts occur over calm waters in places where the temperatures are high and thunderstorms are frequent.

A storm or a hurricane seems such a wild, uncontrolled thing that it's hard to believe it is following a definite path. Yet, as we know, when the hurricane season starts, the hurricanes are given names and their courses are often predicted very accurately!

DO HURRICANES MOVE IN DEFINITE DIRECTIONS?

In most parts of the world, most storms do move in definite directions. In the United States, for example, most big storms are vast circular whirls of air that rotate counterclockwise about a central point of low atmospheric pressure. The reason they rotate counterclockwise in the United States is that, as winds flow in toward the center of low pressure, the earth's rotation deflects them toward the right (in the Northern Hemisphere).

Now, what about hurricanes? First of all, did you know that hurricanes, cyclones, and typhoons are practically the same? In the United States they are called cyclones, in South-east Asia and in the South China Sea they are called typhoons, and in the West Indies and in the Gulf of Mexico they are known as hurricanes.

North of the equator, typhoons and hurricanes commonly originate in late summer or fall over warm tropical waters. They move westward and northwestward through the trade-wind zone in a path curved to the right.

In subtropical latitudes, such storms curve strongly to the east as they enter the zone of westerly winds. In the Southern Hemisphere, a similar curved course is followed, except that the storm track curves to the left.

Even though the path of a hurricane can be carefully plotted and all kinds of warnings given to people and ships at sea, a tremendous amount of damage is done by them. A hurricane may move forward at a speed of up to 125 miles per hour!

Most winds, of course, don't have names. You just say, "It's windy," or "The wind is blowing." Sometimes we might say, "The north wind is blowing." But many of the winds do have special names.

WHY DO WINDS HAVE DIFFERENT NAMES?

Those winds which have special names have acquired them for different reasons. For example, you know how it feels when you have the doldrums. You feel listless and without energy. Well, certain winds are actually called the doldrums! They are found near the equator where there is a great belt of rising air and low pressure. When you are caught in the doldrums in a ship, you are becalmed.

Winds that blow from above and below toward the equator are called the trade winds. Strong and steady, they got their names because in the days of sailing vessels they were a great help to navigation.

There are also some special winds. Monsoon winds, for example, are winds that change their direction with the season. In India, the monsoons blow south as hot, dry winds in the wintertime, and blow north in the summer, bringing heavy rainfall.

In southern France a cold, dry, northerly wind, the mistral, is dreaded by everyone. It blows steadily from the sea for days at a time and makes everybody irritable and uncomfortable!

On a windy day, it may seem to you that the wind is moving at tremendous speed. Then you hear the weather report, and it says, "Winds of 10 to 15 miles per hour." It's easy for us to be fooled about the speed

HOW IS THE SPEED OF WIND MEASURED?

of the wind. But the exact wind speed is important to many people, so there are scientific ways of measuring the wind.

The first instrument for measuring the speed of the wind was invented in 1667 by an Englishman named Robert Hooke. The instrument is called an anemometer. There are many kinds of anemometers, but the most common type now used has a number of aluminum cups on a spindle. They are free to turn with the wind, and the harder the wind blows, the faster the cups will turn. By counting the number of turns made by the cups in a given time, the speed of the wind may be calculated.

When men began to fly, it was necessary to measure the winds at high altitudes. This was done by sending weather balloons up into the atmosphere and watching them with a special kind of telescope called a theodolite. But this wasn't much good when clouds hid the balloon. In 1941, weather radar was invented. And now a radar set can observe the balloon even through clouds and measure the winds in the upper air!

People have long been interested in knowing the direction of the wind. As long ago as A.D. 900, wind vanes were put on church steeples to show the direction of the wind!

In a certain section of the country where thunderstorms occur rather frequently, one storm in eight hundred produces hail as large as walnuts, and one storm in five thousand produces them in tennis-ball size.

WHY DO HAILSTONES DIFFER IN SIZE?

And as you may know from your own experience, hailstones come in many sizes in between.

Hailstorms usually occur during the warm weather, and they are generally accompanied by thunder, lightning, and rain. Hail is formed when raindrops, on their journey to the earth, pass through a belt of cold air and are frozen.

Single raindrops form very small hailstones. Larger stones begin in the same way, but as the small hailstone falls, if it meets a strong rising current of air, it may be carried up again to the level where raindrops are forming. New drops then cling to the hailstone. As it falls once more through the cold belt, they spread into an enveloping layer and freeze about it, making the stone larger.

This rising and falling of the hailstone may be repeated time after time until it has added so many layers that its weight is sufficient to overcome the force of the rising current of air, and it falls to the ground. In this way, hailstones measuring 8 to 10 centimetres in diameter and weighing as much as 0.5 kilograms are occasionally built up.

Snow, too, freezes around hailstones when they are carried into regions where it is forming. So the hailstones are frequently made up of layers of ice and snow.

Hail does enormous damage every year. It beats down such crops as corn, wheat, cotton, and tobacco. It may strip trees of their leaves, break glass in windows, and even injure poultry and livestock!

Many a student who goes to college complains, "Why do I have to study physics and science, I'll never use these things." Of course, such people are quite wrong about "not using" physics and science. The fact

WHY DOES ICE CRACK PIPES?

is that whether we know it or not, we all use the laws of physics in everyday life many, many times.

Any person who lives in a climate where it gets cold in winter, knows that he must put anti-freeze in the radiator of his car, and close off and empty any pipes that might have water in them. He knows that if he doesn't, the radiator will crack and the pipes might burst. The laws of physics explain why such things happen.

For example, when most substances change from a liquid to a solid state, they shrink. But exactly the opposite happens with water! Instead of shrinking, it expands. And it doesn't expand by just any amount; it expands by about one ninth of its volume.

This means that if you start with nine litres of water and this water freezes, you'll have 10 litres of solid ice! Well, now just picture the water in an automobile radiator, or a pipe, freezing up. Ten quarts of ice need more room than nine quarts of water. But radiator pipes and water pipes can't stretch. There just isn't any more room. So when the water freezes, it makes more room for itself by cracking the pipes.

One of the amazing things about this process of nature, is the tremendous power it has. Pipes are made of pretty strong metals, as you know. In places like Finland, this power is actually put to work.

This is how they do it. In the quarries, they fill the cracks in the rock with water and allow it to freeze. The freezing water acts as a wedge and loosens the rock so that great blocks of rock are broken loose by the freezing power!

Even though ice takes up more space than water, it is lighter than water and floats upon it. This is the reason why large bodies of water never freeze solid. The sheet of ice on top protects the water beneath.

WATER   ICE

Even though stone and wooden houses have become more popular among the Eskimos, they still construct the igloo for special occasions or while on a journey. It is quickly built and it defies any kind of weather.

WHY DOESN'T AN IGLOO MELT INSIDE?

A trench is cut about 1.5 metres long and 50 centimetres deep in a new snowdrift. Then, from the face of the trench, blocks are cut with a knife. These are shaped so that they lean inward when set on edge.

A circle of these snowblocks is laid and then shaved down so that as the Eskimo builds there will be a narrowing spiral. The material is cut from the inside of the house as the man works. Then a keystone, with edges wider above than below, is dropped into the space at the top. Then all the cracks are filled in with soft snow. A small igloo can be built in this way in a couple of hours.

When the house has been built, the woman takes over. She lights her blubber lamp and makes it burn as hot as possible. Then she closes the door with a block of ice and makes everything airtight. Now the snow begins to melt. But because the dome's roof is curved, it doesn't drip. Instead, it soaks gradually into the blocks so that they are nearly wet through.

When the blocks are sufficiently wet, she puts out her lamp and opens the door. The intensely cold air rushes in, and in a few minutes, the house is transformed from a fragile building of snow to a dome of ice! It is now so strong that a polar bear can crawl over the roof without breaking it in. And because it is so solid and hard, it doesn't melt and provides a snug shelter.

Of course, when the winter ends and the temperature rises, the igloo does begin to melt, and it is usually the roof which first caves in.

An avalanche is a sliding mass of snow, or ice, or wet earth and stones. An avalanche of earth and stones is a kind of landslide. It can happen even in regions without snow. A steep mountainside or bluff becomes

WHAT IS AN AVALANCHE?

thoroughly soaked with water, or is weakened in some other way. The earth can no longer stand in such a steep slope without sliding, and an avalanche begins.

This kind of avalanche is most common in the spring, when winter snow and ice melt and soak the ground below. It may also occur where a river wears away its banks, or where man digs a roadway or mine along the base of a steep mountainside. This kind of landslide has often blocked mountain valleys and thereby created large lakes.

A snow avalanche occurs when snow will no longer remain on the mountain slope beneath without sliding. Old, packed, crusted snow will often remain quite firm on even very steep slopes, but fresh, loose, powdery snow may slide very easily on even a gentle slope.

When a small slide of snow begins, it often dislodges larger masses below, and as the avalanche descends, it grows in size and destructiveness. In places where the snow is so situated that it will barely support itself without sliding, even the sound of a voice may disturb it sufficiently to start an avalanche! This is because the sound sets up vibrations, and the vibrations start the snow sliding downwards.

In the Alps, when mountain-climbing parties are crossing dangerous slopes, the guides will often insist that everyone remain absolutely silent in order not to set up the vibrations that may cause an avalanche.

Perhaps you think of a crystal as a rare and beautiful mineral or gem. You are partly right. Emeralds and diamonds are crystals. But not all crystals are rare and beautiful. Each tiny particle of salt and sugar is also a crystal! Many of the common substances around us are crystals.

WHAT ARE CRYSTALS?

A crystal is the solid form of a substance. It has a definite shape and a definite number of faces because of the arrangement of its atoms. All crystals of the same substance have the same shape, though they may differ in size.

In nature, there are hundreds of substances which form crystals. Water is one of the most common. When water freezes, it turns into frost crystals or snowflakes.

Mineral crystals are also formed in certain rock-making processes. Great quantities of hot and melted rock material deep down in the earth are actually solutions of minerals. When these masses of molten, or melted, rock materials are forced upward into the earth's crust, they begin to cool.

They cool very slowly. The minerals become crystals when they change from the hot liquid to the cool solid form. For example, the rock granite contains crystals of the minerals quartz, feldspar, and mica. Many millions of years ago, this granite was a molten mass of minerals in solution. In the same way, there are today within the earth's crust masses of molten rock material which are slowly cooling and forming mineral crystals of many kinds.

Crystals take many shapes. All the crystals known in the world can be grouped into 32 forms, which are in turn grouped into six systems. Crystals can also be of many sizes. Some minerals form crystals that can be seen only through a microscope. Others form crystals that weigh several hundred pounds each.

SNOW CRYSTALS

EMERALD CRYSTALS

QUARTZ CRYSTALS

Coral is one of the most curious and fascinating objects in the world! To begin with, red coral has been prized for jewelry since ancient times. But even more interesting is the amount of supersition that has existed concerning coral.

WHAT IS CORAL?

Romans hung pieces of it around their children's necks to save them from danger. They believed it could prevent or cure diseases. In some parts of Italy, it is still worn to ward off "the evil eye." And most fascinating of all—coral has actually changed the geography of the world!

What is coral? It is the skeleton of the coral polyp, a tiny, jelly-like sea animal with many small tentacles. The polyp secretes a limey substance of which the skeleton is composed. It is formed like a cup beneath and around the outside of the polyp.

The polyp first attaches itself to a rock beneath the surface of the water, and young polyp buds grow out from it. When the old polyp dies, the living polyps remain attached to its skeleton, and in their turn produce buds. Thus the process of building goes on as new generations of polyps rise above the skeletons of the old.

As layer upon layer of coral is built up, it actually forms reefs and islands in the ocean! These animals flourish in warm or tropical waters. Coral is found principally in the South Pacific, in the Indian Ocean, in the Mediterranean Sea, and in the waters off the coast of Florida, of Mexico, and of the West Indies.

The most important coral formations are called fringing reefs, barrier reefs, and atolls. Fringing reefs are underwater coral platforms attached to a body of land and extending into the ocean. Barrier reefs are not attached to the mainland but rise from the ocean at some distance from shore. And atolls are coral islands, shaped like a ring.

The Great Barrier Reef, which lies off Queensland, Australia, extends 1,260 miles.

48

In ancient times, amber was thought to have magical powers. The ancient Greeks and Romans believed it could protect people against sorcerers and disease, so they wore it.

WHAT IS AMBER?

The reason amber was believed to have these mysterious powers was its ability to become electrified. When a piece of amber is rubbed briskly, a charge of electricity is produced. This makes amber attract light articles, such as bits of paper.

The Greek name for amber was elektron, and this is the origin of our word "electricity."

Amber is a brittle, yellow, translucent substance. It is hard enough to be cut into beads and ornaments, but it is not as hard as marble or glass.

Ages and ages ago, a certain resinous substance oozed from the pine trees that were then growing on the earth. Great amounts of it gradually accumulated on the ground, and as the earth's crust changed, this was buried under the ground or under water. In the course of millions of years, this substance became fossilized or hardened into the amber we see today.

Because amber was originally a soft, sticky substance, many insects became stuck and caught in it. Over the millions of years, as this substance hardened, the insects remained preserved in the amber. Today, we can find pieces of amber with ants and flies entombed in them, and these insects often look just as if they had been caught yesterday!

The pine trees which produced amber grew chiefly in the area that is now the Baltic Sea and the North Sea. This part of the earth's crust gradually became submerged. In ancient times, the only amber found was obtained when violent storms disturbed these waters, and pieces of it would be washed ashore. Today, amber is obtained by mining.

Amber is usually found in small pieces, though some lumps weighing up to 8 kilograms have been found. The chief uses for it today are in mouthpieces for pipes and cigar-holders, and as beads and small ornaments.

Nature is a master baker. Deep inside the earth is her oven, heated thousands of years ago by great rising masses of molten rock. In this oven she baked, and with tremendous pressure turned limestone into hard marble.

WHAT IS MARBLE?

In its purest form, marble is white. Different impurities often give it shades of pink, red, yellow, or brown, or form wavy lines or patches in it. Different colored crystals caught in the marble sparkle and flash in the sun's rays. In some marble the remains of fossils add to its beauty.

Many other kinds of rock that take on a high polish and are used in building, such as granite, onyx, and porphyry, are often called marble. Real marble, however, is limestone that has been crystallized by nature's process.

When marble is quarried a machine called a "channeler" cuts a series of channels or slots in the face of the rock. Some of these slots may be 2 to 3 metres deep and run from 18 to 24 metres long. Blasting cannot be used because it would damage or shatter the marble. The blocks are lifted out carefully by large derricks.

A great toothless saw is set to work on the rough stone, while a stream of water containing sand is kept running over it. The friction of the steel blade and the sand soon cuts the marble into the desired sizes. Sometimes a wire saw is used instead of a solid blade.

Pieces of marble are then placed on a circular rubbing bed and held stationary. Sand and water flow over the rotating bed surface, rubbing away the marble to an even level. Then still more grinding is done to give it a smooth surface.

The last fine polishing is done by a mixture of tin oxide and oxalic acid applied to the surface of the marble by means of a buffer wheel.

Why is a diamond so precious? Diamonds, of course, are rare, and anything rare has a high value. But rarity isn't enough. A thing must also be desirable, and diamonds are very desirable, indeed.

WHAT MAKES DIAMONDS PRECIOUS?

A diamond's capacity to reflect light gives it an appearance unlike anything else in the world. The diamond is also the hardest substance known to man. A thing of beauty that can last for thousands of years, it has come to be a symbol of enduring love and loyalty.

Diamonds are not naturally beautiful. They have to be worked on to be made beautiful. Diamonds in the rough form are found in all sizes and shapes and are rather dull in outside appearance. Experienced diamond cutters must examine each diamond carefully and decide how to bring out its beauty. Sometimes a diamond is sawed by a fast revolving disc impregnated with diamond dust. Only diamond dust can be used to wear down another diamond.

Most diamonds are sawed in two, and each half is shaped and cut into a round diamond called a brilliant. The facets, or little faces, are ground on a high-speed, cast-iron wheel impregnated with diamond dust and oil.

The facets are placed symmetrically, and the average brilliant is cut with 58 facets. The more facets, the greater the brilliance of the diamond. Diamond cutters have developed a whole series of shapes for cutting diamonds, such as the emerald cut, the baguette, the marquise, and so on.

Diamonds which are sold for jewelry may vary considerably in color and quality. Some colors are rarer than others. The most valuable diamonds are those tinged with red or blue, or those that are clear and colorless.

The first records we have of people deliberately looking for diamonds indicate that this happened in India. Diamond mining as an industry started there more than 2,500 years ago!

WERE DIAMONDS ALWAYS CONSIDERED VALUABLE?

Diamonds were prized from the very beginning. In fact, before the fifteenth century, diamonds were still so rare that only kings and queens owned them.

It was not until 1430 that the custom of wearing a diamond as a personal ornament was introduced. A lady named Agnes Sorel started the fashion in the French Court, and the custom spread throughout Europe. As a result, there was feverish activity in India for more than 300 years to supply diamonds.

Finally, this source became exhausted, and fortunately, diamonds were found on the other side of the world—in Brazil, in 1725. The jungle and tropical climate made conditions very difficult, but for more than 160 years, Brazil was the world's chief source of diamonds.

Today, the capital of the diamond empire is South Africa where, in 1867, important sources of diamonds were discovered by accident. A poor farmer's child found a pretty stone. A shrewd neighbor who recognized it as a gem diamond bought it, and when he sold it, diggers of all ages and nationalities flocked to the scene.

Within a year, three great diamond fields were found and the city of Kimberley, the heart of a great diamond empire, was born.

The only difference between an industrial diamond and any other kind of diamond is that the industrial diamond is of an inferior grade. If it were of perfect quality, beautiful in color and without a flaw, the diamond would, of course, be used in jewelry, where it brings higher prices.

WHAT IS AN INDUSTRIAL DIAMOND?

It may seem astonishing to you that something as precious as a diamond is used in industry at all, but the diamond has been called the "emperor of industry!"

Our word "diamond" comes from the Greek word *adamas,* which means "unconquerable." A diamond is truly unconquerable, for nothing in the world can cut it—except another diamond!

So three fourths of all diamonds that are found don't go into jewelry at all. They are used in industry. And they are used because of their extreme hardness. For instance, about 20 per cent of all industrial diamonds are mounted in drills and used by mining companies to drill through rock.

Diamonds are crushed to dust and this diamond dust is used in making diamond-grinding wheels. These wheels sharpen certain tools and also grind lenses. Other diamonds are used in dies. Without diamonds, some of our most important industries would have to shut down.

If you're a prospector looking for gold, knowing the answer can be the difference between being immensely wealthy and immensely poor! Many a miner has come upon what he thought was gold, only to discover that his dreams of wealth vanished when his "find" was analyzed.

WHAT'S THE DIFFERENCE BETWEEN GOLD AND FOOL'S GOLD?

What has come to be known as fool's gold is a mineral called iron pyrite. Since it is a yellow mineral with a brilliant luster, it can easily be mistaken for flakes of native gold in a rock.

Another reason the mistake is often made is that gold itself is frequently found where there are iron pyrites. Native gold is found mostly in quartz veins or in masses of iron pyrites. The water and wind wear away the quartz and pyrites, and the gold has weathered out of the rocks. This means that the pieces of rock around the lumps of gold have been washed away, freeing the lumps or nuggets of nearly pure gold.

The nuggets are washed down to the bottom of the valleys and become mixed with sand and gravel. In this form it is called alluvial or placer gold. The first gold that man found was placer gold.

But gold is also often found in the ores of other metals. Silver ore nearly always contains some gold. Copper ores quite often are combined with gold. Even sea water contains gold! The quantity, however, is so small compared with the amount of sea water that no one has been able to separate the gold from the sea. Yet, our oceans are so vast that the total amount of gold they would yield has been estimated to be about 9,070,000,000 tonnes. Now there s a nice project for some chemist of the future—to get the gold from the sea.

Man discovered copper before any other metal except gold. Before the dawn of history, it was used by Stone Age men.

WHAT IS COPPER? Copper is found in a fairly pure state, in lumps and grains of free metal. Probably men first picked up the lumps because they were pretty. Then they made the great discovery that these strange red stones could be beaten into any shape. This was an easier method of making weapons and knives than chipping away at flints.

Much later, other men discovered that they could melt the red stones and form the softened mass into cups and bowls. Then they started to mine for copper and to make all sorts of implements and utensils out of it.

For thousands of years, copper remained the only workable metal known, for gold was not only too scarce to be considered but also too soft to be practical. Copper tools were probably used in building the great Egyptian pyramids.

When bronze, an alloy of copper and tin, was discovered, still greater quantities of copper were mined. But after the discovery of iron, copper was little used, except among semi-civilized peoples, until the present age of electricity. Because copper is such a good conductor of electricity, it is a very important metal in modern industry.

Few people ever see pure copper or would recognize it if they did. It is a shining, silvery substance delicately tinted with pink that turns a deeper red when exposed to the air. The copper we generally see has a dull reddish-brown surface. This is an oxide formed when the metal combines with the oxygen of the air.

Most of the world's copper exists in combination with other substances from which it must be separated before it can be used. Often it is found combined with sulphur in what we call a sulphide ore. This sulphide ore may be combined with such substances as iron and arsenic and this makes the separation of the copper difficult.

Copper has many other virtues besides that of outlasting most other metals. It is tough, yet soft enough to be pulled and pounded and twisted into any shape. It is an excellent conductor of heat as well as of electricity. It can be carved or etched, but is not easily broken. And it can be combined with other metals to make such alloys as bronze and brass.

Nickel forms many alloys which are used in hundreds of industries in many ways. It is one of the most useful metals known to man. But in early times, when chemists first tried to work with it, it gave

WHAT IS NICKEL?

them a great deal of trouble. In fact, the word nickel is derived from the German word for "imp!"

Nickel is found in meteorites, and it is sometimes found in the free state in small quantities. But the greatest supply of nickel is obtained from certain ores, especially one called pyrrhotite, which is a mineral containing iron, copper, and nickel. Canada is the greatest of all nickel-producing countries.

The ore containing nickel is usually heated in a blast furnace to obtain a rich mixture called a matte. This is then reduced to nickel by mixing it with coke and heating it in a blast furnace.

Nickel is silvery, lustrous, hard, and malleable, which means it can be easily worked and shaped. And nickel is one of the most magnetic materials known, unless heated.

We seldom see pure nickel except when it is used as a coating on other metals. This is then called nickel-plate. It protects other metals from rust or tarnish, and gives them a better wearing surface.

Most of the nickel produced is used in alloys, or in a mixture with other metals. For instance, when alloyed with copper, it is used in coins. The U.S. five-cent piece is called a nickel for that reason. When it is alloyed with three parts of copper and one of zinc, nickel forms a bright silvery metal known as German silver or nickel silver. This is used for making tableware and as a base for silverplated ware.

But these uses of nickel are relatively minor. Most nickel goes into the making of nickel steel, an alloy which can withstand repeated strains. It is used in structural work, bridges, railroad rails at curves, rivets, locomotive boilers, automobile gears and axles, and the dipper teeth of steam shovels.

Magnesium is one of the most amazing metals known to man. It is so light that it is only two-thirds as heavy as aluminum, and you know from your experience with kitchen utensils how light aluminum is! In fact, magnesium is the lightest metal used in industry.

WHAT IS MAGNESIUM?

In addition to its lightness, magnesium has another unusual property. It has a tendency to burn. In the form of dust or fine shavings, it catches fire very easily and burns violently.

Otherwise, the properties of magnesium are similar to those of other metals. It has a silvery-white luster, is slightly harder than aluminum, and quickly corrodes or wears away in moist air.

To increase its strength, hardness, and resistance to corrosion, magnesium is usually mixed, or alloyed, with zinc, manganese, and aluminum. The alloys of magnesium have many important uses. They are made into sheets, plates, tubes, rods, and wire. The extreme lightness of magnesium makes it especially useful in airplanes and other fast moving machinery. Sometimes the pure metal, because of its ability to burn, is used in flares, rockets, and tracer bullets.

Magnesium, in the form of its salts, is used in medicine and chemistry. Epsom salt is magnesium sulphate, and milk of magnesia is a suspension of magnesium oxide.

At one time, magnesium was just a curiosity of the chemical laboratory. As far back as 1808, Sir Humphry Davy was able to determine some of its properties, even though he couldn't obtain pure magnesium. Gradually, scientists began to work with this strange metal and learned how to obtain it in pure form and how to use it with other metals in alloys. It took almost a hundred years for the first magnesium alloy to be produced.

Magnesium is so active chemically that it doesn't occur in a free state in nature. But in combination with other elements, it actually forms more than two percent of the earth's crust! Magnesium is obtained by separating it from the minerals with which it is found mixed in nature. These are chiefly magnesite, dolomite, carnallite, and natural salt brines.

The crust of the earth, the ground on which people walk and live, is very largely made up of a substance called silicon!

WHAT IS SILICON?

Silicon is the second most abundant element on earth, but it is never found in the free state. This means it is always combined with one or more additional elements. Silicon is the major element in all of the rocks except certain ones called the carbonates. Clay, for example, contains an average of 50 percent silicon, and you can be pretty sure that most of the rocks you see have equally large amounts.

Silicon has been found on the stars and even in plants. A large amount of the silicon in the world is found in the form of silica, which is a compound made of oxygen and silicon. Quartz, jasper, opal, and sand are all forms of silica. Ancient peoples used silica to make glass.

Silicon exists in two forms, crystalline and powder. Pure silicon is not very useful, so it is seldom produced. Compounds of silicon, however, have a great many uses in industry.

When sand is combined with coke, it produces silicon carbide. The common name for silicon carbide is carborundum. An extremely hard substance, it is used in grinding and polishing metals.

Silicon is also added to steel because it gives the steel many desirable properties. Steel may contain from 2 to 6 percent silicon. When steel is used to make equipment for chemical uses, it contains 6 percent silicon. It thus resists corrosion much better than any other steel.

When 2 percent silicon is added to steel, it becomes ideal for electrical equipment, because less power is then needed to magnetize the steel. The chemical industry uses silicon compounds of all kinds for a great many purposes.

Was there a time when there were no plants on earth? According to the theories of science, the answer is yes. Then, hundreds of millions of years ago, tiny specks of protoplasm appeared on earth. Protoplasm

WHERE DID PLANTS COME FROM?

is the name for the living material that is found in both plants and animals. These original specks of protoplasms, according to scientists, were the beginnings of all our plants and animals.

The protoplasm specks that became plants developed thick walls and settled down to staying in one place. They also developed the green coloring matter known as chlorophyll which enabled them to make food from substances in the air, water, and soil.

These early green plants had only one cell, but later they formed groups of cells. Since they had no protection against drying out, they had to stay in the water. Today, some descendants of these original plants still survive, though they have changed quite a bit, of course. We call them algae. Seaweeds are an example of these plants.

One group of plants developed that obtained its food without the use of chloropyhll. These non-green plants are called the fungi, and they include bacteria, yeasts, molds, and mushrooms.

Most of the plants on earth today evolved from the algae. Certain of these came out of the sea and developed rootlets that could anchor them in the soil. They also developed little leaves with an outer skin covering as protection against drying. These plants became mosses and ferns.

All of the earliest plants reproduced either by simple cell division (as in the case of bacteria and yeast) or by means of spores. Spores are little dustlike cells something like seeds, but they contain no stored food in them as seeds do. As time went on, some of these plants developed flowers that produced true seeds.

Now we are pretty far advanced in the development of plants. Two different types of plants with seeds appeared; those with naked seeds and those with protected seeds. Each of these two types later developed along many different lines. In this way, we have traced the plants existing on the earth today back to an original speck of protoplasm that appeared long, long ago. At least, this is the theory of modern botanical science.

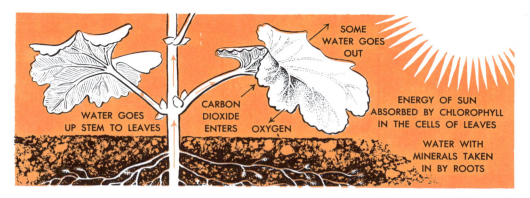

SOME WATER GOES OUT

ENERGY OF SUN ABSORBED BY CHLOROPHYLL IN THE CELLS OF LEAVES

WATER WITH MINERALS TAKEN IN BY ROOTS

WATER GOES UP STEM TO LEAVES

CARBON DIOXIDE ENTERS   OXYGEN

We must not forget that plants are living things. They eat, drink, and breathe, and without plenty of good food, they die. With the exception of two classes of plants, all plants manufacture their own food. Let's see how they go about doing this.

HOW DO PLANTS TAKE IN THEIR FOOD?

The marvelous substance called chlorophyll in the cells of the leaves and often in the stem and flowers helps the living tissue of the plant to absorb the energy from sunlight. This energy transforms dead (inorganic) chemicals into life-giving (organic) chemicals. The name for this truly amazing process is photosynthesis.

But to build living tissues, carbon is required. The plant obtains this carbon from the air. (It exists in the air combined with oxygen in a form called carbon dioxide.) Once the plant takes in the carbon, it must combine it with other substances to build various parts of the plant.

The most important of these is water, from which the plant takes hydrogen. In the water, there must be certain minerals which the plant needs. These are mostly compounds of nitrogen, sulphur, phosphorous, potassium, calcium, magnesium, sodium, and iron.

The plant gets this water and minerals through its roots. One of the reasons roots become long at their tips is so that they can keep coming in contact with new parts of the soil in their search for minerals and water. Thousands of tiny root hairs project from the surface of the young roots, growing about soil particles and absorbing materials from them. Part of the water taken in through the roots is used to make sugar. The rest is given off from the leaves. A plant wilts when water goes out of the leaves faster than it comes in through the roots.

Did you know that no two leaves are exactly alike, even if they have the same shape and color?

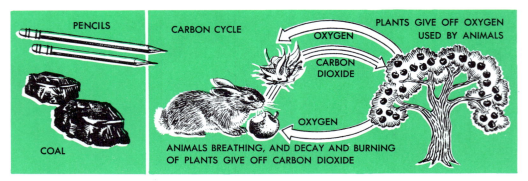

PENCILS

CARBON CYCLE

PLANTS GIVE OFF OXYGEN
USED BY ANIMALS

OXYGEN

CARBON
DIOXIDE

OXYGEN

COAL

ANIMALS BREATHING, AND DECAY AND BURNING
OF PLANTS GIVE OFF CARBON DIOXIDE

Of all the chemical elements known to man, perhaps the most interesting one is carbon. Did you know, for example, that in the form of crystal it gives us one of our most valuable gems, the diamond? As graphite, carbon forms the lead of lead pencils. And coal, the source of much of the heat and power of this machine age, is mostly carbon.

WHAT IS THE CARBON CYCLE?

But even more important is the fact that carbon is so vital to life. The bodies of all living things are made up of compounds containing carbon. In fact, scientists believe that where carbon is found in any quantity in the earth, there life has probably existed.

The carbon cycle is the process in which carbon is continuously being removed, used, and replaced by living things. Here is how it works. There is carbon dioxide in the air. Plants secure carbon from this gas and use it in building up their roots, stems, and leaves. Animals get carbon for food from the plants, in the form of vegetables, fruits, or cereals. At the same time, carbon dioxide is being returned to the air, especially by animals' breathing, and by the burning or decay of plants. The carbon cycle is thus completed.

When elements combine, we have a compound. The number of carbon compounds that we know so far is enormous — more than 200,000 of them! All the other elements together do not form nearly as many compounds as the single element carbon. The reason for this is that the carbon atom can join with the atoms of other elements in so many different ways and can form rings and chains in combination with other carbon atoms.

You come in contact with or use carbon compounds constantly in your daily life. You breathe in a little carbon dioxide and breathe out much more. And most fuels, foods, drugs, plastics, perfumes (and dozens upon dozens of other products) are carbon compounds!

All living things need nitrogen in a form their bodies can use. It is important to plants and animals as well as to humans. It is a necessary part of the protein substance which is man's body-building material.

WHAT IS THE NITROGEN CYCLE?

Without this substance, no one could grow or repair damaged or worn-out tissues.

While oxygen makes up only 21 per cent of the air we breathe, nitrogen makes up 78 per cent. There are about 7,200,000 tonnes of nitrogen above a square kilometre of the earth's surface. It is a colorless, odorless, tasteless gas that dissolves only slightly in water.

It would seem easy for living things to get the nitrogen they need since it is all around them in the air. But human bodies cannot use pure nitrogen. When breathed in, it dilutes the oxygen. So it is useful only when combined with other chemicals to form compounds. In nature, only a few plants, the legumes, such as beans, peas, and clover, are able to use pure nitrogen from the air. But all plants can use the simple nitrogen compounds of the soil in which they grow.

A nitrogen cycle is thus set up in nature which enables plants and animals to maintain life. Plants get simple nitrogen compounds from the soil and unite them with carbon to make proteins. Animals get the nitrogen they need by eating the plants. The nitrogen is returned to the soil as waste. Certain bacteria turn this waste back into simple nitrogen compounds, and the plants are able to use it again. So the cycle is complete. The supply of nitrogen is also replenished by bacteria which take nitrogen from the air and "fix" it in the ground.

Man's relationship to bacteria is a very interesting one. We all know that many bacteria are harmful. Diseases such as typhoid fever, cholera, diphtheria, pneumonia, and all infections that occur in open wounds

WHAT ARE BACTERIA?

are each caused by a particular kind of bacteria. So man wages war on these bacteria.

Yet, without the action of other types of bacteria, life would be impossible on earth! In fact, man actually cultivates certain bacteria because he needs and uses them.

Bacteria are usually considered the lowest members of the plant kingdom. Each bacterium is a single bit of living matter without a nucleus. They average about 0.001 millimetres in diameter. Some are so small they can't even be seen under an ordinary microscope.

Bacteria are usually found in one of three shapes: They are the ball-shaped cocci; the rod-shaped bacilli; or the corkscrew-shaped spirilla. They reproduce by simply splitting in two. Under favorable conditions, they increase at a very rapid rate. Luckily, nature has several ways of checking this increase. Otherwise, bacteria would soon cover the entire earth.

The bacteria that brings about the decay of dead plants and animals are very useful to man. Not only do they destroy dead tissues and break them down into the simple compounds out of which they were made, but without decay bacteria, the earth would become so cluttered with useless dead matter that there would be no room for living things.

Certain other bacteria are useful by causing fermentation. The souring of milk and of sweet fruit juices are the most familiar kinds of fermentations caused by bacteria. Various industrial processes owe a great deal to this fermenting action of bacteria. The ripening of cream, which flavors good butter, is due to bacterial fermentation. Many of the finer cheeses owe their flavors, at least in part, to bacterial products.

And as we know, plants could not live without the bacteria that combine nitrogen with other elements to make nitrates which plants can use.

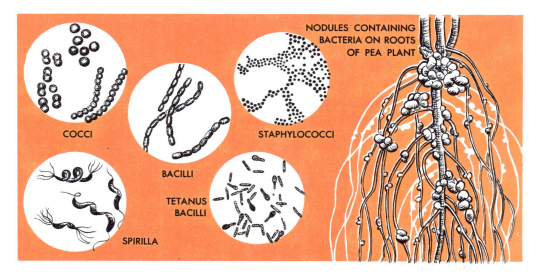

NODULES CONTAINING BACTERIA ON ROOTS OF PEA PLANT

COCCI

STAPHYLOCOCCI

BACILLI

TETANUS BACILLI

SPIRILLA

Is there anybody in your family on a diet? Then you've probably heard them say as they turned down a certain dish, "Not for me! Too much starch!" Of course, if there are growing children in a house, they are usually fed plenty of starch to "build them up."

WHY DO PLANTS MAKE STARCH?

Starch—whether people try to cut down on it or to get all they can—is one of the most important substances in the world. The human race gets more food from starch than from any other single substance!

We get our starch from plants, where it is found in the form of tiny grains. How do plants make starch? With the help of sunshine and chlorophyll, plants combine the water they have absorbed from the soil and the carbon dioxide they have taken in from the air into sugar. This sugar is changed by plants into starch.

Plants store the starch away as small granules in their stems, roots, leaves, fruits, and seeds. The potato, maize, rice, and wheat contain large amounts of starch.

The reason plants manufacture all this starch is that it serves as food for the development of seedlings or the new shoots until they can manufacture their own food materials. So when you see a plant beginning to spread out, you know that stored-up starch is providing the food for that growth.

For people and animals, starch supplies an energy-producing food. Like sugar, it is made up of carbon, hydrogen, and oxygen. It is not sweet; generally, it is tasteless. Certain chemical substances in the mouth, stomach, and intestines change the starchy food to grape sugar, which the body can use easily.

The way we get starch from the plant is to crush those parts of the plant where the starch is stored. The starch is washed out with water and allowed to settle to the bottom of large vats. The water is then squeezed out of the wet starch and the mass is dried and ground to a powder, which is the form in which starch is usually manufactured.

Starch has many unusual uses. It is used in laundering, as an adhesive, in the manufacture of cloth, and as the basis for many toilet preparations.

ENLARGED VIEW OF YEAST CELLS BUDDING   UNRISEN BREAD   RISEN BREAD   BAKED BREAD

If a weak sugar solution is exposed to the air, in several days a light, frothy scum appears on the surface and the liquid begins to smell of alcohol. This change takes place because tiny plant cells called yeast have settled from the air into the liquid. They have found conditions favorable to their growth.

WHAT IS YEAST?

Man has long known that this process takes place and he has used it for thousands of years to make alcoholic beverages of all kinds. Sugar solutions made from molasses, potatoes, rye, corn, malt and hops, apples, and grapes have been exposed to the air to make alcohol, whiskey, beer, ale, cider, wine, and other beverages.

Probably through accident, it was also discovered that if bread dough were allowed to stand for some time before baking, very often a peculiar change took place. The flat lump of dough began mysteriously to swell and rise. It developed a strange but pleasant odor. When this dough was baked, instead of making a flat, heavy slab, it made a light, porous, soft bread!

In 1857, Louis Pasteur announced that he had discovered the explanation for these changes. He said they were due to the presence of tiny, one-celled plants called yeast. Yeasts belong to the fungi family, and are tiny, rounded, colorless bodies. They are larger than most bacteria, but still so small that it would take from 1,200 to 1,600 of them laid side by side to make a centimetre.

Yeast cells reproduce by budding. This means they send out projections which become cut off from the parent cell by a cell wall. Finally, these projections grow to full size. As they grow, they form substances called zymase and invertase.

These substances are called enzymes, and they have the power to ferment starch to sugar, and sugar to alcohol and carbon dioxide. As fermentation takes place, carbon dioxide is formed and rises to the top. Then it escapes, leaving the alcohol. Beer, ale, wine, and cider are fermented beverages in which yeast has changed some of the sugar to carbon dioxide and alcohol.

In breadmaking, the carbon dioxide collects in bubbles in the dough, which makes it rise. Heat later drives off the carbon dioxide, thus making the bread porous and light.

The technical name for this plant is the agave, and it is called a century plant because of a mistaken notion! It is commonly believed that this plant blooms only when it has reached the age of 100 years. The truth

HOW DID THE CENTURY PLANT GET ITS NAME?

is that when it blooms depends on the individual plant itself and the conditions under which it is growing.

In very warm countries, flowers will appear on the century plant in a few years. In colder climates, the plant won't mature until it's about 40 to 60 years old.

The agave, or century plant, grows chiefly in Mexico, but it also occurs in southern and western United States and in Central and tropical South America. The plants have a large "rosette" of thick fleshy leaves which end in a sharp point. The stem itself is usually quite short, so that the leaves seem to spring from the root.

When the century plant flowers, a tall stem or "mast" grows from the center of the rosette of leaves and bears a large number of short flowers. After these flowers are developed, the plant usually dies down. Apparently this flowering is quite an effort for the plant, and during all the years it is growing, it is storing nourishment in the fleshy leaves so that finally the flowering can take place.

The unusual type of growth of this plant makes possible an interesting use of it. The stalk of the plant develops very rapidly, and when this happens, there is a rush of sap to the base of the young stalk. In Mexico, people remove this large bud just as it is ready to emerge. Then they scoop out a cavity in the heart of the plant and gather a large quantity of the sweet sap.

This sap is called aguamiel, and it is brought in pigskin bottles to a central repository where it is allowed to ferment. This makes it thick and milky. The sugars in the sap have been changed to alcohol and the resulting liquid is sold as *pulque,* the national drink of Mexico, considered by many people to be a wholesome and nourishing drink.

The marshmallow you eat today as candy has nothing to do with the marshmallow! At one time, this candy was actually made from a plant called a marshmallow, which is how it got its name.

WHAT IS MARSHMALLOW?

Today, marshmallows are made by whipping a combination of sugar, corn syrup, gelatin, flavors, and egg whites. Marshmallows have a light, fluffy texture. The most popular kind is white marshmallow which has been covered with sugar. But there are also marshmallow "peanuts," marshmallow "bananas," and marshmallow "eggs." Some kinds are made by coating the marshmallow with toasted coconut and chocolate.

The mallow family of plants, of course, has nothing to do anymore with the candy we have described. In the mallow plant family are included the cotton plant, okra, the marshmallow (the one that once was used for candy), and other mallows used for fiber, glue, and food.

One kind of mallow has sweet-smelling seeds from which perfume can be made! The leaves of a Chinese species of mallow are used for shoeblacking. Many mallows have beautiful showy flowers of white, rose, yellow, or red. The hollyhock and the rose of Sharon, common garden flowers, are mallows. There are others that grow wild, including the wild swamp mallow which is found all along the Atlantic Coast of the United States.

Do you remember seeing pictures of visitors to Hawaii being greeted with flower necklaces, called *leis?* Well, the orange flowers used for making these *leis* come from a certain mallow plant native to Hawaii. Another mallow, the roselle, is used for making jams and a refreshing drink.

Altogether, the mallow plant family is quite a family—with more than 900 different species of mallows in it!

When you look at the unopened pod of the peanut, you can see that it closely resembles the pea or bean. In fact, it belongs to the same family. The peanut plant is a bush, and its blossoms resemble those of the pea.

HOW DO PEANUTS GROW?

After the petals fade, a part of the pod elongates very greatly and its tip becomes buried in the soil. There this tip enlarges and the seeds mature. So if you want to gather peanuts, you have to dig them out of the soil!

Where did peanuts come from?—Probably the original home of the peanut was South America. It is a very ancient plant. In prehistoric graves in Peru, peanuts have been found along with pottery decorated with peanut designs! From there it was probably transplanted to Africa, and then to the United States.

Today the peanut is raised in the southern United States from Florida to California and as far north as Washington, D. C. It is also cultivated in Latin America, Asia, and Africa. Common varieties of peanuts are the large-podded, red-skinned Virginia peanuts, and the smaller Spanish and North Carolina types.

Peanuts need a long, frost-free season to grow well. The peanut plant can survive long dry periods, and it is a profitable crop, yielding an average of 100 to 150 hectolitres per hectare.

Peanuts are planted late in the spring, and are dug by machinery before the frost comes. After the vines are dried, the peanuts are picked by machine. Sometimes hogs are turned directly into the fields to root out the nuts.

You enjoy peanuts as peanut butter, salted or roast nuts, and in candy bars. But peanuts have many other uses. Their oil is used in salads, vegetable shortenings, soaps, and oleomargarine. Peanut meal feeds hogs and cattle. Other products include dyes, printing inks, and rubber substitutes.

Did you know that about one-half of all the people in the world live almost entirely on a rice diet? Most of these people live in Asia, but rice is also important in the Western World.

HOW IS RICE GROWN?

There are thousands of varieties of rice, and they vary in many ways. Wild rice grows in the shallow water of lakes in northeastern Canada and in the United States. It is only distantly related to cultivated rice, the rice that most people eat. And there is hill, or upland, rice which can be grown on dry upland fields like other grains.

But most rice, called lowland rice, is grown on flat, alluvial soil, the soil that has been brought there by water. Such soil is usually found along the shores of lakes or the banks of rivers. The soil is not only moist, but can be flooded during the growth of the crop.

In growing rice, first the seed is broadcast (scattered) in specially prepared seed beds. Later, the plants are transferred into flat fields, surrounded by dikes, which are called paddies.

The fields are then flooded by letting in water from the canals or the river through gates in the walls which surround each field. The rice-grower must keep at least 13 centimetres of water on fields during the growing season.

When weeding is necessary, the water is drained off and weeds are pulled by hand. Then just before the leaves turn from green to yellow, the fields are drained again for harvesting. So you can see that growing rice is a job that takes plenty of work.

Nobody knows where rice grew originally, but it is one of man's oldest crops. The Chinese were growing rice more than 5,000 years ago! But rice may have originated along the shores of lakes in India, and spread from there to other countries. The first time rice was grown in Europe was in the fifteenth century in Italy.

A seed, as you know, is one of the ways in which a plant produces another plant of its own kind. But seeds need special conditions to grow. They need moisture, oxygen, and warmth. If a seed doesn't start to grow within a certain time, the seed will die.

HOW DOES NATURE SCATTER SEEDS?

So it's pretty important for a seed to get to the right place in the right time. Luckily, there are at least eight different ways for seeds to be scattered. Let's take a look at each one.

One type of seed may be called a "hitch-hiker." The outer covering of this type of seed has hooks, barbs, or spines. They catch on the fur of passing animals and on the clothing of people, and get carried about this way.

Other types of seeds are "stickers." The seeds grow inside sticky berries. When the berries are eaten by birds, some seeds stick to the bird's bill and thus get carried off.

The seeds of plants that grow in or near the water often fall into mud or water. As birds or animals walk along the shore looking for food, mud sticks to their feet, and this mud often contains the seeds that have fallen into the water.

Some seeds are actually the food of various animals. Squirrels, birds, and insects eat certain kinds of seeds. Since not all the seeds picked up by them are eaten, the rest are carried about to different places and thus scattered.

Man himself scatters many seeds without intending to. Grain contains many smaller seeds that are not cleaned out, and when grain is shipped, these seeds go along for the ride.

Some seeds get to new places by "flying" there. They may have fluffy attachments that are easily caught up by the wind. Maple seeds, for instance, come in pairs, each with a wing attached. Dandelion seeds are shaped like parachutes and are carried by the wind.

Certain seeds are "floaters." They fall to the water and the wind "sails" them away. Finally, there are seeds that are scattered by explosions. Certain seed pods open suddenly as they dry and crack, throwing the seeds as much as several feet away!

In millions of homes in Europe and the United States, the mistletoe is hung up at Christmastime. According to a happy custom, when a girl is standing under the mistletoe, a man is allowed to kiss her.

WHAT IS MISTLETOE?

Curiously enough, the use of the mistletoe on holidays and ceremonial occasions goes back to quite ancient times. When the Romans invaded Britain and Gaul (now called France), the people who lived there were called Celts. These Celts were organized under a strong order of priests called Druids.

The Druids taught that the soul of man was immortal. Many of their rites were connected with the worship of trees, and they considered that whatever grew on a tree was a gift from heaven. Among the most sacred of these "gifts" was the mistletoe. They would cut the mistletoe with a golden knife and hang it over their doors to ward off evil spirits. According to them, only happiness could enter under the mistletoe. This was actually the beginning of the tradition of the kiss under the mistletoe!

Among the Scandinavian people, too, the mistletoe was considered lucky. They gathered it up during their winter festivals and each family received a bit of it to hang up over the entrance to their home. This was supposed to protect the family from evil spirits.

One reason the mistletoe came to be considered sacred is that it is a plant that has no roots in the earth. It grows on the branches of other trees. When the mistletoe is very young and just developing from a seed, it produces tiny outgrowths. These pierce the bark of the limb on which the seed fell. After they have grown through the bark to the wood, they spread out and in this way absorb a part of the moisture and the food which the tree contains.

The food and moisture go to nourish the young mistletoe plant, which then grows as most other plants do. So you see it has no direct connection with the soil and it doesn't need any! Sometimes, the mistletoe grows so abundantly it kills the tree that has given it life.

The mistletoe grows on oak and other kinds of trees in many parts of Europe and the U.S.A. The berries which the plant produces are loved by birds. When they eat them, the sticky seeds cling to their beaks. In trying to remove them, the birds rub their beaks on other trees and so spread the seeds!

Lumbering was one of the earliest industries to be started in America. In fact, there is a legend that Leif Ericson, who was supposed to have visited North America about the year 1000, brought back a cargo of

HOW DOES A TREE BECOME LUMBER?

timber from the new world! We do know that one of the first products shipped to England from the Jamestown colony was timber from the Virginia forests.

There are many trees used for building and other purposes. The leading softwood trees include pine, Douglas fir, hemlock, spruce, white fir, cypress, and redwood. Hardwood timber or lumber used for furniture making, flooring, and certain other special purposes comes from such trees as oak, gum, maple, poplar, and walnut.

After a tree is cut down, handsaws or power saws are used to cut the trunk into logs. Then the logs are hauled to a sawmill, or, where there is water transportation, they are floated to the mill.

When a log first enters a large mill, it may be cut into two or more lengths. The log is then rolled onto a carriage, which is mounted on wheels and runs on a track. While the log is held fast, the carriage moves toward one end of the track. This brings the log into contact with a saw which cuts off a slice from one end to the other. This is continued until the log is cut into several slices, each of a desired thickness.

The rough boards are then trimmed, planed smooth, and sorted. Now they must be dried before they can be used as lumber. This is because the weight of a newly cut board is almost two-thirds water! If it were used at once, it would dry out later, and it would warp and shrink as it dried.

Some lumber is dried by being piled in the open air, which may take from one month to more than a year. But this way of drying still leaves a water content of from 15 to 20 percent. Another method of drying uses heated rooms called kilns. Here a load of lumber can be dried in two days to two weeks, and its water content is reduced to a very small percentage. For floors and furniture, it is important to have a lower water content, though for most construction purposes, 15 percent is considered all right.

By the way, of the lumber that is used in the United States, 18 percent is used as fuel!

Anyone who travels across our country sees so many forests everywhere that he might well wonder why we have to worry about protecting them. Don't we have too many forests with too many trees right now?

WHAT IS FORESTRY?

Actually, about a third of all the land area in the United States is forest land. That's more than 250,000,000 hectares. One of the most important things we can do for the future of our country is to see that our forests are properly cared for! This is being done in Britain and elsewhere.

First, just imagine all the products we obtain from trees. Fruits, nuts, and sugar are only some of the foods. Buildings, furniture, and boats come from trees. Paper, rayon, toys—the list is almost endless.

Secondly, forests reduce the danger of damaging floods and help regulate our water supplies. Under a good forest, there is porous soil which easily absorbs heavy rains or melting snow. If this water didn't seep slowly into the soil, it would rush off to cause floods and erosion of the soil. And, of course, our forests provide wonderful vacation lands for millions of people.

The care of forests is called forestry, and it has been practiced in some European countries for hundreds of years. More than 400 years ago, England began to issue laws about the cutting down of forests, and in the eighteenth century, England actually began buying trees from other countries for replanting!

In most forests, it is important to harvest trees when they are mature. Otherwise, the old trees would take up space that could be better used for fast-growing younger trees. Also, unharvested old trees eventually decay and become useless.

After a tract of mature lumber is cut, the area is often replanted by hand. In very many places, however, we usually let nature do the replanting. But great care and skill are needed in harvesting and replanting trees to make sure that there'll be a good new growth of the right kinds of trees. This is why forestry has now become a science.

The country with the largest forest area is not the United States but the Soviet Union. Brazil ranks second, Canada third, and the United States fourth. Did you know that despite all the efforts to prevent them, about 200,000 forest fires occur each year in the United States?

Can one kind of tree produce the fruit of another kind of tree?—Yes! Grafting makes it possible. If a bud from a twig of a pear tree is carefully inserted in a slit made in the bark of a quince bush, a pear twig will grow. The quince bush will bear both pears and quinces!

WHAT IS GRAFTING?

In the same way, an almond tree can be made to produce both peaches and almonds. Or a crab apple tree can be made to bear a crop of fine cultivated apples. Sometimes grafting is used to produce freak trees and bushes, but it has nevertheless an important place in agriculture.

The first advantage of grafting is that it makes it possible for a nurseryman or gardener to be sure that his young trees or shrubs will bear the same quality and variety of fruit as the parent tree. A twig taken from a tree and grafted into another tree will produce the same type of fruit borne by the tree from which it was taken.

There are many methods of inserting the budded twigs, or scions, as they are called, into the stock of the other plant, but two rules must always be followed: First, only related species of trees or shrubs can be grafted. This means that apples can be grafted on pear and quince trees, and peaches can be grafted on apricot, almond, plum, or other stone fruit trees. But it is impossible to graft apples on peach trees, for example.

The second rule is that the cambium layer which carries the vital sap of the scion must touch the cambium layer of the stock on which it is grafted. Otherwise, the grafted twig cannot grow.

There are many different kinds of grafting. It can range from inserting a single bud under the bark to grafting long twigs across the wound of a tree in order to heal wide wounds in the bark.

Interestingly enough, grafting is being applied to animals, too. Eyes, for instance, have been replanted in such creatures as frogs, toads, rats, and rabbits. Surgeons have learned from these experiments how to help people who have been injured or disfigured. Bone taken from the ribs has actually been grafted onto the nasal bone to form a new nose, and skin has been grafted onto burnt tissue to remove scars!

TWIG GRAFTS

BUD GRAFT

The little boy who brings his line to the old fishing hole uses a piece of cork as a "floater" without ever wondering what keeps that piece of cork bobbing on top of the water. But the capacity of cork to float has

WHY DOES CORK FLOAT?

been known since ancient times, and cork life-preservers saved many a life thousands of years ago!

Cork is much lighter than water. The reason it floats is that water does not easily penetrate the walls of the cells, which are filled with air. This prevents the cork from becoming water-logged and sinking.

Cork is the outer bark of the cork oak tree. Two-thirds of the world's cork supply comes from Spain and Portugal, where the cork oak is cultivated extensively.

The cork oak grows from 6 to 12 metres tall and can measure as much as 1 metre in diameter. The bark of this tree is usually first stripped when the tree is about 20 years old. This doesn't injure or kill the tree; instead, the stripping actually benefits it.

About nine years later, another stripping is taken. The cork obtained from these first two strippings is coarse and rough. Later strippings, which are made about nine years apart for about a hundred years, give cork of a finer quality.

After stripping, the cork is stacked for several weeks to season, and then boiled to soften it and to remove the tannic acid. After boiling, the cork lies in pliable flat sheets, which are dried and then packed for shipping all over the world.

There are two kinds of raw cork: One is known as corkwood. This is the material used to make cork stoppers, floats, and life preservers. The second kind of raw cork is called grinding cork. It is ground up and then baked, some of it with binder materials. This is made into pipe covering, shoe fillers, automobile gaskets, and liners such as you find in the crown of bottle covers.

One of the greatest uses of cork today is for soundproofing rooms, and for insulating warehouses, freezer rooms, and refrigerators.

DATE PALM COCONUT PALM

Most of us probably think of the palm tree as purely decorative. We have seen pictures of these stately trees lining the streets in certain cities, or growing near tropical beaches.

HOW MANY KINDS OF PALM TREES ARE THERE?

Actually, there are about four thousand different species of palm trees and they are among the most useful trees known to man. Their fruit, their stems, and their tender leaves provide food. Their leaves, branches, and trunks furnish strong wood, cane, thatch, and twine. Their bark and leaves are used in making rugs, paper, cloth, baskets, hats, and brushes. The nuts of the ivory palm are carved into buttons. The sap of some palms is made into sugar, or wine, or honey.

Most palms have the same general shape. The majority of them have straight, slender, unbranching trunks with a cluster of leaves at the top. Others have branching stems and at least one is a trailing vine. They vary from a few centimetres to 23 metres tall. They are called palm trees because their leaves resemble a hand.

The shiny, leathery leaves are either fan-shaped or feather-shaped. Their measurements range from a few centimetres to 3 metres wide and 9 metres long. The fruit of a palm tree may be the size of a bean or as large as a football, as in the case of a coconut. It may be soft like a date, or have a woody covering.

There are palms in the southern United States, Mexico, South America, Asia, Africa, and Europe. In the tropical islands of the Pacific Ocean, there are great quantities of palms. Some grow in dry desert sand and some grow in rich damp earth.

While palms are mainly tropical, there is one species that grows at 3,960 metres in the northern Andes! The many varieties include: oil palm, sago palm, palmyra palm, cabbage palm (native to Australia), button-nut palm, petal-nut palm and coconut palm. Raffia for basket-making is made from the leaves of a malagasy palm.

The pomegranate is a fruit with a very interesting background in history. According to a legend of the ancient Greeks, the pomegranate was the fruit which Persephone ate while in Hades. Because she swallowed six of the seeds, she was forced to spend six months of each year in the underworld! To the Greeks, the juicy, many-seeded pomegranate always symbolized the powers of darkness.

WHAT IS A POMEGRANATE?

In China, the pomegranate was a symbol of fertility. King Solomon, according to the Bible, had an orchard of pomegranates. When the children of Israel wandered in the wilderness, they longed for the pomegranates they used to have in Egypt. Mohammed advised his followers, "Eat the pomegranate, for it purges the system of envy and hatred."

So you see the pomegranate was an important fruit in the East in ancient times. It is supposed to have originated in Persia, but from very ancient times, it has been grown in the warm countries of southern Asia, northern Africa, and southern Europe. Now it is common in South and Central America and in the southern United States.

The pomegranate grows as a bushy tree, or shrub. It grows from 1.5 to 6 metres high. Its leaves are glossy and at the ends of its thin twigs grow its coral-red, waxlike flowers.

The fruit is about the size of an orange. It is leathery-skinned and is colored a deep yellow, tinged with red. Inside this fruit are many small seeds. They are covered with a sweet, red, juicy pulp, which is often made into refreshing drinks. There is something about its taste that makes it especially agreeable to people who live in hot, dry regions.

There are many varieties of the pomegranate. In fact, a Moor who wrote about it 700 years ago described 10 different kinds which were grown in Spain at that time! In the United States, three leading varieties have been cultivated. They are called the Wonderful, the Paper-Shell, and the Spanish Ruby.

Bamboo is one of the most phenomenal examples of plant life. It shoots upward at a rate of 41 centimetres a day and can grow to 36 metres. It spreads so rapidly that if there is a road running through a growth of bamboo, that road may disappear completely in a month if it is not kept open!

WHAT IS BAMBOO?

There are about five hundred kinds of bamboos. They all have smooth, hollow, jointed stems with a strong, watertight partition at each joint, and all grow very rapidly. While most bamboos flower every year, there are some that bloom only three or four times in a century. The flowers are like those of grains and grasses. The fruit is usually like grain, and in some kinds, like nuts.

The bamboos are tropical and subtropical plants. They grow in Asia, in South America, and a few species grow in Africa. About thirty kinds of tall bamboos from other parts of the world have been successfully introduced into California and Florida.

The uses of bamboo are so numerous it is almost hard to believe. In the United States, bamboo is chiefly used in fishing poles, walking sticks, and phonograph needles. But it is in the Oriental countries that bamboo is really put to use.

People build entire houses with it, using large sections for posts and the split stems for rafters, roofing, and floor planks. They strip off the hard outer layers for mats and lattices to separate the rooms. The joints of the largest kinds are used for buckets and those of smaller ones for bottles.

There are even certain kinds of bamboos so hard that they can be made into crude knives, and beautiful and strong baskets are woven of strips from the outer coverings. In Japan, gardeners use hollowed bamboo stems for water pipes. In China, the inner pulp is made into the finer grades of native paper. The Javanese make bamboos into flutes. And many Oriental people eat the tender shoots of bamboo as a vegetable. So you see how valuable the bamboo is in certain parts of the world.

Amazingly enough, bamboo is a grass. It is the largest member of the family of grasses, though most people think of it as a bush or a tree.

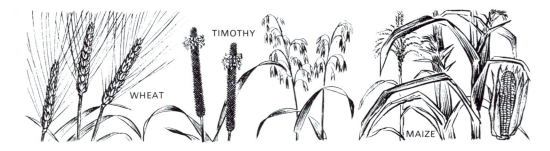

If you go to the store and want to buy some grass seed, you'll probably have a choice of a dozen kinds. That seems like quite a variety of grasses—but it doesn't give you any idea at all of the true picture.

HOW MANY KINDS OF GRASSES ARE THERE?

True grasses, as they are classified scientifically, include such things as corn, wheat, rye, barley, rice, and oats! As a matter of fact, there are actually about 4,500 kinds of grasses.

We know that the tallest of grasses, the bamboo, grows in warm climates to a height of more than 30 metres. The shortest grass, a pygmy variety of the Arctic Regions, may be only 5 centimetres tall.

The true grasses are distinguished from other plants in that the leaves are arranged in two opposite rows on the stem, with a single leaf at each joint. The leaf veins run in a regular, more or less parallel, arrangement. The flowers are usually not brightly colored.

In the United States alone, there are more than 1,500 varieties of grasses! A common cultivated grass is timothy, which is grown for hay and pasturage. Timothy grows in meadows and fields and along waysides throughout nearly all of North America.

One of the most famous and important American grasses is Kentucky bluegrass (June grass, spear grass). Its nutritious leaves and stems make it a rich pasture for stock. The quality of the bluegrass of Kentucky and the surrounding regions has made this region famous as a horse-breeding center. Because of its blue-green beauty and because it makes a dense, hardy turf when closely clipped, this grass is popular for lawns, parks, and golf courses in the northern United States.

When you realize the great variety of grasses that exist, it is not surprising that many of them serve as important sources of food and other purposes. In fact, most of the world's sugar comes from a grass, the sugar cane.

The rose has been the favorite flower of man for hundreds of years. No other flower has been mentioned so often by the poets of all ages and all countries. In the language of flowers, its blossoms have always been the symbol of love.

HOW MANY KINDS OF ROSES ARE THERE?

The rose has even played its part in history. In England, when the Houses of York and Lancaster were fighting for power, they chose white and red roses respectively for their emblems. The flowers gave their name to the War of the Roses!

Roses have been cultivated for many hundreds of years. So many varieties have been produced that it is impossible to tell just how many species exist. The estimate runs from 30 to more than 200! The rose is not limited to any one country. It can be found throughout the Northern Hemisphere, and will even grow in the mountain districts of the tropics.

The colors of roses vary from white through all the shades of pink, yellow, and orange to deep crimson and scarlet. The blossoms vary in size from the tiny buttonlike blooms of the ramblers to the widespreading blossoms of the highly cultivated varieties.

In all cases, however, the flowers are borne on sturdy bushes or rambling vines. The stems are generally provided with thorns. These thorns protect the rose from being eaten by various animals who might find it a delicious dish.

Cultivated roses may be divided into two general classes: summer roses, which bloom only once, usually in the early summer; and perpetual roses, which bloom several times during the season, even until late fall.

Summer roses include most of the hardy, old-fashioned roses, such as the damasks, moss roses, climbers, and yellow brier roses. The perpetual roses are usually less hardy. They include the musk, Chinese, and evergreen roses, as well as the beautiful tea roses.

There is a difference between the Arctic Region and the Arctic Circle. The Arctic Circle goes around the northern part of the earth in a perfect circle, 66½ degrees north of the equator. At one time, the

DOES ANYTHING GROW IN THE ARCTIC REGION?

Arctic Region was considered to be all land and water lying north of this circle.

But today, the Arctic Region is considered to be a geographical unit based on the combination of a number of different elements, especially vegetation and climate. It extends south into Canada and includes all of Greenland.

The climate of the Arctic is not continuously cold, nor is the Arctic an area of heavy snow covered by ice. During the short, hot summer, temperatures may rise to 27 degrees centigrade, and in some places, even reach 38 degrees. What makes the Arctic feel so cold is mainly the frequent, strong wind driving the dry crystals of snow before it.

Over much of the Arctic there are less than 38 centimetres of precipitation a year, although southern Greenland may have as much as 100 centimetres, so a great number of plants grow in the Arctic. More than 1,300 different species of plants have been identified there, and more than half of them are of the flowering kind! Large areas are covered with moss and lichens, but in the southern regions of the Arctic, there are fertile valleys and grasslands.

Animals are quite numerous in the Arctic and distributed widely. Land animals include the large herds of caribou or reindeer that perhaps number as many as 5,000,000 to 25,000,000 head. There are also musk oxen, mountain sheep, wolves, foxes, and grizzly bears.

Among the birds found in the Arctic are the eider duck, the goose, the swan, the tern, and the gull. Salmon, cod, flounder, trout and halibut, and, of course, the seal, walrus, and whale live there, too.

Suppose you have two friends who don't know each other. You introduce them and leave them alone. Nothing happens. They can't seem to get together. Then you join the company and, when all three of you are together, your two friends suddenly take to each other.

WHAT IS A CATALYST?

In this situation you have been a "catalyst!" In science, or chemistry, a catalyst is a substance which by its mere presence hastens or slows a chemical change. Suppose a manufacturer wants to produce a certain chemical compound synthetically, that is, by combining simpler substances to form it. He often finds that these simpler substances will not combine at all, or will combine too slowly to be of use. So he adds a catalyst.

A catalyst hastens or slows a chemical change, without changing itself permanently. If it does change for a time, it returns to its original form when the chemical process is completed. A catalyst may help in building up a chemical compound or breaking one down.

Almost any substance may be a catalyst. Water is a common one because many chemical changes take place only when moisture is present. When iron combines with oxygen we have a chemical reaction. But it requires moisture to take place. Water acts as a catalyst in the rusting of iron!

The snow-white, solid cooking fat that mother uses is the result of an interesting example of catalysts. We start with liquid oil, such as cottonseed oil. Hydrogen is forced under high pressure into a vessel containing the oil and the catalyst, which is nickel oxide or nickel. After one to four hours, the oil becomes saturated with hydrogen and changes to solid fat.

When the change is complete, the mixture is run out and put through a press. The catalyst is taken out and it can be used again and again!

Did you ever look at the edge of a mirror, where the glass is cut at an angle, and see all the colors of the rainbow there? The glass was acting as a prism. What was taking place was the "dispersion" of light; what you saw was the "spectrum." Now let's see what all of this means.

WHY DOES A PRISM PRODUCE COLORS?

When light passes from air into water, or from air into glass, it is changed in direction. This change is called "refraction," and you've probably noticed it thousands of times! For example, you've seen a spoon slanting into a glass of water. At the surface, the spoon looks as if there's a sharp bend in its handle. This is because the water has bent the beam of light slightly.

Now let's get back to our prism. When a beam of light strikes the glass at an angle, it is bent. Its speed actually becomes less. This is refraction. But instead of coming out as the white light that went in, it comes out in all the colors of the spectrum! Why is this? It's because white light is not a special kind of light, it is a mixture of all colors.

So when white light enters the prism, all the colors in the light are being bent or refracted. But not all the colors are bent the same way! The red light is bent, or refracted, the least. So it appears at the top of the spectrum, or rainbow of colors. Next to it is the orange, then the yellow, green, blue, indigo, and at the other end, the violet, which is bent the most. And that's why we see all the colors that are in white light coming out separately when light goes through a prism.

Man had known for a long time that this happened, but it was explained by saying that the water or glass changed the light in some way. Then Sir Isaac Newton, in 1666, performed an experiment that gave the correct explanation. Newton let sunlight into a darkened room through a narrow slit, placed a prism in the path of the light, and studied the spectrum thrown on the wall. He called the spreading effect "dispersion," and he proved that white light is a mixture of all colors.

If you put a pencil on a table and give it a twist, it will spin around several times. So will a ball, or in fact, any object that you can make turn. So what makes a top spin, is the force, or energy, you apply to it.

WHY DOES A TOP SPIN?

But what keeps a top spinning? And why does it keep spinning in a certain position?

The scientific principle that explains this is called "gyroscopic inertia." (It explains how a gyroscope spins too.) Any spinning body, if left free to spin, continues its same spin in space because of inertia. This means that if you were to have an imaginary line through its center, it would point in the same direction unless some outside force is applied.

When you throw a football through the air in a spinning motion, it will continue spinning on that axis unless the force of air or a player's blow changes it. As a matter of fact, our spinning earth follows the same principle. It is like a giant gyroscope. The axis runs through the North Pole and the South Pole, and this axis always points the same way—toward the North Star—day and night, year after year.

The spinning of tops has fascinated man since ancient times and in all parts of the world. It is one of the oldest and most popular toys. Eskimos make tops from ice, Indians from bone, South Sea Islanders from palm wood and volcanic ash!

In ancient Greece, men used to enjoy playing with tops. One of the most popular was the whipping top. It was kept moving by a whip wound around the upper part of the top. The lashing of the whip kept the top going around.

Top spinning is very popular in Japan and China, where some men become "experts" at it. In Japan there are tops that play music and tops that spin inside other tops. An African tribe has a top that it can spin in the air with a whip. And South Sea islanders often lie on their backs and spin tops on their big toes!

The most popular top to be found anywhere is probably the peg top. A string, wound around the bottom part, is pulled to make it spin.

If all sound is caused by vibration, why is one sound simply a noise and another sound pleasing or musical? The answer is that it depends on how the sound-making object vibrates. When the vibration is very regular

WHAT IS PITCH?

(that is, when the sounding body sends out waves at absolutely regular intervals), the result is a musical sound. If the vibration is not regular, or very sudden, the effect on our ears makes us call it a noise.

Sounds differ in many ways. We know, for example, when a sound is near and when it's far away. We can also tell that certain sounds are high and shrill and others are deep and low. And we can tell the sound of one musical instrument from another. Well, these three differences between one sound and another are loudness, pitch, and tone quality.

Loudness of a sound depends on two things: the distance from the ear, and the distance the vibrating object moves in its to-and-fro motion. (This is called amplitude.)

Pitch is the highness or lowness of the sound. Pitch depends on the speed of vibration of the sounding object. (This is called the frequency.) The greater the number of vibrations that reach the ear every second, the higher will be the pitch or tone. The quality or timbre (tone quality) of a sound depends on the number and strength of the overtones which are present in the sound. These are higher notes produced when more than one part of the object is vibrating.

Have you ever heard a loud sound like an explosion when a fast airplane was flying overhead? This sound is produced by a plane as it passes the sound barrier. Now what is this sound barrier and why does

WHAT IS THE
SOUND BARRIER?

the plane produce this BOOM?

Sound, as you know, travels at a certain speed. The speed depends on the altitude. At sea level, the speed of sound is about 760 miles (1,220 kilometres) per hour, and at a height of 11,000 metres, it's 660 miles (1,060 kilometres) per hour. When a plane flies at speeds close to the speed of sound, it undergoes certain kinds of stress. When it is flying at ordinary (slower) speeds, the forward part of the plane sends out a pressure wave. This wave travels at the speed of sound.

The pressure wave is produced by the buildup of particles of air as

84

the plane goes forward. The wave moves faster than the plane itself when the plane is flying at ordinary speeds. And the result seems to make the air move smoothly over the wing surfaces of the airplane.

Now let's take a plane that is flying at the speed of sound. The pressure wave ahead of the plane is not formed. Instead, what happens is that the pressure wave builds up in front of the wing (since the plane and the pressure wave are going forward at the same speed).

What happens now is that a shock wave occurs, and this causes greater stresses in the wing of the plane. In fact, the expression "sound barrier" was developed in the days before planes could fly at the speed of sound—and the phrase was supposed to describe the stresses that a plane would undergo at that speed. It was thought of as a "barrier."

But it seems that the speed of sound is not a barrier at all! Engineers and designers of planes have overcome the problems of the new stresses. And all we have left today from the old concept is the BOOM caused by the shock wave when a plane travels faster than sound.

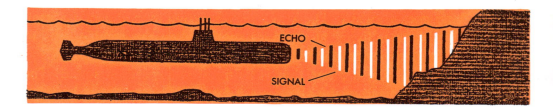

Now that we know something about sound, let's find out what makes an echo and whether an echo can travel through water.

Sound travels outward from its source at a speed of about 375

CAN AN ECHO TRAVEL THROUGH WATER?

metres per second in open air. Sound travels in waves much like the ripples made by a pebble thrown into the water. However, sound waves go out in all directions like the light from an electric bulb.

A sound wave may meet an obstacle and bounce back, or be reflected just as light is reflected. When a sound wave is thus reflected, it is heard as an echo. Therefore, an echo is sound repeated by reflection.

Not all obstacles can cause echoes; there are some objects which absorb the sound instead of reflecting it. If a sound is reflected by some obstacle, only one echo is heard. This is called a simple echo. If the sound is reflected by two or more obstacles, the echo may be repeated many times. The echo, however, becomes fainter each time until it dies away altogether. When repeated more than once, it is known as a compound echo, or reverberation.

An echo cannot be heard as a separate sound unless the sound is made some distance away from the reflecting surface. This allows time between the sound and echo. At a distance of 167 metres from a wall, for example, the echo returns in just one second.

Whether an echo can travel through water depends on whether sound can travel through water—and we know that it can. In fact, sound travels through water at a speed of more than 1,430 metres a second! This ability of sound to produce an echo through water has proven very useful.

Ships are often equipped with devices for sending and receiving sound signals under water. By sending out sharp signals and timing the echoes, a navigator can measure the distance from his vessel to the ocean bottom or to any nearby vessel or obstacle!

Chapter 2

LIVING CREATURES AROUND US

Do you like to read detective stories or watch them on TV? What makes them exciting for you and me is the suspense. We want to find out who did it, or how, or why. But the world around us is full of mysteries, too.

WHAT IS BIOLOGY?

Why do animals behave as they do? What makes plants grow in special ways? How does our body do this or that?

Man has always wanted to solve these mysteries of life. And just the way a detective proceeds on a case, the first thing that had to be done was to gather all the facts. The gathering and the study of these facts was called natural history.

Today we call this science biology. The word comes from two Greek words: *bios,* meaning "life," and *logos,* meaning "a study." So biology is the study of all organisms, plant and animal. What is studied about them is their form, their activities, their functions, and their environment.

But today our biologist-detectives are not satisfied just to collect a lot of facts, helter-skelter. They try to establish some links between the facts, some relationship. For example, they are interested in discovering the relationships that exist between man and the millions of living things that surround him. They want to know what effect these living things have had on man's own development.

Biologists are interested in the greatest mystery of all: how life first started on earth and why it took the forms it did. So they also study all the conditions that are necessary to life. And just as a detective bureau keeps a file, they try to classify every organism which exists on our planet.

In looking for clues that will answer their questions, biologists get a helping hand from nature. They dredge the icy depths of the oceans and scale the peaks of the tallest mountains looking for clues. They hack their way through steaming jungles, and peer for hours into microscopes. Sometimes they perform strange experiments in order to get at the mystery of life.

Biology is a very complex science. It has two main divisions: botany, which deals with plants; and zoology, which deals with animals. And each of these divisions is separated into dozens of subdivisions!

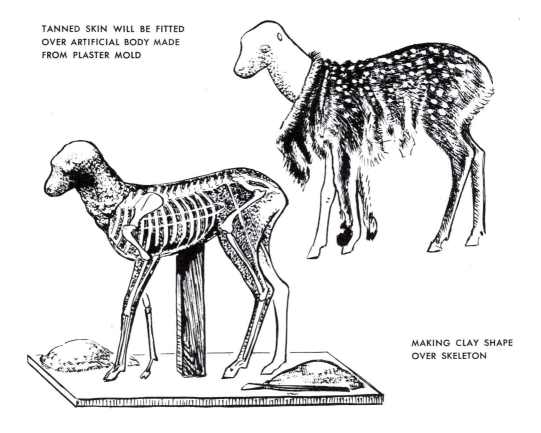

TANNED SKIN WILL BE FITTED
OVER ARTIFICIAL BODY MADE
FROM PLASTER MOLD

MAKING CLAY SHAPE
OVER SKELETON

The animals you see on exhibit in natural-history museums are the product of taxidermy. So are the reptiles and birds, and the fish that proud fishermen display on their walls. We think of them as "stuffed animals," and in most cases, this is just what taxidermy involves.

WHAT IS TAXIDERMY?

Taxidermy is the art of mounting birds, animals, fish, and reptiles. It has been practiced for about 300 years, and the earliest "stuffed animal" in existence is a rhinoceros that was mounted in the sixteenth century.

When an animal is dead, its organs and other parts begin to decay. To preserve the animal so that it looks real and "alive," the insides have to be removed. But the exterior of the bird, fish, or animal can be preserved. A taxidermist has the job of fitting this "outside" of the animal on a framework so that the color, texture, and general appearance will look natural.

Let's see how taxidermy is performed with larger animals, such as a deer. As soon as the animal is collected, measurements are made of different parts of the body and the skin is carefully removed. The skin is well-salted to preserve it for shipping to the taxidermist's studio. The flesh and muscles are cut away. The bones are cleaned and the entire skeleton is saved, if possible. The skin is tanned, or leathered, so it won't crack and cause the hair to fall out.

What the taxidermist gets, therefore, is just the skin and bones of the animal, plus all careful measurements. He poses the skeleton in the position desired, holding it up with rods. Then wet modeling clay is applied over the skeleton. The taxidermist models the exact shape and size of the animal's body in clay.

Then a plaster of Paris mold is made over the clay form. An artificial body is then made inside this mold. Finally, the tanned skin of the animal is fitted into place over the artificial body. Glass is used for eyes, and oil paints are used to restore faded colors. You then have an animal that looks natural and lifelike, ready to be exhibited! The mounting of birds, fish, and reptiles, is done differently, but the basic idea is the same.

WARM-BLOODED   COLD-BLOODED

As we move about from place to place, we may feel changes in the temperature around us, but we don't expect the temperature of our body itself to change. And it doesn't. We are classified as "homeothermic,"

WHAT IS THE BODY TEMPERATURE OF ANIMALS?

and in our class are included all warm-blooded animals, all mammals, domestic animals, and birds.

But there are animals whose body temperature does change with the temperature around them. They are called "poikilothermic," and they include insects, snakes, lizards, tortoises, frogs, and fishes. Their temperature tends to be slightly lower than the temperature of their environment. They are cold-blooded animals.

We know that the normal body temperature of man is considered to be 37 degrees centigrade. But there are many changes in the temperature that occur quite "normally." For example, man's body temperature is lowest about 4:00 A.M.; the skin temperature is lower than the internal temperature; taking in food raises the temperature for an hour or two; muscular work may raise the temperature; alcohol lowers the internal temperature.

The body temperature of animals has quite a range, going from 35 degrees in the elephant to 43 degrees in small birds. Here is how animals may be classified according to their body temperature:

From 35 to 38 degrees — man, monkey, mule, ass, horse, rat, mouse and elephant. From 37 to 39 degrees — cattle, sheep, dog, cat, rabbit, and pig. From 40 to 41 degrees — turkey, goose, duck, owl, pelican, and vulture. From 42 to 43 degrees — fowl, pigeon, and several small common birds.

Animals, like man, have to eliminate excess body heat in order to maintain a constant body temperature. Animals who don't sweat have to do this by panting — which is why your dog often pants on a hot day.

When we use the word "mammoth" today, we mean something that is huge or colossal. But there actually was an animal that lived long ago that is called the "mammoth." It was a kind of elephant that is now extinct and that lived in many different parts of the world during the Stone Age.

WHAT WAS THE MAMMOTH?

Even though this ancient type of elephant is called the "mammoth," it was about the same size as the Indian elephant that exists today. It had a kind of pointed skull and very unusual tusks curved in a spiral with the tips pointing to each other.

What made this elephant unique and quite different from the elephants we know today is that it was covered with long hair. In fact, the hair was so long that it almost reached the ground. The body was shaped into a great hump at the back of the neck, and the ears were small.

The whole body of this creature was covered with an undercoat of yellowish-brown wooly hair, and the long, black thicker hairs came out through this undercoat. The hair also grew on the ears. The first thing you'd probably say if you saw a mammoth today would be: "Get a haircut!"

Obviously an animal with so much hair on it would be more comfortable in a cold climate. And the mammoth is the only kind of elephant ever to exist that felt at home in a cold or Arctic climate. So it lived in Siberia quite comfortably, and probably survived there until a fairly recent period.

In other parts of the world, such as France and England, it survived only as long as the glacial period, or ice age, lasted. In fact, when things warmed up in England between glacial periods, the mammoth moved up north, following the retreating ice.

There were also mammoths in North America during that age, and some of these reached a height of 4 metres. Mammoths, because of their great weight, often sank into ice-cold mud which later became frozen. That's why frozen mammoths are still sometimes found very well preserved in places like Siberia.

TASMANIAN WOLF

KANGAROO

WOMBAT

OPOSSUM

When European explorers visited the New World, they often brought back with them whatever they considered strange and new. Thus the South American opossum was brought back from Brazil in 1500, and

WHAT ARE MARSUPIALS?

Captain Cook in 1770 told about seeing kangaroos in Australia. Nobody in Europe had ever known about such creatures before — they were marsupials.

The marsupials are a separate order of animals. The name comes from the Greek word *marsupion,* which means "pouch." What sets these animals apart is that their young, after they are born, live and are fed in a pouch on their mother's body.

This is necessary because young marsupials are so tiny and helpless when they are born that they cannot take care of themselves. They do not even know how to eat. Even after they have grown to a fair size, young kangaroos and opossums run back to hide in their mother's pouch when they are frightened.

Judging from the fossils found in rocks, marsupials were once common in all parts of the world. Today almost all of them are found in Australia and the nearby islands. The only other true marsupials are the various species of opossums which live in North and South America.

Australian marsupials range in size from tiny molelike creatures only a few inches long to the giant kangaroos. Some of them, such as the bandicoots, look like rabbits. Others, such as the wombats, look like beavers. Still others, such as the thylacines and the Tasmanian wolves, look like wolves.

They may live on the ground or dwell in the trees like monkeys. Some of the phalangers, which are one family of marsupials, can even glide from tree to tree like flying squirrels. The food of marsupials is quite varied. Some eat only vegetables, others are meat-eaters or insect-eaters, and some eat anything they can find.

A bloodhound, of course, is a breed of dog. But how did it develop? Where did it come from?

The history of the dog itself goes back many hundreds of thousands

WHAT IS A BLOODHOUND?

of years. Some scientists believe that dogs are the result of the mating of their cousins, the wolves and the jackals. It is generally believed however that our modern dogs and the wolves are descended from a very remote common ancestor.

During the many years that dogs have been tamed, men have developed more than 200 breeds of dogs. Sometimes they have bred dogs for strength, like that of the mastiff; for speed, like the greyhound; or for keenness of scent, like that of the bloodhound.

The bloodhound is typical of the breed of dog known as the hound. It is probably a descendant of the dog which at one time was called the "St. Hubert." Hounds generally have smooth coats, are heavy, and have drooping ears and upper lips.

Like all hounds, the bloodhounds follow the quarry by scent—keener in them than in any other dog. They are slow put persistent, and if they lose the scent they cast back until they find the trail again. It is these two qualities, their keen scent and their ability to be persistent, that make bloodhounds ideal for tracking down escaped criminals and for other use by police.

There are many other interesting types of hounds. For example, otter hounds, harriers, beagles, and bassets are all smaller than blood-hounds and are used in hunting small game, such as rabbits.

The pointer is a hound that is one of the best bird dogs. It was given its name because it "points" at the game.

WHY DO DEER SHED THEIR ANTLERS?

Deer are vegetarians who feed on moss, bark, buds, leaves, or water plants. They are usually very timid animals, and they depend on their speed for safety. They generally feed at night. They have very good eyesight, and their senses of hearing and smell are so sharp that they are able to detect danger easily. Deer vary in size from the little pudu, which is only a foot tall, to the great moose, which may weigh more than 450 kilograms.

The chief distinguishing marks of the deer are the antlers. Nearly all the males have antlers, and in the case of the caribou and reindeer, females have them too. The antlers are not hollow, like the horns of cattle, but are made of a honeycomb structure. Each spring, the male deer grows a new pair of antlers, and each winter he loses them after the mating season is over. In some varieties of deer, the antlers are single shafts, in others there may be as many as 11 branches to each antler!

Since the number of branches varies with age, you can tell how old a deer is from its antlers.

The first year, two knoblike projections appear on the deer's forehead. These are called the "pedicles," and they are never lost. The antlers break off from the pedicle each spring and new antlers are grown during the summer. The second year, a straight shaft grows out of the pedicle, and in the third year, the first branch appears.

When the antlers are growing, they are covered with a sensitive skin called the "velvet." This is filled with blood vessels which feed the antlers and build up the bone. When the antlers have reached their full size, after a period of two to four months, the blood supply is cut off from the velvet by the formation of a ring around the base of the antlers. This makes the velvet wither and dry up, and it finally falls off. Usually, the deer help by rubbing their antlers against trees.

Because a bear can stand up on its hindlegs, and because some bears are pretty huge, indeed, all kinds of exaggerated tales have sprung up about them. There are legends about great hunters who fought with or killed giant bears.

HOW BIG IS THE BIGGEST BEAR?

The bear family does include some pretty big fellows. The largest of all flesh-eating animals are certain bears. A lion, for example, seldom weighs as much as 230 kilograms. The biggest tiger may weigh 270 kilograms. But a good-sized polar bear or grizzly bear may get up to as much as 400 or 450 kilograms.

The biggest of all bears are the Alaskan brown bears. Some of the males weigh over 680 kilograms and when standing up they may be three metres tall. That's a lot of bear! And just to give you the other end of the picture, there are bears (the Malaysian bear) that weigh less than 45 kilograms when full-grown.

There are two curious ideas that people sometimes have about bears. One is that they are awkward or clumsy, and the other is that they are stupid. Neither is true. A bear seems clumsy because of the peculiar way he walks. Bears are flat-footed, which means the heel of the foot rests on the ground like a man's.

When a bear walks, he moves both legs on one side of the body forward at the same time. So he seems to have a rolling motion. But don't let that fool you. A bear galloping along on all fours can beat any human runner!

Because bears seem so slow and awkward, people imagine that they're not very bright. But ask any zoo keeper and he'll tell you the bear is among the cleverest and most intelligent of animals. Besides, in Europe, bears are often trained to perform amazing tricks in the circus.

In North America, there are four distinct types of bears: the black bear, the grizzly bear, the Alaska brown bear, and the polar bear. Of these, the grizzly bear is the toughest. In fact, it's the most dangerous American mammal. In olden days, the Indians considered it one of their greatest enemies, and the warrior who was able to kill a grizzly bear was regarded as a great brave!

One of the gentlest of all animals is the hare. When you consider how mild, timid, and defenseless this creature is, you might wonder how it can survive in a world full of enemies. But then you've also probably noticed its strong hindlegs. Those legs give it plenty of speed and endurance. And, of course, you know how rapidly hares and rabbits breed.

WHAT'S THE DIFFERENCE BETWEEN RABBITS AND HARES?

That's another reason why they manage to survive.

Hares and rabbits are rodents, which means they have long, sharp front teeth. Their hindlegs are longer than their forelegs, so that they actually run faster uphill than downhill! When they are pursued, they resort to some clever tricks. One is to crisscross their tracks, and the other is to take huge leaps in order to break the scent. They can also signal danger to each other by thumping the ground with their hindfeet.

Hares and rabbits are purely vegetarians, but they can live very well on the inner bark of trees. There are many differences between hares and rabbits. Hares are larger, and their feet and ears are longer. Hares do not dig burrows or live in groups, as do rabbits. Hares are born open-eyed and furry, while rabbits are born blind and hairless. Hares and rabbits never mate.

North America is the home of many different types of hares. One of the best known is the jack hare, which is usually mistakenly called "jack rabbit." It is found throughout the West. Jack hares are more than

0.5 metres in length and have enormous ears. They are so fast that they can sometimes make a leap of 6 metres. They are a great nuisance to farmers in the West, and are often rounded up and killed by thousands.

The March hare, whom we know from "Alice in Wonderland," is a common European hare. In March, its mating season, it disregards caution, coming out at all times of the day, and performing amusing acrobatic feats.

Rabbits came originally from the western shores of the Mediterranean. They are social animals, living together in burrows, called "warrens." A rabbit may mate when it is six months old. Its young are born within a month. There may be from three to eight in a litter and a female rabbit may bear from four to eight litters in a year. So if the rabbit has no natural enemies, it can become quite a nuisance. In Australia for instance, three pairs of rabbits were introduced many years ago, and today the rabbit is a great national pest!

One of the most interesting animals to be found anywhere is the mole. Moles live in every part of the United States and there are about 30 different species. But they are so seldom seen by people that they have become a kind of mysterious creature.

CAN A MOLE SEE?

You can find a mole by looking for the long ridges of cracked earth it makes across fields. This is the roof of its tunnel, for the mole spends its whole life in darkness under the ground.

A mole grows to about 15 centimetres long. It has a fine, velvety fur, the color of a mouse, and a tail about 3 centimetres. It has no neck at all, and its ears are tiny openings hidden in the fur. A mole does have eyes, but they are tiny points covered with fur and skin. This is why it was once believed that moles are blind. A mole can see, but very poorly.

If you picked up a mole and put it down on the ground, it would race about until it found a soft spot and would begin to dig at once. A mole is one of the most efficient diggers in nature. Its forefeet are powerful and shaped like spades. It can dig a burrow and disappear into it in less than one minute! In a single night, it can dig a tunnel 68 metres long.

Moles usually live in a colony in a sort of fortress undergound. From the surface, we see a little hillock of earth called a "molehill." Right under it, there are two circular galleries or passageways, one above the other. Vertical passageways connect them, so the mole can move up and down. The upper gallery has five of these openings which go down to a central chamber where the mole rests.

A whole series of complicated tunnels lead from these galleries and from the central chamber to the feeding grounds, to the nest, and even to an "emergency" exit. These underground tunnels are so well built that field mice and gophers often use them to get roots and plants for food. But it isn't too safe for other animals to venture into a mole's home. It has such sharp front teeth that it can fight viciously and kill mice much bigger than itself. Its chief food, however, consists of insects and earthworms. A mole is so greedy that if it is unable to get food for 12 hours it will die!

The porcupine has always been considered an annoying, disagreeable animal. In fact, even Shakespeare described it that way. In Hamlet, there is the line: "Like quills upon the fretful porcupine."

DO PORCUPINES SHOOT THEIR QUILLS?

Actually, the porcupine is quite a harmless' animal, who simply likes to be let alone. During the winter, it curls up in a hollow log or cave and sleeps most of the time. In the summer, it moves slowly through the woods in search of bark, twigs, roots, and leaves of trees and shrubs.

Porcupines can be found in Europe, Africa, India, and South America as well as in the United States and Canada. The American species of porcupine is nearly 1 metre long and weighs from 7 to 13 kilograms. Its quills are about 18 centimetres long and yellowish-white, with black tips. The quills grow among the softer hairs of the porcupine, and consist of a shaft with a hard point.

When the porcupine is born, the quills are fine and silky. It takes them several weeks to thicken into hard quills. When a porcupine is attacked, it bristles up its coat of quills and curls into a bristling ball.

These quills are fastened rather loosely into the body of the porcupine. Since the porcupine will sometimes swing its tail into the face of an enemy, the quills come out easily during such an action. This is what has made people think a porcupine "shoots" its quills. It doesn't. They just fly out.

The porcupine usually sleeps during the day and comes out to feed at night. It uses its long, sharp claws to climb trees, and then it sits on a limb to gnaw away at the bark and twigs. It crams bark, twigs, leaves, all into its mouth at once. Because of its liking for bark, the porcupine does much damage to forests. A single porcupine has been known to kill 100 trees in a winter!

Another strong liking the porcupine has is for salt. It will walk boldly into camps and gnaw any article that has been touched by salt or even by perspiring hands!

Some people believe that raccoons wash all their food before eating it. There is some truth to this. Most raccoons do wash their food, and there have been cases where raccoons refused to eat food when they couldn't find any water nearby!

DO RACCOONS WASH THEIR FOOD?

But on the other hand, raccoons have been known to eat food even when they were some distance from water, though perhaps they weren't too happy about it. And some raccoons have been observed to eat without ever washing their food.

Nobody really knows why raccoons wash their food. It isn't because of cleanliness, since they may wash it in water that is actually dirtier than the food! Besides, they will wash food caught in the water, which certainly doesn't need washing. So the reason is probably that the raccoon enjoys feeling the food in water. It seems to make it tastier!

The name "raccoon" comes from the Algonquin Indian word *arakhumen*. The raccoon lives from southern Canada to Panama, except in the high Rockies. Raccoons vary in size from about 65 to 90 centimetres long. In weight they can range from 1 to over 11 kilograms. The general color of the fur is grayish or brownish. The 25-centimetre tail is dark brown with four to six yellowish rings. The eyes are covered with a black mask. The ears are medium-sized, the nose pointed, and the front feet are used like hands.

Raccoons live in places where there is water and trees for dens. Their food, which they hunt at night, is principally crayfish, clams, fish and frogs, which they catch in the muddy water. In season raccoons also feed on nuts, berries, fruit, and paticularly young corn.

The year-round home, or den, where the young are born is usually in the hollow limb or trunk of a tree. Raccoons give birth to young but once a year, with four or five to a litter. By fall, the young raccoons are large enough to start their life alone.

Do you know what the word "armadillo" means? It's a Spanish word meaning "the little armored one." And that's just what an armadillo is, a little mammal with a bony covering that is like armor.

WHAT IS AN ARMADILLO?

There are ten different kinds of armadillos living from southern United States to southern South America. The upper parts of armadillos are covered with bony shells. These include one on the head and two solid pieces on the back. These two pieces are connected by a flexible center section made up of movable bands. This enables the armadillo to twist and turn.

The number of these bands in the center is sometimes used as a name for the armadillo. For example, there is the seven-banded the eight-banded, and the nine-banded armadillo. The nine-banded armadillo is the only one found in the United States. The tail of the armadillo is also completely covered by armor—except in the case of one kind, and naturally it's called the soft-tailed armadillo!

A very curious thing about the armadillo is that its teeth are simple pegs without enamel. It's one of those contradictions that nature seems fond of. A shell of armor on the body—and soft teeth! Most of the animals have just one set of teeth they are born with, and that's all.

As a result of having such teeth, the armadillo has to eat soft food such as ants, termites, larvae, grubs, and bugs. As you know, such food is found in leaves and the soft ground, so to get at it the armadillo has to dig for it. Nature made up for the soft teeth by giving the armadillo long, strong claws and powerful forearms. An armadillo can dig faster than a dog! And it uses the claws and forearms to dig its burrow or to make itself a hole quickly into which it can escape from its enemies.

The way most armadillos escape from their enemies is by digging or running away. Only one kind, the three-banded armadillo, rolls itself into a ball. Its shell is much heavier than that of the others, so this becomes a good way of protecting itself.

When man gets hungry and the supply of food is limited, he seems able to eat just about anything! You might consider the armadillo to be pretty good proof of this.

ARE ARMADILLOS EDIBLE?

Here are creatures about as repulsive as can be, yet the natives of Central and South America are known to eat them! The armadillo is like a pig with armor. Its whole back and the sides of its body are covered with bony plates, jointed together.

The reason for these plates is obvious. They protect the armadillo in time of danger and from attack by its enemies. In fact, some types of armadillos can roll themselves into a tight round ball when they are attacked. The only thing that shows then is the armor plate.

Oddly enough, the armadillo is a very timid creature. It has such poor eyesight that it must depend entirely on its sense of smell and its hearing to know where it is and where it's going. The legs of an armadillo are very short, but when it is frightened it can scamper away with amazing speed. It also has very powerful digging claws, and when it decides to bury itself, it seems to disappear before your eyes.

Armadillos are usually brownish-black in color, with yellowish markings above and a yellowish-white underbelly. They are constantly digging away and they make their homes in burrows in the dry soil of arid regions. Some armadillos are found as far north as Texas and others as far south as Argentina.

The great armadillo has a body 1 metre long and a tail almost as long. But there are some that are only 13 or 15 centimetres. Fossils of armadillos have been found nearly 2 metres in length, and they must have looked like giant turtles. Armadillos feed at night on insects, worms, roots, and fruit.

Kangaroos are one of the strangest and oldest species of animals on earth today. We know that there was a kind of kangaroo in existence hundreds of thousands of years ago which was nearly as large as a horse!

HOW FAR CAN A KANGAROO JUMP?

Today kangaroos are found in Australia, which is sometimes called the "Land of the Kangaroo," and even has this animal on its national coat of arms.

The kangaroo is the best-known of the marsupials, which means "animals with pouches." The mother kangaroo has a fur-lined pouch between her hind legs in which she carries the young and nurses it. A young kangaroo lives in this pouch until it's a pretty good size.

When a baby kangaroo is born, it's a tiny, pink, naked mass, not much over an inch long! The mother places it in the pouch right after birth and the baby is quite helpless for some time. But by the time it's six months old, it's as large as a puppy. It rides around inside the pouch with its head sticking out. When mama stops to feed on tree branches, the young baby pulls off leaves at the same time and feeds itself.

Even after a young kangaroo has been taught to walk and run by its mother, it likes to stay in the warm, safe pouch. And when danger threatens, the mother hops over to it, picks it up in her mouth without stopping, and drops it safely into her pouch.

A full-grown kangaroo stands about 2 metres tall. It has short

front legs with small paws, and very long hind legs. These powerful
hind legs enable a kangaroo to take jumps of 3 to 4.5 metres at a
time! The kangaroo uses its big, long tail to rest and to balance itself
when jumping.

In Australia, kangaroos are hunted because they kill the crops.
But they also make good eating, and their skin produces good, strong
leather. The kangaroo's protection is its speed and its ability to hear
an enemy at a great distance. When a kangaroo is cornered by hunting
dogs, it can seize a dog with its forefeet and kill it with one swing
of its hindfoot!

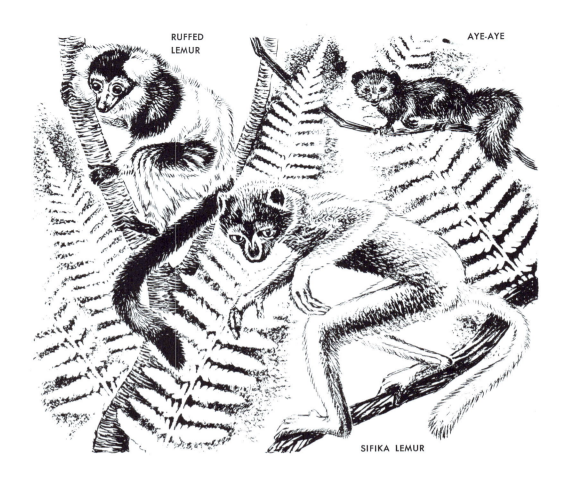

RUFFED LEMUR

AYE-AYE

SIFIKA LEMUR

The lemurs are the most primitive members of the order Primates, which includes the monkeys. Today, lemurs are found in Madagascar, Africa, and parts of Asia. At one time they also lived in America and Europe where their fossil remains have been found.

WHAT IS A LEMUR?

Lemurs differ from other Primates in having a long foxlike face, and a long claw instead of a nail on the second toe. All the lemurs are arboreal (live in trees). You don't very often see a lemur in a zoo, because apparently they don't survive too well in captivity.

Lemurs live on a mixed diet which may include fruit, seeds, insects, birds' eggs, or meat. Some of them are diurnal (active in the daytime) and some are nocturnal (active at night).

There are many different kinds of lemurs and some of them are quite interesting. One large lemur lives in Madagascar and is called the "sifaka." It is brightly colored—white with black, red, or brown markings. There is a fold of skin between its arms and body that is probably a help to it in its long leaps from one tree to another.

Another group of lemurs is called the "true lemurs," of which 13 kinds live in Madagascar. They have long tails and vary greatly in color. The smallest of the lemurs is 13 centimetres in length and has a tail of 15 centimetres. It is known as the "mouse lemur". These little animals store fat around the base of the tail in good times. During the dry season when food is scarce, they sleep in a hollow tree, living off the fat in the tail.

The aye-aye is very different fom other Madagascar lemurs. It has very large ears, long coarse fur, a long bushy tail, and long fingers. Its big toes have nails, but the other fingers and toes have claws. One kind of lemur, the tarsier, has a neck so flexible that, without turning its body, it can turn its head to look backwards!

WOOL

The wool that grows on a sheep is like the hair that grows on your head. It grows the same way and is the protective covering of the sheep against cold weather.

DOES A SHEEP GROW WOOL EVERY YEAR?

Once a year, usually in the spring when warm weather is ahead and the sheep no longer needs its "protection," the sheep are given a haircut and all the wool is sheared off. It is usually full of burrs, thorns, and natural oil which is called "lanolin." It comes off almost whole, like a hide, and is then rolled up and tied with wool twine.

After that the wool is cleaned, at which time it is called "scoured wool." Then, the wool is combed to straighten out the curls. Next, it is spun into yarn. The wool yarn is then made into cloth by weaving or knitting.

Nobody knows when man first tamed the sheep. But primitive man kept the same sheep for both wool and meat. Then, through centuries of breeding, different types have been developed, some especially valuable for their wool, others for their meat. One type, called the "Merino," which originated in Spain or Africa, is practically a mop of wool with a nose and four legs protruding!

In Australia and the United States, there are varieties of the Merino type which produce great quantities of wonderful wool. In fact, sheep raising and wool production are among the earliest American enterprises. When Columbus returned to America in 1493, he brought sheep with him to what is now Santo Domingo and Cuba. Until the middle of the nineteenth century, there were huge sheep flocks in New England. When the West was first settled, the great ranges had flocks of thousands of animals.

Today, the United States produces about 48,000 tonnes of wool a year. Australia is the largest wool-growing country in the world with a yearly wool clip of about 700,000 tonnes. New Zealand is another major producer of wool with an annual wool clip of about 380,000 tonnes.

Thousands of years ago, many kinds of giant monsters roamed about the great forests then covering the earth. Even though these beasts were immense in size, they were not able to endure the hardships they

WHERE DID ELEPHANTS ORIGINATE?

had to undergo, brought about by changing climate and disappearance of food.

One by one they perished, until of all those huge animals, there are only two species remaining, the African and Asiatic elephants. The ancestors of the elephant were great monsters, known as "mammoths." Their skeletons can be seen in museums, and they are quite awesome sights! Their bones have been dug up in caves and river beds in North America and Europe. In far-off Siberia, the carcass of one was found frozen hard in ice, perfectly preserved even to its eyes!

Although elephants seem to have once inhabited many parts of the earth, they are now found in their wild state only in Africa and tropical Asia.

ASIATIC ELEPHANT

AFRICAN ELEPHANT

Elephants are the largest land animals, and in many ways, among the most interesting. They are mild and gentle, and quite intelligent. They are more easily trained than any other beast except the domestic dog.

The shape of the elephant's legs, like four huge pillars, is necessary to support its immense weight. Its ivory tusks are really overgrown teeth. These tusks are used to dig up roots for food and also as weapons for defense. The brain of the elephant is comparatively small, considering the size of the animal.

The most remarkable part of the elephant's body is its trunk. It is an extension of the nose and upper lip, and it serves the elephant as hand, arm, nose, and lips, all in one. There are about 40,000 muscles in the trunk, so it is very strong and flexible. The tip of the trunk ends in a sort of finger which is so sensitive that it can pick up a small pin!

When most people say "Cat," they are thinking of the small, domesticated cat. But the cat family is really quite an amazing one, and includes leopards, lions, tigers, and jaguars!

HOW LONG HAVE CATS BEEN PETS?

All cats, large or small, have the same general proportions of body, and the same food habits. All cats are meat eaters and kill their own food. Depending on the size of the cat, this food ranges from small mice and birds up to large zebras, deer, antelope, and cattle.

A cat has soft cushioned toes on which it moves very silently. It also has five sharp pointed claws on each of its front feet and four on each of its hindfeet. The sounds made by cats are mewing, purring, howling, and screaming. Some of the large cats, such as the lion and tiger, often roar. By the way, because of the formation of certain bones in the throat, none of these four cats, the lion, tiger, leopard or jaguar, are able to purr.

Cats have been around in the world since the beginning of time. Fossils of cats have been found which are millions of years old! But the domestication of the cat took place only a short time ago in terms of the history of man.

It is now believed that cats have been domesticated for about 4,500 or perhaps 5,000 years. Probably one of the small wildcats of Europe, North Africa, or Asia was the original ancestor of the domestic cat.

We know that the Egyptians had tame cats 4,000 years ago, and they worshipped the cat as a god. Their goddess Bast, or Pacht, was shown in pictures with a cat's head, and sacrifices were offered to cats. The cat also represented their chief god and goddess, Ra and Isis.

In Egypt, when a house cat died, the family and servants shaved their eyebrows and went into mourning. The death of a temple cat was mourned by the whole city. Many mummies of cats have been found, prepared in the same way as the mummies of kings and nobles. The penalty for killing a cat was death!

The tame cat appeared in Europe about the year A.D. 1000, and it was usually believed to be an evil spirit rather than a god!

The squirrel is such a familiar sight to us in parks or in the country that we might imagine that our own land is its home. Actually, there are squirrels in every part of the world except Australia!

ARE THERE SQUIRRELS IN OTHER COUNTRIES?

In fact, there are very many different kinds of squirrels. They may be as large as cats or as small as mice. They may have soft, warm fur or prickly spines. They may scamper through the branches or glide easily through the air from treetop to treetop on flaps of skin that are like parachutes. Some of them even live in the ground. But almost all of them are friendly, chattering little animals with long bushy tails and bright beady eyes.

Squirrels form a separate family of rodents, or gnawing animals. They are divided into two general groups: the ground squirrels and the tree squirrels. In the same family as the ground squirrels are wood-chucks, chipmunks, and prairie dogs. The best known tree squirrels are the little red squirrels, the gray squirrels, the fox squirrels, and the tufted-ear squirrels.

Tree squirrels, as a rule, spend the winter in some hollow tree trunk, which they line with leaves and twigs. In the spring, they often build another home high up in the treetops. There they raise their families of from four to six young.

The harmful red squirrel often eats the eggs and young of birds. However, most tree squirrels feed almost entirely on nuts, acorns, and pine cones. The squirrels must store up enough food in the fall for their use during the cold months.

The flying squirrels differ from all other squirrels in having the skin on their sides enlarged into flaps. When the animals stretch out their legs, these flaps, like the planes of a glider, help them to shoot through the air. Flying squirrels live in warm parts of North America, Europe, and Asia. They are seldom seen, for they usually sleep during the day.

Another interesting squirrel is a certain Asiatic squirrel which changes its coloring during the mating season, just as male birds do!

GRAY SQUIRREL

FLYING SQUIRREL

There are few animals that have played as important a role in history as the horse. This is because the horse has been so useful in warfare. Can you imagine what wandering tribes, invading armies, knights,

WHO FIRST TAMED THE HORSE?

and soldiers all over the world would have done without the horse during the last few thousand years?

We can trace the ancestors of the horse back millions of years. But who first tamed the horse, the animal that we know? It is impossible to say. We know that prehistoric man used the horse as one of his chief sources of food. This was probably long before he thought of using the horse for riding.

The earliest pictures and carvings of horses were made by European cave men about 15,000 years ago. The horse in these pictures is very much like today's Mongolian pony. In these pictures and carvings there are marks that suggest a bridle, so perhaps the horse was already tamed!

It is probable however, that the wandering tribes in central Asia were the first to tame the horse, and from there the horse came to

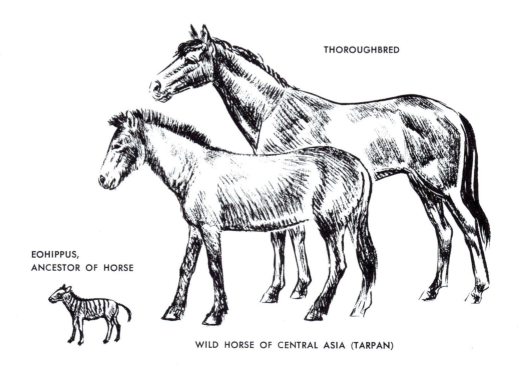

THOROUGHBRED

EOHIPPUS,
ANCESTOR OF HORSE

WILD HORSE OF CENTRAL ASIA (TARPAN)

Europe and Asia Minor. We know there were horses in Babylonia as long ago as 3,000 B.C.

Because the horse was tamed before historic records began, it is very difficult to trace the origin of any of the modern breeds. The oldest and purest breed of saddle horse is the Arabian. They have been bred for at least fifteen centuries! They are small horses, their legs are slender, and their feet are small. Their backs are short and strong.

When Julius Caesar invaded England he found horses there. In his time, they were probably small, hardy animals. Later on, during the days of the knights, horses were bred chiefly for size and strength, and used as war horses. Then when gunpowder was invented, speed became more important than strength or size, so faster horses were bred.

As horse racing became more widespread, horses from the Arabs, Turks, and Persians were brought into England. Our modern thorough-bred horse is descended from these combinations.

A thoroughbred, by the way, is any horse eligible to be registered in the General Stud Book. It was begun in England in 1791 and traces the pedigree of horses, going back to about 1690!

Men have ridden horses for thousands of years. Yet, as you can probably remember from the first time you tried to ride a horse, there's quite an art to riding.

WHY ARE HORSES RIDDEN WITH A SADDLE?

There's more to riding a horse than avoiding sores and aches and pains. The chief marks of good riding are ease and grace, combined with straightness of posture. When people are trained from earliest childhood, these things come naturally. The cowboys of the West usually get this kind of training, and they can ride without lifting from leather, which means they never bounce on the saddle.

The type of saddle that is used can make quite a difference in riding. In modern rodeos, the saddles used most often have a horn, or high pommel, and a cantle. A pommel is the knob in the front of the saddle and the cantle is the hind bow of the saddle.

The army uses a different kind of saddle with a medium-height pommel and cantle. On this saddle, the rider posts or lifts himself in the stirrups to avoid part of the up and down jolting of a trot.

At horse shows and for most pleasure riding, the English or "postage stamp" saddle is used. This is a light leather pad, with only the slightest suggestion of a pommel and cantle. It can only be used on well-trained horses.

With all saddles, the rider generally grips the leather with his thighs, allowing the lower parts of his legs to hang free in the stirrups. Just the balls of the feet are in the stirrups. The feet are held straight along the horse's sides. The reins are held in the left hand, the left rein between the little finger and the next finger. The right rein is looped over the index finger.

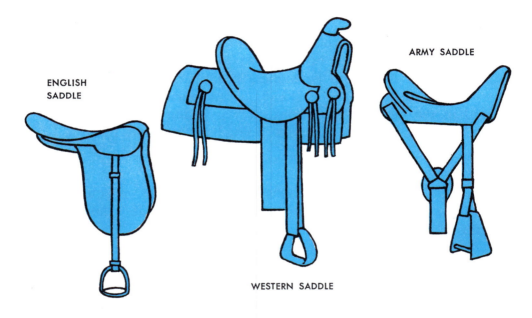

ENGLISH SADDLE

ARMY SADDLE

WESTERN SADDLE

Guiding the horse is accomplished first by pulling one or the other of the reins, or by kneeing or neck-reining. The horse must be trained for either of the latter two methods. The off-rein or off-knee (the one farthest away from the direction of turn desired) is pressed against the horse's neck or shoulder to signal the turn. Neck-reining is considered much better horse show style than pulling on a rein.

Of course, the art of riding a horse gracefully must be learned with much training and practice. Without it, you're likely to discover that it's not only painful, but you look quite awkward.

116

It would probably be hard to convince anyone that the buffalo on the United States five-cent piece is not really a buffalo. Yet it's a fact. The so-called American buffalo is not a true buffalo, but a bison.

ARE A BUFFALO AND A BISON THE SAME?

It belongs, however, to the wild-ox family and so is a near relative of the true buffaloes, chiefly in their proportions and in having 14 pairs of ribs, not 13.

The American bison has huge shoulders and shaggy hair covering its head and forequarters. In comparison with the head and the forequarters, the rest of the body looks almost naked. Males are considerably larger than females. A bull may weigh as much as 900 kilograms.

To the Indians of the plains, the American buffalo meant food, clothing, and shelter. The buffalo furnished excellent meat, which the Indians ate not only fresh, but also sun-dried. The hides were made into winter clothes, tepees, horse trappings, shields, and coverings for boats. Even the bones, sinews, and horns were used.

The buffalo has had a narrow escape from extinction, which almost resulted from the butchery it suffered within a period of less than 20 years. Herds of buffaloes once roamed the region between the Alleghenies and the Rocky Mountains. But by 1800, there were almost no buffaloes east of the Mississippi.

The Western plains however, were still black with herds made up of thousands, sometimes millions, of buffaloes. The size of these herds was almost unbelievable. They covered the prairie as far as the eye could see. Steamboats on rivers were sometimes halted by swimming herds, and trains were stopped for hours while an army of these animals crossed the tracks.

Whole herds were shot by hunters to feed the thousands of men building the new railroads, and hundreds of thousands were killed for their hides alone. Between 1865 and 1875, some 2,000,000 buffalo hides each year were sold at about $1 apiece. By 1889, in the whole of North America, there were only 835 buffaloes at large and 256 in captivity! Today, there are about 15,000 buffaloes living in the United States and Canada.

If you live on a farm or have anything to do with cattle, then you've probably heard people talk about this disease, also called foot-and-mouth disease. It is a highly contagious disease that affects practically all cloven-footed animals.

WHAT IS HOOF-AND-MOUTH DISEASE?

When an animal gets this disease, it develops blisters on the tongue and lips and around the mouth, on parts of the body where the skin is thin, and between the claws of the feet.

The disease appears suddenly and spreads very quickly. It causes tremendous losses among cattle. If the disease strikes in a serious form, it may kill off as many as 50% of the animals that catch it! And even those animals that do survive are in great trouble. They lose a great deal of weight because they cannot eat. Cows have their milk cut down considerably.

The horse, by the way, does not catch hoof-and-mouth disease. This helps in diagnosing the disease. Suppose, for example, that on a farm the horses, the cows, and the swine all develop fever. Then we know it is not hoof-and-mouth disease. But if the others develop fever and the horses don't, then we know it is this disease.

This disease is caused by a virus that presents quite a problem. For one thing, it is the smallest virus known. The virus that causes smallpox, just to give you an idea, is 10,000 times larger! Another problem is that this virus can resist being destroyed if the conditions are right. It can remain active in hay for 30 days. It can remain active for 76 days at freezing temperature! And it can resist a great many antiseptics.

Still another complication is that there are six types of virus that cause hoof-and-mouth disease. So if an animal develops an immunity to one of these viruses, it may still get the disease from any of the other five!

SEAL

SEA LION

WALRUS

Because we have all seen trained seals in the circus, and because seals are such fun to watch in the zoo, they have a kind of fascination for us. Yet surprisingly little is known by most people about these creatures.

CAN SEALS LIVE UNDER WATER?

The order of seals includes the fur seals, the sea lions, hair seals, sea elephants, and the walrus. Seals are mammals, and they stand halfway between typical mammals such as cows and dogs, and such sea mammals as whales.

Actually, seals are descended from land mammals, which means that at one time they had to adapt themselves to living in the water. They have not lived in the water for as long as whales have. The result is that seals are not nearly so well adapted to aquatic life as whales are.

Seals cannot live under water all the time. Not only that, but their young must be born on land. In most cases, the babies must be taught to swim by their mothers! So you can see why a seal is halfway between a land mammal and a sea mammal.

As they adapted themselves for life in the water, certain changes took place. They developed webbed hind-limbs and paddlelike fore-limbs to be able to swim fast. They acquired a layer of blubber to keep them warm. They have also either lost or reduced the size of their external, or outside, ears in order to lessen water resistance. And they began to feed on such sea creatures as squid, octopuses, and fish.

Although nature has changed the seal greatly for water life, seals spend a good deal of time on land. They like to sun themselves or sleep on beaches or ice floes. On shore, they move either by wriggling along or by dragging themselves with their fore-flippers.

In the United States, the most familiar seals are the California sea lions. They are active and intelligent. They can be trained easily to do tricks, such as juggling and balancing balls on the ends of their noses.

The habits of seals make them an easy prey for man. This is especially so during their breeding season when they can be approached on the beaches or ice floes. For centuries, the Eskimos have used seals for food, clothing, and their oil for cooking and light.

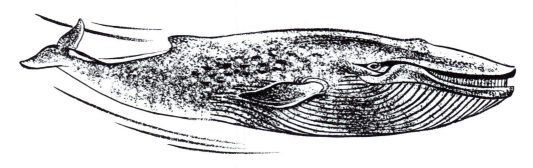

A mammal is a warm-blooded animal whose young are born alive and fed with mother's milk. Strangely enough, there are quite a few creatures who live in the sea who are mammals.

IS THE WHALE THE ONLY SEA MAMMAL?

A zoologist groups these creatures under the name "Cetaceans." They include the whales, the porpoises, and the dolphins. By studying their skeletons and other parts, we can determine that the ancestors of these animals lived on land in very ancient times.

When they began to live in the water, the form of their body gradually changed and became fishlike, because they had to live like fishes. The hair which used to cover their bodies disappeared and their skin became smooth. The hind legs they used to have disappeared, too, and they developed powerful flat tails. The forelimbs became paddles.

Fish have gills for breathing, but whales have lungs and breathe air. This is why they must come to the surface every half-hour or so and take in more air. At the moment they emerge from the water, the pent-up air from their lungs is released. It comes out through the nostrils at the top of the nose and not from the mouth. Whales can swim with their mouths open because their nostrils are connected directly with the windpipe. Therefore, when water enters their mouth, it doesn't choke them.

We all know that the dinosaurs were huge creatures, but even the biggest dinosaur was smaller than certain types of whales. In fact, the blue rorqual whale, also called the "sulphur-bottom," is probably the biggest animal that ever existed on this earth. Some of them are more than 30 metres long, while the biggest dinosaur we know of was only about 24 metres long. The average weight of one of these monsters is 68 tonnes. A new-born blue whale is bigger than a full-grown elephant! While its mother is nursing it during the first year, it reaches a length of about 18 metres.

It is hard to believe that the porpoise is not a fish, but a mammal. Yet it is just as much a mammal as the cow in the fields. Porpoises, dolphins and whales form the order called "Cetacea" of the group of aquatic mammals.

IS THE PORPOISE A MAMMAL?

Actually, dolphins belong to the whale family and porpoises are a variety of dolphins. All these animals may be given the general name of whales, or cetaceans.

There are a great many differences between porpoises and other whales and fish. The baby porpoise is fed on its mother's milk like other little mammals. It is not hatched from an egg, but is born alive. Porpoises have no gills and breathe air through their lungs. Internally, porpoises have a skeleton, circulatory system, brain, and vital organs that are quite unlike those of fish.

Another important difference is the existence of blubber. Mammals are warm-blooded animals, and blubber conserves their animal heat in the cold waters.

The common porpoise is about 1.6 metres long. The head is round in front, and the underjaw projects slightly. It has a wide mouth with between 80 and 100 teeth. A porpoise is black or grey in color above, and white below, with black flippers.

The porpoise prefers to live in waters near the coast rather than the open sea. It inhabits the North Atlantic but is quite rare in the Mediterranean. Porpoises live in great herds and seem to delight in following ships. There are some species of porpoises that appear in the South Atlantic and the Pacific Oceans.

Porpoise oil, which is obtained from the soft fat of the head and jaw, is used as a lubricant in the manufacture of watches and other delicate instruments because it doesn't gum up and can resist very low temperatures.

When the average person thinks of a reptile, he thinks of a snake. But actually, this class of animals includes many other creeping and crawling creatures.

WHAT IS A REPTILE?

In the animal kingdom, reptiles rank between the amphibians and the birds. Amphibians are animals that can live both on land and in the water. As a matter of fact, scientists believe that birds developed from the reptiles several million years ago. At that time, the reptiles were the the ruling class among animals, and they were often of giant size. But these giant reptiles died out, and the reptiles that are living today are comparatively small. The largest of these are crocodiles and the python snakes.

In many ways, reptiles are much like amphibians. All are cold-blooded, creeping animals with backbones. They are distinguished mainly by their lungs and their skin. Amphibians breathe through gills when they are young, and later many kinds develop lungs. Reptiles, on the other hand, breathe by means of lungs all their lives.

SNAKE

ALLIGATOR

LIZARD

TURTLE

The skin of amphibians is smooth and clammy, being kept moist by special slime glands. Water passes easily through this skin; therefore, most amphibians dry out and die if kept out of water for long. Reptiles have no slime glands, and their skin is dry and scaly. Because water cannot pass out through their skin, reptiles are able to live entirely on land.

The reptiles living today are divided into four main groups: the turtles, the crocodilians, the lizards, and snakes, and the strange lizard-like tuatara of New Zealand.

Turtles and tortoises differ from other reptiles in having their bodies surrounded by a bony shell covered with horny shields. All turtles and tortoises lay eggs. Many of the turtles live in or near bodies of fresh water, while tortoises live entirely upon land.

The alligators and crocodiles and their relatives are long, four-limbed animals having scales or plates covering their bodies. Alligators and crocodiles are so much alike that it may take an expert to tell them apart. In the United States, however, the alligators have a shorter and broader snout than crocodiles. Australia has crocodiles, no alligators, but many lizards. Lizards and snakes belong to the highest order of reptiles. The main difference between lizards and snakes is in the structure of the jaws. In snakes, both upper and lower jaws have movable halves with sharp recurved teeth.

BRONTOSAURUS

STEGOSAURUS

The best way we have of knowing what creatures were alive on this earth millions of years ago is from studying fossils. Fossils are animal and plant remains buried in the rocks. These remains, which have in most cases petrified (turned to stone), may be of shells, insects, leaves, bones, whole skeletons, or simply the tracks made by ancient animals on the shores of swamps.

WHERE DID THE DINOSAURS LIVE?

From such evidence, scientists believe that dinosaurs roamed the earth about 180,000,000 years ago, and that they died out about 60,000,000 years ago. What fossils have been found that make these scientists believe this?—The most common ones are bones, teeth, and claws. From these, skeletons can be reconstructed so we can tell how the body was built. In other cases, there have been trails and footprints.

In the Gobi Desert of Asia, nests and huge bones of dinosaurs have been found. Scientists have even found potato-shaped fossil eggs laid by dinosaurs with dinosaur "chicks" almost ready to hatch! In fact, dinosaur fossils have been found on all the continents, including North America. So we must conclude that the dinosaurs lived in practically every part of the world millions of years ago.

124

Certain conditions were necessary, however, for the dinosaurs to exist. The dinosaurs were reptiles, which means they were cold-blooded. Their body temperature changed with the air temperature. Many of them lived in swamps, where the luxuriant vegetation provided them with food.

But the climate of the world underwent a great change about 60 million years ago. Swamps dried up. Lowlands became mountains. The climate became colder and drier. So the dinosaurs not only lost their homes—the swamps and lowlands—but the cooling climate made them sluggish. It also killed off much of the vegetation they lived on.

In time, the dinosaurs, who were unable to adjust to the new conditions, died out and became extinct. They were replaced by warm-blooded animals with larger brains and the capacity to get along under the new and changing conditions.

There are few animals on earth which have as frightening an appearance for their size as some lizards! Yet of all the more than 2,500 different kinds of lizards, only two are actually poisonous. These are the Gila

ARE LIZARDS POISONOUS?

monster, which lives in American deserts, and the beaded lizard of Mexico.

Lizards are closely related to snakes, and, like snakes, are cold-blooded reptiles with scaly skins. Unlike the snakes, however, their long bodies are usually divided into three distinct parts; head, trunk, and tail. Most species have four legs.

With so many different kinds of lizards, we naturally find many exceptions. For instance, some lizards have no legs at all and look exactly like snakes. They also have a peculiar power, common to many lizards, which is quite useful in a fight with the enemy. They are able to break off their tails! This often enables a lizard to escape while the enemy stops to chew up the tail. Later, the lizard grows a new tail!

Although most lizards are hatched from eggs, a few are born alive. Most lizards feed on insects, but a few of the larger species eat birds and small animals. Lizards are most common in the tropical regions, but they can be found all over the world with the exception of the Arctic regions.

Wherever lizards live, they adapt themselves remarkably well to their natural surroundings. For example, the lizards which live among grass or trees are brightly colored, while those which live in the desert are colored dull gray or brown to match the sand. The chameleon, which is a kind of lizard, can even change its color to match its surroundings.

Lizards vary greatly in size. There are some which live in Central America which are less than 8 centimetres long. There are others called 'monitors', which are more than 2 metres long. In the East Indies there are lizards called "dragons", which are as much as 3 metres long, and must be a frightening sight, indeed. These dragons can easily kill a large animal with one lash of their long, strong tails.

Lizards love the burning heat of the sun. So those that live in cooler climates simply sleep through the winter, hiding themselves away to escape the cold.

Turtles, tortoises, and terrapins all belong to a group of four-legged reptiles that have hard outer shells, scaly skins, and horny beaks. Most people use the three words—turtle, tortoise, and terrapin—interchange-

WHAT'S THE DIFFERENCE BETWEEN A TURTLE AND A TORTOISE?

ably. Scientists, however, sometimes make this distinction: a turtle is a sea reptile; a tortoise is a land reptile; and a terrapin is a fresh-water reptile.

It is correct to call all three turtles. They all breathe air through lungs and have shells that are made up of a "bony box" covered with horny plates or with soft skin. These shells are divided into two parts. One part covers the back; the other covers the underpart of the turtle's body. Through the openings between the two parts, the turtle can thrust out its head, neck, tail, and legs.

Turtles have well-developed senses of sight, taste, and touch, but their hearing is quite poor. Most turtles eat all kinds of food. Female turtles are able to make a hissing sound, while the male turtle is able to give a kind of "grunt." Some of the giant land turtles are even able to bellow!

The largest of living turtles is the leatherback, which is a sea turtle. It usually weighs about 450 kilograms, and the biggest specimen on record is over 2 metres long and weighs 680 kilograms.

Turtle soup is made from the flesh of the green turtle, which is also a sea turtle. It is usually found in tropical seas, and may weigh as

ALLIGATOR SNAPPING TURTLE

GOPHER TORTOISE

GREEN TURTLE

much as 225 kilograms. Tortoise shell is quite expensive and is obtained from the hawksbill turtle. It is the smallest of the sea turtles and is rarely more than 1 metre long. Its horny shell consists of separate, clear, horny shields of dark brown, richly marbled with yellow.

The biggest North American turtle is the alligator snapping turtle. It can weigh 70 kilograms and lives in the Mississippi region. Snappers, which are fresh-water turtles, have long, large tails and very strong, sharp jaws.

The most common North American land turtle is the wood, which has brick-red skin. It can become quite a friendly pet and will learn to take food from one's fingers. Turtles hibernate during the winter months, hiding either in the bottom of ponds or in holes in the ground. Turtles sometimes live for 200 years or more!

Have you ever seen a salamander? They're not very pleasant-looking creatures. Their slender bodies, long tails, and sprawling legs make them look like lizards. And probably because they have a smooth, shiny

CAN SALAMANDERS LIVE THROUGH FIRE?

skin that always looks wet, a legend has arisen about them—that they can pass through fire without being harmed.

But this isn't true at all. Salamanders' natural home is in the water or in cool, moist places. When they are removed from this kind of environment, they die. Salamanders are amphibians, which means they can live both in water and on land.

Strictly speaking, the only true salamanders are found in Europe. But there are many creatures like the salamander in other parts of the world. Salamanders usually lay their eggs in water. The young have gills, like genuine water animals. When full-grown, the salamander usually develops lungs, loses its gills, and lives on land.

There is a Japanese giant salamander, which grows to be 1.5 metres long, that keeps both gills and lungs. The ugly black hellbender of the eastern United States also keeps both gills and lungs. The black hellbender is a great nuisance for fishermen because it greedily snaps up their bait.

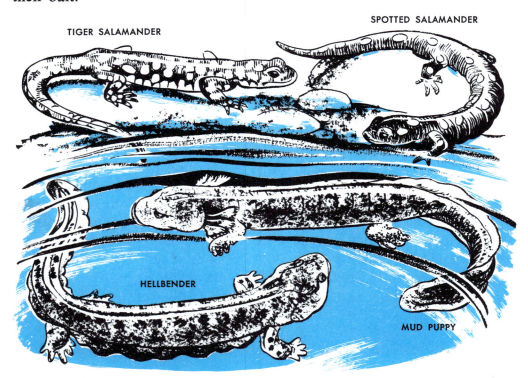

Other salamander-like animals never develop lungs at all, but spend their entire lifetime as water animals. Among these are the mud puppy, the congo snake of the southeastern United States, and the axolotl of Mexico.

The newts of Europe and America differ from other salamanders in that they return to the water and change again into water animals after living on land for about two and a half years. The best known of the true European salamanders is the spotted salamander. It is about 23 centimetres long and it gives out a poisonous fluid when frightened.

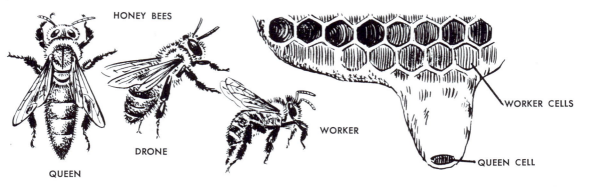

HONEY BEES

QUEEN

DRONE

WORKER

WORKER CELLS

QUEEN CELL

In order for there to be a "queen bee," there must be a colony of bees. But not all bees live in colonies. There are species of bees called "solitary" bees. Among them there are only two kinds of bees, the males and the egg-laying females.

WHAT MAKES A QUEEN BEE A "QUEEN?"

But bees that live in colonies, called "social bees," have a third form of bee known as "workers." The workers are really female bees that ordinarily don't lay eggs. So in a colony of social bees we have the workers, the males, who are called "drones," and the one egg-laying female, the mother of the colony, who is called the "queen."

Here is how a queen bumblebee spends her life. She passes the winter in a hole dug in a sandbank or other suitable place. She is the only member of the colony that lives through the winter! In the spring, she starts a new colony.

She first looks for a home, perhaps a deserted mouse nest. She heaps the soft material of the nest together and hollows out a place under it to serve as a nursery. Then she visits flowers for pollen and nectar and places a lump of beebread in the dry hollow she has prepared. She lays some eggs on this lump, covers them with wax, and sits over them, keeping the cold air away with her body.

Near her she has made a large waxen cell, called a "honeypot," which she has filled with enough honey for food to last until her eggs hatch. As soon as her first brood of young have grown big enough to use their wings, they take over most of mother's work. They prepare wax, make the beebread, and keep the honeypot filled to use in bad weather.

During the early part of the season, the only bees born are the workers. But before the summer is over, young queens and males, or drones, will also grow up in the colony. In the fall, the colony breaks up. All that the queen bee has done all summer long is lay eggs!

Among the honeybees, the queen lays all the eggs, but she cannot care for them. She may lay more than 1,500 eggs per day and about 250,000 in a season! She lays fertilized eggs that develop into workers or queens, depending on the needs of the colony. The unfertilized eggs develop into drones.

Young queens are reared in special queen cells. Before they emerge, the mother queen and about half the workers swarm off to start the new colony. The first young queen to emerge kills her sister queens in their cells and thus becomes the new mother queen!

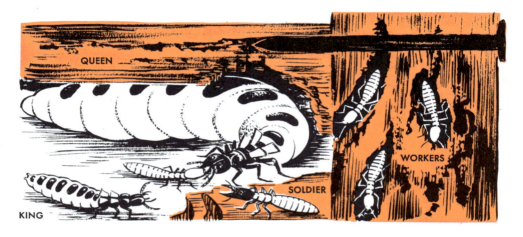

In the United States alone, termites do millions of dollars worth of damage a year! Strangely enough, these creatures which are such a problem to man today, have existed for millions of years. Primitive

WHAT ARE TERMITES?

termites probably lived during the age of dinosaurs!

Today, they are found in every state in the United States and in southern Canada. The greatest number are to be found in the rainy tropical regions around the world. There are more than 2,000 kinds of termites, about 50 of which are found in the United States.

Termites are insects that look like ants, but which are quite different from them. They have thick waists, a light color, and evenly curved feelers, or antennae.

Termites live in colonies in wood. They cut out the wood and form rooms for the colony. A colony of termites will consist of a king and queen, soldiers, and workers. The soldiers protect the colony from its enemies. They do not have wings and are blind, but they are the fighters.

The job of the workers is to feed the colony. They eat the wood and then feed this digested wood to all the other termites. In the hind intestine of a worker is a liquid. When this liquid is looked at through a microscope, thousands of single-celled animals, or protozoans, are seen. The protozoans turn the celluose of the wood into sugar. The sugar is digested by the worker and fed to the others.

Wood can be so treated that termites will not attack it. One method is to soak it with coal tar creosote under pressure, so that the creosote reaches the center. When building a house, care should be taken not to let untreated wood be closer than 60 centimetres from the ground. Although moist soil is necessary for the life of most termites, there are dry-wood termites in the South that can live without such soil.

EGGS   EGGS

Every now and then great swarms of grasshoppers have appeared in certain places and devastated the land. They are mentioned in the Bible among the seven plagues of Egypt. But every year, in most parts of the world, they do thousands of dollars worth of damage to crops.

WHERE DO GRASSHOPPERS LAY THEIR EGGS?

There are many varieties of grasshoppers but they look very much alike. They all have strong jaws, three pairs of legs, and usually have two pairs of wings. The first pair of wings is leathery and straight, while the second pair is membranous and folds underneath the first pair. The hind pair of legs, which are used for jumping, are usually long and well developed.

The female grasshopper has an organ for laying eggs at the tip of her abdomen. This organ is called an ovipositor. Katydids have long sword-shaped ovipositors. Some locusts poke holes in the ground with their ovipositors, lay their eggs there, and cover them with a gummy

131

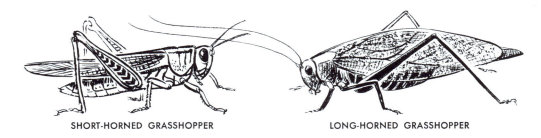

SHORT-HORNED GRASSHOPPER   LONG-HORNED GRASSHOPPER

substance. Some katydids cut slits in stems for their eggs, and some lay their eggs in rows on leaves.

Grasshoppers are divided into two general groups: the long-horned and the short-horned. The short-horned grasshoppers are sometimes known as "locusts" and include the common brown field grasshoppers. They have short antennae, short ovipositors, and three-jointed feet. They "sing" by rubbing their hindlegs across their forewings. Their "ears" are on their abdomens at the base of the hind legs.

The long-horn grasshoppers, which include the green meadow grasshoppers, the noisy katydids, and the cricket-like, wingless kind, have antennae which are much longer than their bodies and four-jointed feet. Only the males "sing," producing the sound by rubbing the bases of the forewings together.

In a few countries, grasshoppers are used as food, but most people try to get rid of them.

There is hardly a place in the world you can go where you won't find spiders. They can be found at sea level and on Mt. Everest, in forests, meadows, swamps, deserts, and in caves underground.

WHICH SPIDERS ARE POISONOUS?

Many people have a fear of spiders, because some types are known to be poisonous. All spiders, except two species, have poison glands. But this doesn't mean that the spiders with poison glands can harm man.

The poison glands in spiders are controlled by them and used in special ways. For example, spiders who spin nets to catch their prey do not use their poison. Those who hunt for their prey or hide in flowers and capture insects by grasping them with their fangs, kill their victims with poison.

All spiders, however, use their poison in self defense. When they are trapped and escape is impossible, the poison will be used as a last resort.

Very few spiders are poisonous to man. The only one in the United States that is dangerous is the black widow. Its body is about 1 centimetre long and shiny black, and it has a red hour-glass shaped mark on the underside.

The bite of this spider may cause severe pain and illness. Some spiders whose bite is poisonous to man live in Australia. The large so-called "deadly" tarantulas and banana spiders have never actually killed any person. They may cause one's arm or whatever is bitten to swell greatly and to ache for a few days.

The majority of spiders are no more dangerous to man than wasps or hornets. In fact, a great many spiders won't bite even if you hold them in your hand. So unless you know the spider is a black widow, you can feel pretty safe with one.

The most amazing thing about spiders of course, is their ability to spin webs. The silk of spiders is manufactured in certain of their abdominal glands. The silk is forced through many tiny holes from the spinning organs at the tip of the abdomen. It comes out as a liquid which becomes solid on contact with the air.

There are many kinds of silk, depending on the type of spider, and there is a great variety of webs, including one built underwater!

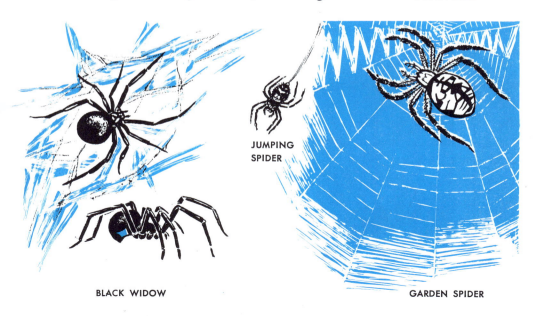

JUMPING SPIDER

BLACK WIDOW

GARDEN SPIDER

Did you ever dance the tarantella, or see it being danced? Did you know this dance originated with a belief that people had about the tarantula?

The tarantula is a large, fierce, hairy spider. In the Middle Ages it

ARE TARANTULAS POISONOUS?

was thought that people bitten by a tarantula became ill with "tarantism." The patients were supposed to fall into a dull, unhappy state. The only way to stir people out of this state was with music, and they were supposed to dance until they were completely worn out and collapsed from exhaustion. After that they would become well.

From this belief a dance called the "tarantella" developed. It is a very lively Italian dance that gets faster and faster until the end. While the bite of the tarantula is fatal to insects and small animals, there is no evidence that it is poisonous to man. But the fear of the tarantula is still strong among the peoples where it is found.

True tarantulas are found only in southern Europe and are named after the city of Taranto in Italy. They have hairy bodies about three quarters of an inch long. Like some other spiders, they don't spin webs. Instead, they dig deep burrows, which they line with silk. During the winter they shut themselves up in their houses with a silken door and hibernate until spring.

Tarantulas wait for their prey somewhat like tigers. They lie hidden among leaves or rubbish, or within their burrows. When an insect comes along, they rush out, bite it, and then drag it into their burrows. That bite either kills the insect or paralyzes it so it is helpless.

The spider then eats at its leisure. Tarantulas do not chew or swallow their victims. They suck out the blood and body juices. But when it comes to their own young, tarantulas are very considerate. They keep their cocoons in their houses, and carry them when they go out. When the young hatch, they ride around on the mother's back for a week or so.

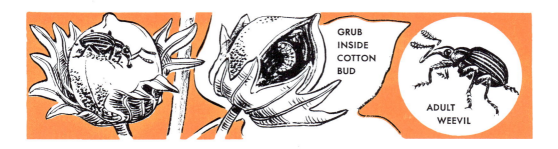

GRUB INSIDE COTTON BUD

ADULT WEEVIL

When the presence of the boll weevil within the United States was first discovered, cotton growers refused to believe that this little brown beetle could cause serious damage. The discovery was made about 1892, in southern Texas. About 30 years later, it was estimated that the boll weevil had decreased the annual cotton crop by more than 6,000,000 bales!

WHAT IS A BOLL WEEVIL?

The boll weevil is a native of Central America. It worked northward through Mexico, and crossed the border into Texas at Brownsville. Like most insects, it has a keen sense of smell. Experiments have shown that the boll weevils which have just come forth in the final, or beetle stage of their development can head straight for a cotton field several miles away!

When full-grown, the beetle is about a quarter of an inch long. Its jaws are at the tip of a snout well arranged for boring holes in cotton buds. The beetle sleeps all winter under dry grass and leaves, or in cracks in the ground. In the spring, when the cotton buds are starting to form, it begins its destructive work.

The female insect bores into the buds and lays her eggs in them. Within three or four days, the eggs hatch, and the small grubs feed on the inside of the bud.

The young "squares," as the flower buds are called, are the favorite breeding places; but when squares can no longer be found, the beetles attack the cotton bolls or fiber-filled pods. The worms remain inside the bolls during the period when they are changing into beetles.

There are four or five generations of weevils during a season, so it is easy to understand what a large amount of damage they can cause. The infested buds usually drop off without maturing, and the cotton fibers of infested bolls are useless.

One of the most fascinating and remarkable creatures in the world is the ant. There are more than 3,500 different kinds of ants, and they are found almost everywhere in the world.

WHAT ARE ARMY ANTS?

All ants are very much alike except in size. Ants may be as tiny as 1.5 millimetres or as long as 50 millimetres. All ants live in colonies. But there are tremendous differences in their way of life and their habits.

One of the most interesting types of ants, for example, is the "army ant." It eats living things! In Africa, there is a type of army ant called the "driver" ant. These ants go out in armies of many thousands. They kill and eat everything in their way.

Now you might wonder, "How can a little insect like the ant eat and kill everything in its way?" Well, there are thousands and thousands of them. Even the largest animals run away when they are coming. And if a creature cannot run—then good-bye! The army ants will kill and eat it, whether it is a fly or a crocodile or a wounded lion!

Army ants in the Americas eat only small things. They are called "legionary" ants. They may be found in the southern United States, and in Central and South America. Legionary ants travel in lines of thousands of individuals. In Mexico, people move out of their houses when they come. The ants eat all the roaches, rats, mice, and lizards that may be in the houses. Then the people move back to vermin-free houses!

Did you know that there are also ants who own slaves? These are the Amazon ants. The Amazon workers are all soldiers, and so they cannot gather food or tend to the young. So they must raid other ants to get slaves who will do this work.

They raid the nests of certain small, black ants. They kill any ants who try to resist them. Then they take the cocoons and larvae to their own homes. When the black ants come out of the cocoons, they will work in the Amazon colony, just like slaves!

Have you ever turned over a flat stone or a rotting log, and seen a little wormlike creature running quickly away from the light? The chances are it was a centipede.

DOES A CENTIPEDE REALLY HAVE A HUNDRED FEET?

Of course you didn't actually have a chance to count all its feet to see if it really had a hundred of them! The name "centipede" means "100-footed," and some species of this creature actually have 100 feet. Some, in fact, even have more legs than that! And some have only 30 legs.

While it seems rather amazing to us that any living thing can have so many feet, such creatures are not as rare in nature as we might think. There is a whole group of animals called "Myriapoda." This means "many-footed," and it includes not only the centipedes, but also the millepedes. Can you guess what "millepedes" means? You're right if you said 1,000-legged! So the centipede is not the champion when it comes to greatest number of legs. Incidentally, this type of creature is one of the oldest in existence. According to scientists, there have been centipedes and millipedes for millions of years!

While some human beings have trouble not stumbling with just two feet—a centipede can manage his hundred or so feet quite easily. The legs are arranged in pairs, and each pair grows out of a segment of the centipede's body, which is flat and has many joints.

On the section next to the head of the centipede, there are two long feelers and two poison-bearing claws. The poison of most centipedes is harmless to man, but in the tropics there are certain species, 20 to 25 centimetres long, whose bite may be serious. Such centipedes have been known to kill small birds!

Centipedes develop from eggs laid in the open. Some kinds are hatched with their full number of legs. Others start with seven pairs and add a new set each time they shed their skin, until they are full-grown. Centipedes come out at night to hunt their food, and during the day they hide under rocks or in dead wood.

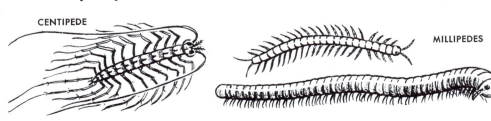

CENTIPEDE

MILLIPEDES

Have you ever been out camping or walking in a beautiful country spot, when suddenly everything was spoiled by a swarm of mosquitoes? These little creatures cannot only ruin our pleasure, they can make us quite miserable with their stubborn attacks.

DO ALL KINDS OF MOSQUITOES CARRY DISEASE?

For a long time, man considered mosquitoes annoying and troublesome—but that was all. It wasn't until the end of the century that we began to discover they were dangerous, too.

A few scientists had suspected that mosquitoes were carriers of disease, but no actual proof had been found. Then it was proven that certain species of mosquitoes carry the worms which cause elephantiasis, a horrible tropical disease, and that other mosquitoes spread malaria and yellow fever.

As a result of these discoveries, scientists really went to work to study the mosquito. They have studied their species, learned all about their life history, and developed ways of controlling them.

For example, we now know that there are about 1,000 species of mosquitoes. While mosquitoes are found all over the world, some species are found everywhere and other species are found only in certain regions.

One of these is the Anopheles mosquito, and several species of this type are known to be carriers of malaria. An Anopheles has black spots on its wings. It stands, when at rest, with its head down and its bill and body in a straight line.

There is another mosquito that is quite dangerous, and this is the Aedes mosquito. It carries yellow fever. This mosquito has white stripes around its legs and crosswise on its back. It rests with its bill at an angle to its body.

The best thing to do about mosquitoes is to eliminate them! The systematic draining of marshland and use of insecticides have done much to defeat this pest.

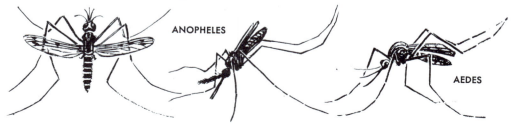

ANOPHELES

AEDES

It's a natural thing to consider the housefly a nuisance. It makes an irritating buzzing sound; it annoys you when it crawls on your skin; and so on. For ages that's what man considered the fly to be—just a nuisance.

WHY DO FLIES RUB THEIR LEGS TOGETHER?

It wasn't until the twentieth century that we found out that the innocent-looking housefly is one of man's worst enemies. It was discovered that these flies carried disease germs that cause the death of millions of people every year!

When you see a fly rubbing its legs together, it is just cleaning itself, and scraping off some of the material that has gathered there. But how dangerous that material may be! It may be the bacteria of such diseases as typhoid fever, tuberculosis, or dysentery. Flies get such germs from garbage and sewage. Then, if they happen to touch our food, the germs spread to the food, and if we eat it, we may become infected.

How does the fly carry these germs around? If you were to look at a fly under the magnifying glass, you would notice that the fly's body isn't smooth at all. Its whole body, its claws, and its padded feet, are covered with bristling hairs. The fly's tongue is also coated with sticky glue.

This means that practically any place the fly stops for even a moment, it's going to pick up things that stick to its body, its feet, or its tongue. In fact, each foot on its three pairs of legs has claws and two hairy pads—so it can make plenty of "pick-ups!" By the way, a sticky liquid is secreted by the fly's pads, and it is this which enables the fly to walk upside down on the ceiling, or any surface.

Did you know that flies are among the oldest insects known? Fossil remains of flies have been found that are millions of years old. Will we ever get rid of flies altogether? The only way we can bring this about is to prevent them from breeding. And for this to be done, conditions have to be made very sanitary all over the world!

SOLITARY WASP
AND CICADA

SOCIAL WASPS
AND CATERPILLAR

Almost all insects have interesting ways of caring for their young, but few of them show as much skill as the wasps. Some wasps build little houses of mud for their babies. Others make nests of paper. Some

WHAT DO WASPS EAT?

dig caves in the earth, and some saw out little cells in wood.

When the house is built, each mother goes out to hunt for food to stock the house. Young wasps are very particular about their diet. Some will eat only spiders, some beetles, some flies, and many of them will eat nothing but living food.

The females in each species travel long distances to find just the right insect. Then they seize it with their powerful jaws and carefully insert their poison-laden stings into the nerve centers of the insect. This poison does not kill the insect, but paralyzes it completely so that the meat will keep fresh until the young wasps are ready to eat it.

Wasps belong to the same group of membrane-winged insects as the bees and ants. Their many species are divided into two groups. Social wasps work together to build homes and supply food for their young. Solitary wasps always work alone.

These two groups can be distinguished by the fact that the social wasps carry their wings extended like fans, while most solitary wasps let them lie flat on their backs.

All wasps look somewhat alike. They all have four transparent wings and three pairs of legs. The females always have long, slender stinging organs attached to the lower parts of their bodies.

Their mouths are fashioned both for chewing and for sucking, for they live on the juices of fruits and on the bodies of other insects. Some wasps live entirely on honey.

In the Bible, we read of plagues of locusts descending upon a people and causing great suffering. Of course, in those times such a plague was considered a punishment from God, just as floods, droughts, and disease.

WHAT CAUSES PLAGUES OF LOCUSTS?

But plagues of locusts have appeared in other times and in other lands, too. In the western United States, there was such a plague from 1874 to 1876 that did more than $200,000,000 worth of damage!

The word "locust" has been applied to many members of the grasshopper family. A locust is actually any of a group of insects that belong to a family called "Acrididae." The so-called 17-year locust is not really a locust but a cicada.

Many scientists have been studying the question of why these insects descend on a region in great swarms at certain times, and seem to disappear between those times.

It seems that the species of locust that produces the "plague" exists in two phases, or periods. The two phases are solitary and gregarious, or in groups. In these two extreme phases, the locusts are quite different. They differ in color, form, structure, and behavior.

In the solitary phase, the locusts do not congregate and are sluggish in behavior. Their color matches that of their surroundings. In the gregarious phase, the locusts have a black and yellow color, congregate in great groups, are very active and nervous, and they even have a higher temperature. There are other differences as well. The solitary phase is the normal phase for the locusts.

When, for some reason, crowding is forced on the locusts in the solitary phase, they produce locusts of the gregarious type. These locusts are restless and irritable; they begin to wander; they are joined by others; a great swarm develops, and soon millions of them are ready to descend on a region in the form of a plague!

Not everybody accepts the theory of evolution, but those who do have a theory to explain how birds came to be. There are many different parts of birds that are quite specialized because they have developed

ARE BIRDS DESCENDED FROM REPTILES?

the ability to fly. They became warm-blooded because warm-blooded animals can change food into energy quickly. They have feathers, not only to keep warm, but because feathers make lightweight flying surfaces. They lost their teeth, because teeth are made of heavy bone. They have developed legs that act as shock-absorbers. Their eyesight is very sharp.

When all these specializations came into being is uncertain, but it is known that birds developed from some primitive reptiles millions of years ago. The group of reptiles from which birds are probably descended lived in the Triassic Period about 130,000,000 years ago. This is known from fossils which have been found.

These first birds already had feathered wings, but they probably were not strong fliers. The tails were long with many bones, and the feathers grew from each side. In today's birds, there is only one tail bone and the feathers grow fanlike from this bone. The old birds had many small sharp teeth.

About 10,000,000 years later some birds still had teeth, but most of the others had already lost them. Fossils of birds from this time show that there were already some birds that had the same size, wing shape, and possibly habits that a bird like the tern has today.

The strange thing is that today we can go over each part of the body of a bird and find traces of the time when birds were reptiles— but each part has been adapted to the special needs of the bird.

Perhaps the most important of all these changes was the change from a cold-blooded to a warm-blooded animal. This meant that the eggs of the bird had to be kept at a constant temperature and the young too, had to be kept warm. As a result, birds had to build nests, care for their young, and develop many other functions which are part of the bird's life today.

The migration of birds has fascinated man since the very beginning of history. Did you know that Homer wrote about it in 1000 B.C.; it's mentioned in the Bible; and the great Greek philosopher, Aristotle, studied the question?

HOW DO BIRDS KNOW WHEN TO MIGRATE?

And yet, so many thousands of years later, we still don't have the complete answers to the fascinating phenomenon of the migration of birds. By this migration, we mean the movement of birds south in the fall and north in the spring, or moving from lowlands to highlands, or from the interior to the seacoasts.

We can have a pretty good idea as to why it's good for the birds to migrate. For example, they go to warmer climates because some of them couldn't survive winter conditions. Those birds that feed on certain insects, or small rodents, wouldn't find any food in winter. Oddly

143

enough, temperature alone wouldn't make most birds migrate. Did you know that your canary could probably survive outside in the winter in temperatures 45 degrees below zero, centigrade, if it had enough food?

Whatever the reason for the migration (and there are many), how do birds know when it's time to take off on their long flights? Well, we know that they migrate quite punctually every year when the season is changing. And what is the surest, unmistakable clue to the fact that the season is changing? The length of the day! It is believed that birds can tell when the days get shorter (and longer in the spring), and this is the best "alarm clock" they have to tell them to get along!

Since birds breed in the summer, this is also connected with migration. Only in this case, it's migration northward. Certain glands in the bird begin to secrete chemicals that have to do with breeding. This happens in the spring. The bird feels the need to breed and heads north where it will be summer.

So the change in the length of days and the disappearance of food tell the bird to head to warmer places. And the breeding instinct in the spring tells them to head north. There are many other factors involved, of course, and many things we still don't understand, but these are certainly among the chief clues to bird migration.

HOW DO MIGRATING BIRDS FIND THEIR WAY?

In the late summer, many birds in various parts of the world leave their homes and fly south for the winter. Sometimes they travel to other continents, thousands of miles away. Next spring, these birds return not only to the same country, but often to the very same nest in the same building! How do they find their way?

Various interesting experiments have been made to try to find the answer. In one of these, a group of storks was taken from their nests before the time of the autumn migration and moved to another place. From this new location, they would have to travel in a new direction to reach their winter feeding grounds. But when the time came, they took off in exactly the same direction they would have followed from their old home! It seems as if they have an inborn instinct that tells them to fly off in a certain direction when winter approaches.

The ability of birds to find their way home is equally amazing.

Birds have been taken by airplane from their home to places 400 miles away. When they were set free, they flew back to their home!

To say they have an instinct to "go home" doesn't really explain the mystery. How do they find their way? We know that young birds are not taught the road by their parents, because often the parents fly off first on the annual migrations. And birds who fly home often fly by night, so they can't see landmarks to guide them. Other birds fly over water, where there are no landmarks of any kind.

One theory is that birds can sense the magnetic fields that surround the earth. Magnetic lines of force stretch from the north to the south magnetic poles. Perhaps the birds direct themselves by these lines. But this theory has never been proven.

The fact is, science just doesn't have a full explanation of how birds find their way when they migrate or fly home! An interesting bit of history is related to the migration of birds. When Columbus was approaching the American continent, he saw great flocks of birds flying to the southwest. This meant land was near, so he changed his direction to the southwest to follow the direction taken by the birds. And that's why he landed in the Bahamas, instead of on the Florida coast!

Everybody knows that birds migrate. In fact, people use the disappearance and then the re-appearance of certain birds as a sort of way of telling the change of seasons. But no one fully understands why birds make such long journeys.

HOW FAR DO BIRDS MIGRATE?

We cannot explain it by difference of temperature alone. The feathery coats birds have could protect them very well against the cold. Of course, as cold weather comes there is a lack of food for the birds, and this may explain their flight to places where it can be found. But then why do they migrate north again in the spring? Some experts think there is a connection between the change in the climate and the breeding instinct.

For whatever reason they migrate, birds certainly are the champions of all migrating animals. And the champions among the birds are the arctic terns. These amazing birds will travel in the course of a year, going back and forth, as much as 22,000 miles!

The tern nests over a wide range, from the Arctic Circle to as far south as Massachusetts. It takes this bird about 20 weeks to make its trip down to the antarctic region, and it averages about 1,000 miles a week.

Most land birds make rather short hops during their migrations. But one bird, the American golden plover, makes a long nonstop flight over the open ocean. It may fly from Nova Scotia directly to South America, a distance of about 2,400 miles over water without a stop!

Do birds start and end their migrations on exactly the same day each year? A great deal has been written about this and many people believe it happens. But no birds actually begin their migration the same day each year, though there are some who come pretty close to it. The famous swallows of Capistrano, California, are supposed to leave on October 23 and return on March 19. Despite all the publicity about it, their date of departure and arrival has been found to vary from year to year.

GOLDEN PLOVER

VARIEGATED CHOPPER YELLOW ROLLER

Finches form a large family belonging to the perching order of birds. They include common British birds (e.g. sparrows, yellow-hammers and linnets, most of which are poor songsters), but also canaries.

WHERE DO CANARIES COME FROM?

Canaries are now bred and raised in many parts of the world, but their original natural home was the Canary Islands, the Madeiras and the Azores. In the wild state, canaries, which are finches, are about 14 centimetres long and are olive-green in color, streaked with brown above, and greenish-yellow beneath.

Canaries were first caged in the sixteenth century, and the tame birds of today differ quite a bit from the original wild ones. This is because for many generations men have bred them to bring out certain qualities and check others. Some breeds are especially noted for song, some for shape, and some for color.

The most popular of all are roller canaries, which are bred for their singing. People in America are now able to breed roller canaries with great success, but probably the best known songsters are the birds from the Harz Mountains in Germany.

Did you know that young canaries imitate the notes of other birds? So to teach young canaries to sing, the best singers among the adult birds are used. Sometimes canaries can even be taught to sing like nightingales by playing them records of nightingale songs!

Canaries are easy to care for. Their cages should have loose clean sand in the bottom. The birds should have fresh drinking water and a lukewarm bath daily. For food, they should be given mixed birdseed and some green stuff, such as checkweed or lettuce leaves. They should never be fed acid fruits. They like to peck at a cuttlefish bone, from which they get the lime they need.

Canaries are very sensitive to drafts, so in winter their cages should not be hung near windows. They like to stretch their wings from time to time by flying, so they should be let out in a closed room occasionally. When the canary's nails grow too long, they should be trimmed.

Because of its name, and because this bird does have a remarkable ability to imitate the songs and cries of other birds, most people think of it only in this way.

DOES THE MOCKINGBIRD HAVE A CALL OF ITS OWN?

As a "mocking" bird, this creature is amazing. There is a case where an observer once heard a bird mimic the notes of 32 different birds within 10 minutes! The mockingbird may improve on the other bird's song by making up trills and runs of its own.

Did you know that sometimes a mockingbird will even try to imitate sounds it hears around the farm—such as the cackling of a hen, the barking of a dog, the screech of a wheelbarrow, or the whistle of a postman?

This doesn't mean, however, that this clever bird doesn't have a distinctive song of its own. In fact, it has a very lovely one. The song of the mockingbird is one of the delights of the South*, where the bird is found by the thousands. It sings from time to time through the winter. By the first of March, it is singing throughout the day and often during moonlit nights. It seems to be proud of its ability to sing. Many times you get the impression that one bird is trying to out-sing another!

But this isn't the only thing about the mockingbird that makes

* "South" refers to the southern part of the U.S.A. It is essentially a bird of the North American continent.

148

people love it. It is sociable and trusting by nature, and seems to want to live near man. Sometimes it nests in the vines or shrubbery growing around house doors. At other times, it builds a nest in a fence corner, in a brush heap, thicket, or some other familiar place.

The nest is made of string, rags, bark, feathers—and anything else that seems handy. It is well put together, and lined. And when the baby birds are hatched, a mockingbird will put up quite a fight to defend them. It will attack birds twice its size, cats, dogs, or even man himself. Here is really a creature that is willing to die, if necessary, to protect its home and family!

Although the mockingbird prefers the South, it occasionally goes north as far as Maine. In the summer, it is found all along the Gulf Coast.

Parrots are one of the oldest types of birds known to exist. Fossil remains of parrots show they have been around since prehistoric times, and they haven't changed for thousands and thousands of years.

WHERE DO PARROTS COME FROM?

Today, there are more than 600 species of parrots, but they are limited almost entirely to the tropics. Parrots are common in southern Asia, North Africa, Australia, and the Malaysian Islands.

Parrots are very hardy birds and generally live for a long time. They easily adapt themselves to any sort of living condition. This is one of the reasons why sailors have always liked to take parrots along as companions. They are colorful and amusing, and, of course, when they learn to "talk" they are fun to have around.

Even though the parrot is a tropical bird, it gets along comfortably in captivity and can be happy even in cold climates. At home, parrots prefer the forest and live in great flocks.

A little known fact about parrots is that they are very brave and loyal birds. If a danger appears, the whole flock stands by and fights together to overcome it.

Parrots are vegetarians, and will eat fruits, tender buds, palm nuts, and figs. When they search for food, they swing from one limb to another like monkeys. The reason they can do this is that they use the bill as well as the feet when they swing among the branches. If you've

MACAW

COCKATOO

TRUE PARROT

ever seen a parrot eat, you know that it can sometimes use the feet like hands. It will sit and hold a choice piece of food in its claws and enjoy it at leisure.

Parrots make their nests in the holes of trees. The eggs are always white. The parents take good care of their young, and will sometimes go on long trips in search of food. Parrots don't like to walk, but they climb and fly very well indeed. The best talker of all among parrots is the African gray parrot, which is also one of the most intelligent of all birds.

No bird has been written about so much by poets as the nightingale. Its song is supposed to be the most beautiful of all and nobody has been quite able to describe it. As a matter of fact, this attempt at describing it goes back to Aristophanes, the ancient Greek writer!

DOES THE NIGHTINGALE SING ONLY AT NIGHT?

According to the poets, the nightingale sings only at night and at almost any season of the year. But this isn't true. The nightingale is a migratory bird and in England, for example, can only be heard between the middle of April and the middle of June. The nightingale does not visit Ireland, Wales, or Scotland. On the continent of Europe it is quite abundant in the south, and even goes as far as Iran, Saudi Arabia, Ethiopia, Algeria, and Ghana in West Africa.

Only the male nightingale sings. His melody is the song of courtship to his mate, which remains silent in a neighboring bush or tree. He sings during the day as well as at night, but because of other birds, his song is not noticed so much then.

The male keeps singing until the female has hatched out her brood. Then he remains quiet so as not to attract enemies to the nest. He stays on guard, and his notes are short calls to tell his mate that all is well, or to warn her of some danger.

While the nightingale sings one of the most beautiful songs of all birds, its plumage is very inconspicuous. Male and female are very much alike—a reddish-brown above and dull grayish-white beneath.

The nest the nightingales build is somewhat unusual. It is placed on or near the ground. The outside of the nest consists mostly of dead leaves set up vertically. In the midst of this is a deep cuplike hollow, neatly lined with fibers from roots. It is very loosely constructed and a very slight touch can disturb it. There are from four to six eggs of a deep olive color.

For thousands of years, the owl has been a creature to which people have attached special significance. Primitive people have many super- stitions about the owl, chiefly because of the peculiar cries it makes.

HOW CAN AN OWL SEE AT NIGHT?

In many parts of Europe when an owl is heard to hoot, it is considered a sign of death. In ancient Greece, the owl was a symbol of wisdom.

Owls of one species or another are found in all parts of the world. In the frozen arctic districts, owls have snowy-white plumage which blends in with their surroundings and keeps them safe from their enemies. In parts of Texas there are owls so tiny they are no bigger than a sparrow, and they feed on grasshoppers and beetles.

The owl is a bird that really comes to life at night, and its whole body is especially suited to this kind of life. First, let's take the owl's hoot. When the owl utters this cry in the night, creatures who may be nearby are frightened by the sound. If they make any motion or sound, the owl hears them instantly with its sensitive ears.

The ears of an owl have a flap on the outside, unlike most other birds. Some owls have a kind of "trumpet" of feathers near the ears to help them hear better. Once the owl has startled its prey and heard its

motion, it can see it even in the dark! There are two reasons for this remarkable ability. The eyeballs of the owl are elastic. It can focus them instantly for any distance. The owl can also open the pupil of its eye very wide. This enables it to make use of all the night light there is. The owl's eyes are placed so that it has to turn its whole head to change the direction of its glance.

Even the owl's feathers help it to hunt its food. The feathers are so soft that the owl can fly noiselessly and thus swoop right down on the animals it hunts. Some owls are helpful to farmers because they destroy rats, insects, and other enemies of crops. But there are other owls that are fond of chickens and other domestic fowl, and these owls cost the farmer quite a bit of money!

One of the strangest-looking of all birds is the toucan. In fact, it's a kind of freak among birds.

WHAT IS A TOUCAN?

To begin with, the toucan has an enormous bill, actually larger than its head! In some toucans, the bill is a third of the length of the entire bird. This bill is shaped like a great lobster claw and is marked with bright colors.

If you were to see a toucan, you would wonder how this bird can maintain its balance with such a bill. The answer is that the bill is very light for its size. It is paper-thin on the outside, and it's reinforced on the inside with a honeycomb of bone. At its base, this bill is as large as the head of the bird. It has an irregular toothed or cutting surface along the edge.

The tongue of the toucan is also very unusual. It has side notches and is flat and featherlike. Another peculiar thing about the toucan is the way the tail is joined to the body. It seems to have a ball and socket joint. The toucan can give this tail a jerk and raise it above its back.

The toucan is a tropical American bird that has a family of its own. It is related to such birds as the jacamars, puffbirds, barbets, and distantly to the woodpeckers. There are about 37 different species of toucans, the largest of which are about 60 centimetres in length.

The toucan's appetite nearly equals its bill. It eats almost anything, and in captivity it has been trained to the most varied diet. At home in the forest it turns with equal greediness to fruits, or to the eggs and young of smaller birds. When feeding, it makes a chattering noise with its great bill. It also has a harsh, unmusical cry.

The toucans live together in small flocks in the depths of the Central and South American forests. Little is known of their life history, but it is believed that they make nests in the hollows of trees. Toucans are easily tamed and thrive in captivity.

The common name for the osprey in the United States is "fish hawk." This is a name that describes the habits of this bird.

It is an amazingly keen-eyed bird of prey. It flies about at a height

WHAT IS AN OSPREY?

of 15 or even 75 metres in the air, and watches the waters below. Suddenly it sees a fish close to the surface. The fish is so neutral in color that a human being on the shore wouldn't even notice it! But the fish hawk sees it and plunges down to seize and hold the wriggling victim in its strong talons. Then the fish is carried away to some tree top to be devoured at leisure.

When hunting, the osprey usually flies back and forth over the chosen spot slowly flapping its wings and occasionally sailing. Its downward swoop is sudden and sure. It strikes the water with a mighty splash, almost going under. It does not dive, for it is not a water bird.

The osprey measures about 60 centimetres long and has a wing spread of about 1.5 metres. It has a rather short curved beak which is not used for seizing or holding. This task belongs to the powerful feet and

claws. The head, neck, and lower parts are a pure white, except for some dark markings or streaks on the head. The back and wings are dark brown.

There is only one species of osprey. It breeds throughout the Northern Hemisphere and in the Malay Peninsula, Australia, and New Caledonia. Since the osprey's only food is fish taken alive, the bird is never found far from water.

One of the peculiar things about the osprey is the huge and unattractive nest it builds. It makes no attempt to hide the nest and adds new material each year to the same old nest. In the course of time there is a huge pile of such material as twigs, small branches, pine bark, and needles. The whole is perhaps 1.8 metres deep and weighs 315 to 450 kilograms. This may be put in plain view on top of a tall pine tree. Or it may be on the sandy beach, or on the roof of a shed. It is always built of a wide variety of materials.

To begin with, the stormy petrel is a bird, but a rather unusual bird. It gets its name ("petrel") from St. Peter. St. Peter is said to have walked on the water, and these birds seem able to do the same thing!

WHAT IS A STORMY PETREL?

All we know is that they are web-footed birds (in fact, the smallest of all web-footed birds) and that they manage in some way to stay above the water as if they are "walking" on it.

The petrel is an oceanic bird; it lives almost its entire life over the ocean and comes to land only during the breeding season. They can be seen by sea travelers circling about the ship or flying close to the crests of the waves. If a storm arises, they can't "walk" on the water, so they are forced to remain in the air day and night!

Several kinds of petrels are called "stormy petrels" and also "Mother Carey's chickens." A petrel is about the size of a swallow. The petrel that appears off the eastern and southern coasts of the United States during the summer is called "Wilson's petrel." It is sooty-black with a white rump-patch. It is about 18 centimetres and has a short bill and long, stiltlike legs. It greets the traveler with a friendly chattering, but it cannot sing.

Another stormy petrel that is seen only in the northern seas, such as the Arctic Ocean and the Bering Sea, is called "Leach's petrel." It is brownish-black in color and builds its nest in holes or burrows in the ground, or in hidden spots among the rocks. When this bird is breeding, it manages to remain completely hidden. Hundreds of birds may be gathered near one spot without being seen!

There are other kinds of petrels, in fact about 80 other species, that range over all the oceans of the world, especially in the southern seas. The largest is the giant petrel, which is 88 centimetres. Another petrel, called the "diving petrel," is from 18 to 25 centimetres long.

All petrels belong to the order Tubinares, because their nostrils are shaped like tubes.

One of the most spectacular sights presented by any bird is that of the peacock displaying his feathers. As you might imagine, such a sight has always impressed people. In fact, in ancient times, both the Greeks and

WHY DOES THE PEACOCK RAISE HIS FEATHERS?

the Romans considered the peacock to be a sacred bird. But this didn't prevent the Romans from serving peacocks for dinner!

The peacock is a native of India and South-east Asia, from which it has been brought to other parts of the world. There are only two species of peacock, and they are related to the pheasant.

Because of the way the peacock displays his feathers and struts around, a common expression has arisen: "Vain as a peacock." Actually, this is quite unfair to the peacock. It is no more vain than many other birds during the mating season.

The male peacock's display of gorgeous plumage is for the sake of the hen and for her alone. Among birds, as you know, it is the male who usually has the brighter colors and more "flashy" appearance. The peacock happens to have more marvelous colors than any other birds.

His head, neck, and breast are a rich purple, splashed with tints of green and gold. His head is also set off with a crest of 24 feathers in paler hues. His back is green, with the wing feathers tipped with copper.

The most remarkable feature of the male peacock of course is the train, or extension of his tail. A peacock is about 2.25 metres long, of which the tail takes up about 1.5 metres.

The tail is a medley of blue and green and gold. Here and there in the regular pattern are "eyes" which change colors. The train is raised and held up by the stiff quills of the shorter, true tail.

The female peacock, the peahen, is slightly smaller and quieter in tone. She has no train, and only a short crest of dull color. She usually lays ten eggs, of a dirty-brown color. Peacocks are generally kept for ornament and for the sake of their plumage.

We have a good feeling about most birds, and like to think they are a friend to man. Yet when it comes to the crow, we have quite a different attitude. We know that the farmer sets up "scarecrows," and hopes to keep these birds as far away as possible.

WHY IS THE CROW A HARMFUL BIRD?

While crows are somewhat helpful as scavengers, they are really quite destructive. To begin with, crows are expert thieves. They not only steal the eggs in other birds nests, but they often carry off the young! They even invade barnyards in search of hens' eggs, and will make off with newly hatched chicks if they can catch them. The worst complaint against crows is the destruction they do to crops. They simply eat up so many crops, and destroy so many cornfields, that the farmer considers crows one of his worst enemies.

The crow is about 48 centimetres, entirely black, including the feet and bill. He is an all-around bird with strong wings, and he can put his stout bill to many uses. His appetite, as has been indicated, is very good and he'll eat fruits, seeds, grains, birds' eggs, insects, or fresh meat which he kills himself. Since he can live on so many different kinds of foods he has no need to migrate, although some crows do move southward in winter.

The crow has exceptionally keen sight and hearing. It is usually seen in flocks, large or small, because a flock of crows can detect danger better than a single crow could. Crows are supposed to be very shrewd,

but several clever ways have been devised to take advantage of them. Crows are devoted to their young. So they will often come close in response to an imitation of a young crow's hoarse, rattling cry. They also sometimes attack hawks and owls, so stuffed hawks and owls are used as decoys to trap them.

Crows breed in the early spring, usually building their nests at least 9 metres high in trees. At this season the flocks are scattered. Soon after the young can fly, the flocks gather in colonies. In winter, all the crows of a wide area may gather together every night in some woodland to roost. They go forth in the morning to seek food and return at sundown.

The number of crows that may gather together in a roost can run as high as 200,000 to 300,000 birds! And somehow, despite all the efforts of men to destroy them, crows continue to increase in number.

HOMING PIGEON WITH MESSAGE

MOURNING DOVE

Pigeons and doves can be found in all the tropical and temperate parts of the world. In fact, there are more than 300 different species of these birds, but only a few of them are found in the United Kingdom.

WHAT'S THE DIFFERENCE BETWEEN PIGEONS AND DOVES?

The names "pigeon" and "dove" are really interchangeable. There is no basic difference between them except that the name "dove" has come to be used more often to describe the smaller species.

One of the most interesting species of pigeon is the carrier, or homing pigeon. When it is released, it has an instinct which guides it back to the home loft. This makes it very useful as a carrier of messages, and apparently man recognized this usefulness a long time ago.

Did you know that some of the Roman emperors used carrier pigeons to send messages to and from their armies in the field? And in the twelfth century, the Sultan of Baghdad maintained a regular postal system by using these birds! Probably their greatest use in modern times has been during wars, and they were found useful for sending messages even in World War II.

The Americans have had a curious and unfortunate experience with one particular kind of pigeon, the passenger pigeon. At one time, this bird could be found all over North America. In fact, during colonial days passenger pigeons were so plentiful that the trees bent beneath their weight. As many as 100 nests were found in a single tree. When a flock would take off, there would be a sound like a whirlwind and the sky would be darkened.

It is hard to believe that a bird so numerous at one time should now be extinct, but that's exactly what happened. These birds were shot, clubbed, netted, and sold in the markets in barrel lots. Year by year, during three centuries of hunting, the flocks grew smaller. Finally, in 1914, the last bird died in captivity in Cincinnati, Ohio. The passenger pigeon was about 40 centimetres long and had a slaty-blue color.

The mourning dove, which is about a foot long and has a very sad note, resembles the extinct passenger pigeon very closely, and is often mistaken for it. Pigeons, by the way, are not gentle birds. At mating time, they often fight and fly at each other angrily.

Many people imagine that this strange bird lives wherever it is cold, near the North Pole, South Pole, and so on. But the penguin inhabits only the Southern Hemisphere. Penguins live along the Antarctic (not

WHERE DO PENGUINS LIVE?

Arctic!) continent and islands. They are found as far north as Peru or southern Brazil, south-west Africa, New Zealand, and southern Australia.

The penguin is famous, of course, because it is like a comic version of a human being. Penguins stand up straight and flat-footed. Often they arrange themselves in regular files, like soldiers. When they walk, their manner seems so dignified and formal that it looks funny to us. Their plumage covers their entire bodies and is made of small, scalelike feathers. It looks like a man's evening dress of black coat and white shirt front.

The penguin that existed in prehistoric times was six feet tall, and you can imagine the effect that penguin would have on us today! There are 17 species of penguins in existence today, and the largest of these, the emperor penguin, stands just over 1 metre high and weighs about 36 kilograms.

Ages ago, the penguin could fly as well as any other bird. But today its wings are short flappers, of no value at all in flying. How did this happen? One of the reasons, strangely enough, is that the penguin had few, if any, enemies. It lived in such remote areas in the Antarctic regions, that there was practically no one around to attack it. So it could safely spend all its time on land or in the water.

As generations of penguins were born and died without ever using their wings, those wings in time became very small and stiff, until today they are useless for flying. But the penguins became wonderful swimmers and divers, and those wings make excellent paddles! Penguins also developed a thick coat of fat to protect them from the icy cold of the regions where they lived.

Penguins are hunted by men today for this fat, and it may be necessary to pass laws to protect them from extinction.

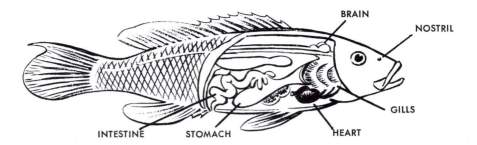

BRAIN

NOSTRIL

GILLS

HEART

INTESTINE   STOMACH

Sometimes it is hard for us to imagine that creatures which are so unlike us have organs very much like ours that function in the same way. Many people think that because a fish lives in the water and is cold-blooded it must lack various organs, or not have certain senses.

DO FISH HAVE HEARTS?

Actually, the anatomy of a fish is very much like that of higher warm-blooded animals. In fact, many scientists believe this similarity is evidence that life on land evolved from life in the sea!

Fishes breathe and digest food. They have a nervous system and suffer pain and physical discomfort. They have a very keen sense of touch. They taste as well as feel with their skin. They have two small organs of smell located in the nostrils on the head. They even have ears, but these are internal. Fish have no external ears. Their eyes are similar to those of other vertebrates, but less complicated in structure.

So you see a fish has "systems" to carry on various processes just as we have. Let's consider briefly just two of these systems—the digestive and the circulatory. A fish's food passes from the gullet into the stomach which contains gastric glands and where digestion begins. Food goes on into the intestine where it is assimilated, that is, passed on to be absorbed by the blood. Different types of fishes have different digestive systems which take care of their special type of food, ranging from vegetable matter to other fish.

But a fish uses food just as we do, as fuel for the power of life, growth, and motion. The blood stream of a fish carries its food, as well as oxygen, to every organ of the body. The pump which controls the flow of blood in a fish, is the heart, just as in humans. A fish's heart is located just behind and below the gills. The heart of a fish has three or four chambers, and it contracts rhythmically, just like ours.

There are thousands of different kinds of fishes, each adapted to a special way of life, but with organs, senses, and systems like our own.

Even though the sea horse is a fish, there is very little about it to suggest a fish. It has a head shaped like a pony. Instead of scales, the body of a sea horse is encased in rigid plates and thorny spikes. And its tail is like a snake's!

WHAT IS A SEA HORSE?

The sea horse doesn't even behave like other fish. It usually curls its tail around a bit of seaweed in the water so that it won't be swept away by the current. When it does swim, it moves about with the help of a single fin which is located on its back, and it moves upright through the water.

The mouth of a sea horse is a pipe-like tube through which it sucks in its food. Unlike other fish, it has a distinct neck and movable horse-like head, which is set at an angle to its body.

Perhaps the most peculiar thing about sea horses is the way they care for their young. The female fish, when she lays her eggs, puts them into the broad pouch beneath the tail of the male. So the father, instead of the mother, carries the eggs about until they hatch. Even after the young hatch out, they remain in the father's pouch for a time until they are able to take care of themselves.

Sea horses can be found in nearly all the warm and temperate seas. They belong to the pipefish family, and their food consists of small sea creatures and the eggs of other fishes. A sea horse never eats a dead thing.

There are about 50 different kinds or species of sea horses. Their size may range from 5 to 30 centimetres.

Sea horses are seen only in the summer and they are known as summer fishes. Nobody knows what happens to them in the winter!

Even though the sea horse hasn't many ways of defending itself against its enemies, it is quite safe from attack. It seems that other fishes in the sea just don't like to eat or attack sea horses!

BROOD POUCH

The starfish is one of the most curious of sea creatures. Among its queer relatives are the prickly sea-urchins, the sea cucumbers, and the sand dollars. There are more than 6,000 of these relatives and they are called "echinoderms," which means spiny-skinned.

DOES A STARFISH HAVE EYES?

The starfish and its relatives all have well-developed nervous and digestive systems. This system follows the same five-armed arrangement which occurs in all echinoderms. The starfish are sometimes divided into three groups. There are the brittle stars, which break off their long snaky rays if they are caught. Their arms may extend 20 to 25 centimetres. There are the feather stars, whose waving rays resemble little plumes. And there are the ordinary sea stars which usually measure about 13 centimetres.

The tough, leathery skin of a starfish is covered with very short spines. In the center of their bodies, on both the upper and undersides, are button-shaped disks. Through these disks they draw in or expel sea water. The disks on the under sides act as mouths. The eyes are at the tips of their arms and are protected by a circle of spines.

Along the underside of their arms are grooves, and along these grooves are arranged little tubelike sucker feet. These are used both for moving about and as organs of smell. Sea stars cannot travel very fast with their little tube feet, but they can do something more remarkable. They can open an oyster! They attach the sucking disks of their feet to either half of the oyster shell and pull at it until the oyster finally opens. Then the starfish turns its stomach inside out, brings it through its mouth, and wraps it about the oyster.

Starfish can also eat by taking food into their mouths in the ordinary way. They can also replace broken arms. They may even grow a whole new body from one arm!

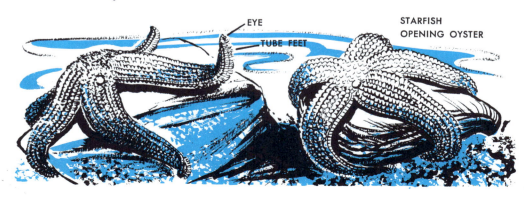

EYE

TUBE FEET

STARFISH OPENING OYSTER

Sardines are small, yellowish-green fish which belong to the herring family. When they are full-grown, usually about 25 centimetres, they are called "pilchards" and are smoked and sold like other herrings.

WHAT ARE SARDINES?

Usually, however, sardines are caught when they are still very small and are prepared for canning. The fish are first put in bins filled with fresh water. Then they are cleaned and scaled and the heads are removed. Next, they are dipped in salt brine and poured into large trays which are passed under an artifical drier.

Finally, they are cooked for about five minutes in boiling oil. When they are thoroughly cool, they are put in small flat tin cans and further soaked with oil to keep them moist.

One kind of sardine, found off the Pacific coast of North America, is the largest catch by weight of all commercial fishes in the world. As much as 560,000,000 kilograms of this fish have been caught during one season!

The sardine which is imported from Europe is found chiefly in the Mediterranean Sea and off the west coast of France. By the way, the name "sardine" comes from the fact that these fish were first caught in large quantities near Sardinia.

Most of the sardines caught along the Pacific coast are not canned at all. The greatest part of the catch is made into oil, used in the manufacture of soaps and paints, and made into feed for poultry and livestock.

A female sardine lays 100,000 to 300,000 eggs a season, chiefly in April and May. The young hatch in three days and in about two months begin to form in schools. They feed on microscopic plants and animals, and they themselves are the chief food of larger fish such as salmon. They travel in tremendous schools near the surface of the water.

One of the most curious creatures to be found in the sea is the lobster. It is a "crustacean," which means a hard-shelled animal, and it is related to the crawfish, the shrimp, and the prawn.

HOW DO LOBSTERS GROW?

There are three species of true lobsters. American lobsters, which live all along the Atlantic coast from Labrador to North Carolina, are the biggest members of the family. Next in size is the European lobster, which is found on the eastern shores of the Atlantic. The smallest lobster is the African species found off the Cape of Good Hope.

The lobster is encased in a suit of armor made of hard shell. This is usually dark green in color but turns red when the lobster is boiled. The shell covering the front part of the body is practically solid. The rest of the shell is divided into seven segments, the last of which forms the tail.

Lobsters have four pairs of walking legs, two pairs of which have small pincers for feet. In front of these are the great claws. They serve as hands rather than as feet. One of them, the club, is very thick and heavy, and is used for crushing tender objects. The other, the fish claw, is more slender, curved, and provided with many sharp teeth. It is used to seize prey or enemies.

Lobsters usually walk about at the bottom of the sea balanced on the tips of their walking legs. When they are alarmed they make huge backward leaps through the water covering as much as 7.5 metres at a time. They dart backward by powerfully jerking their paddle-equipped tails down and forward.

The female lobster lays from 5,000 to 100,000 eggs. She carries them about for some ten months, glued to the swimmerets under her tail. As soon as they hatch, the mother fans the babies away and they start on their own adventures.

If the lobster has a hard shell, how does it grow? All through its life, the lobster molts. This means it sheds its armor whenever it out-grows it. During its first year, it molts fourteen to seventeen times, but when it grows older it molts not more than once a year.

The little lobster swims at the surface for six to eight weeks, during which period it can easily become a meal for some other animal. If it lives, it finally sinks down and makes its home on the bottom, in shallow water.

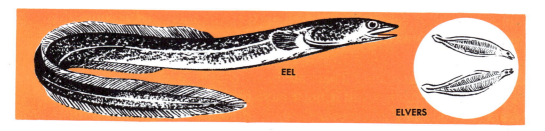

EEL

ELVERS

One of the most curious of all living creatures is the long, slippery, whiplike member of the fish family called the eel.

If it were possible to identify one of the species and follow it in its

WHERE ARE EELS BORN?

travels, it would be found at different times swimming across hundreds of miles of ocean, ascending rivers, and even wriggling through wet grass on land toward the place where its instinct tells it there is a pond rich in food.

Every eel caught in America or Europe, even from streams far inland, was born from one of possibly 20,000,000 eggs laid by its mother at a depth of 180 to 275 metres in a certain area of the Atlantic Ocean near Bermuda!

The common eel, brownish-black in color, has a smooth skin, and is usually without scales, or with embedded ones.

It is only recently that people have learned the origin of young eels, or elvers. Now it is known that they first appear as peculiar, transparent forms floating near the surface of the ocean. After a certain length of time these forms gradually shrink and take on the definite outline of the adult eel. Then the elvers of a certain section of this breeding zone swim by millions toward Europe.

But they do not enter the fresh water of European rivers until they have reached their third year. The elvers of the other section of the breeding zone swim toward America and, when one year old, enter fresh water, ascending all American streams from the St. Lawrence River to the Gulf of Mexico.

After a life of four to twelve years in fresh water, during which they reach an average length of 60 to 90 centimetres, the adults descend the rivers, never to return. They swim back to Bermuda, breed in the depths, and die!

Eels are caught as they go downstream from July to the end of October—sometimes later in the year—on their way to Bermuda. The annual catch of eels for market along the Atlantic coast is more than 900,000 kilograms.

Do you like to eat clams? There are many people to whom the very idea is quite unappetizing. And it must have been this way for thousands of years. Nobody in Europe ever thought of eating this creature until the white man came over to America and saw the Indians doing it!

WHAT DO CLAMS EAT?

Clams have a boneless, soft body which is protected by two hard shells that close over it like the covers of a book. There are two chief kinds of clams, the long, or soft-shelled clam, and the round, or hard-shelled clam.

The soft-shelled clam lives in the ocean mud in a peculiar way. It "stands" imbedded in the mud on end like a book in a bookcase. The upper end is the more pointed. From it, when the shell is open, comes a long siphon which people call the "neck." This siphon squirts out water when some shock makes the clam pull in its neck and close its shell.

Hard-shelled clams are larger than the soft-shelled clam. They lie on the ocean bottom near the shore, more or less buried in sand or mud. Very young hard-shelled clams used for food are called "little-neck" clams. Those not quite so small are sometimes called "cherry stones."

What do clams eat? Their food consists of the tiniest animal life in the sea, and is taken in through the neck. Clams are able to move about: Between the free edges of the two shells of the clam is a foot which the clam uses for burrowing in the mud or pushing itself along the ocean bottom.

The biggest clam of all, the giant clam, has a shell that weighs 180 to 225 kilograms. It lives in the coral reefs of the East Indies.

ROCK BARNACLE

BARNACLES ON WOOD

If you have ever been near the sea and walked along the shore where there are piers, rocks, and breakwater walls, then you've almost certainly seen barnacles. In fact, the "crust" you saw that was formed on the piers and rocks was made up of millions and millions of barnacles!

WHAT ARE BARNACLES?

A barnacle is simply a small shellfish. When barnacles are hatched, they swim about freely. But when they reach adult state, they no longer move about. They attach themselves to any convenient surface and actually lose their power of locomotion.

This habit of attaching to a surface, since it is done by millions of barnacles at a time, is quite a nuisance to man. For example, when barnacles form a crust on the hull of a ship, they can cut down its speed by 50 per cent! In the days of smaller ships, barnacles were a real danger because they made steering very difficult and could delay a ship from reaching its port for quite a while.

The pirates who sailed the Caribbean Sea had to tip over their ships on beaches and scrape off the barnacles. Many an old-time whaler could hardly get home after a two-year cruise because of the masses of barnacles clinging to its hull. Even today, with our modern, powerful ships, barnacles cost the world's shipping industry a lot of money every year because of the loss of time and wear and tear on machinery.

There are many different varieties of barnacles, among them the rock barnacles, which prefer to live on rocks rather than on wood or iron. As we said, when first hatched they resemble tiny crabs or lobsters and can move around. But once a barnacle attaches itself to a surface, it's for life!

An attached barnacle begins to grow a shell which encloses its body completely. The only thing that moves from then on is tentacles or antennae of the barnacle. There are six pairs of these feathery tentacles and they are able to move about to reach and draw in smaller water creatures for food.

FANTAIL GOLDFISH   COMMON GOLDFISH

The ancestor of the goldfish is the carp. In the lakes and rivers of China and Japan, the greenish-gray carp is found in great quantities, and this is where the goldfish was first developed.

WHAT IS THE ORIGIN OF THE GOLDFISH?

The Chinese have been breeding goldfish for centuries, and the Japanese have raised goldfish for more than 400 years! Goldfish weren't known to Europe until a few were brought over about 200 years ago. These were given to Madame Pompadour of the court of King Louis XV of France. Because she was the leader of fashion, other people began importing them.

Goldfish vary from 4 centimetres to about 30 centimetres. The common goldfish, the fantail, the comet, and the nymph, are the breeds best known to the Western world. The common goldfish has a slender body and rather short, tough fins.

The fantail has a shorter, fatter body with double tail and fins. The American-bred comet is slender, with a long, single, deeply forked

170

and free-flowing tail. The nymph is like the comet but has a short, round body.

All these breeds may be kept in an aquarium, and millions of people have them in their homes. If you would like to keep goldfish, there are certain things you should know about them and their care.

The lowering of the back fin of a fish is a sure sign that it is not in good condition. A fungus disease, caused by plant parasites, is also common. In this, a white scum develops on the fins of the fish and extends over the body. If this scum reaches the gills, it keeps the fish from breathing and kills it.

This disease can be cured by giving the fish a salt-water bath, which will also correct the lowered-fin condition. One tablespoon of salt to a gallon of water the same temperature as that in the aquarium may be used for a daily 30-minute bath. The fish should be placed in a shallow basin containing this solution and set in a dim light.

Then the aquarium and plants should be soaked for four hours in a very weak solution of potassium permanganate, washed, and filled with a fresh supply of clean water. In two, or three days, the fish may be put back into it.

Did you ever eat a dish of fried scallops? As you looked at the little squares of food on your plate, did you wonder why you had never seen them in the water? What kind of creature was this that existed in square chunks of meat?

WHAT IS A SCALLOP?

Actually, what are sold as "scallops" and what you eat as "scallops" are only the large muscles of certain mollusks. These muscles are used to open and close the shells, and they are the only part we eat.

The scallop itself is a curious creature. As you probably know, most bivalves (mollusks with two shells) find a place to live and stay there. They may fasten themselves to rocks or to timbers, or form a bed on the bottom of the ocean as the oysters do. But the scallop is quite different.

The scallop likes to wander about. He is constantly moving from place to place. The way he moves is by sucking water into his shell and then squirting it out suddenly. This gives him enough force to push himself forward in zigzag fashion.

Did you know that the scallop became a symbol for travelers because it is always moving? In the Middle Ages, pilgrims wore a scallop shell in their hats to indicate that they had made a long trip by sea.

Scallops belong to the great group of mollusks which includes snails, clams, and oysters. There are more than two hundred different species.

The common scallop lives in bays close to shore, and measures up to 3 centimetres across. The giant scallop is a sea scallop. It is found off-shore in deeper waters and measures about 15 centimetres across.

"Mollusk" sounds like it ought to be the name of some prehistoric animal, but it isn't. Mollusks are a huge division of animals without backbones, and they range from snails to clams, and oysters to octopuses.

WHAT IS A MOLLUSK?

They differ in size from almost invisible creatures to giant squids 15 metres long! They may live in the tropics or in the arctic, in deep seas or on land!

But even though there are more than 60,000 different species of mollusks, they have certain characteristics in common. All mollusks have soft, slimy, boneless bodies which are covered with big folds of flesh called "mantles." In many mollusks, this mantle is covered with a hard shell, such as that of the oyster, while others have no protecting shell at all. Almost all mollusks have a kind of "foot," which is an extension of the mantle and which helps them move about. It may help them swim or walk, burrow in the mud, or tunnel through wood, depending on the species.

There are five groups of mollusks, and the members of three of

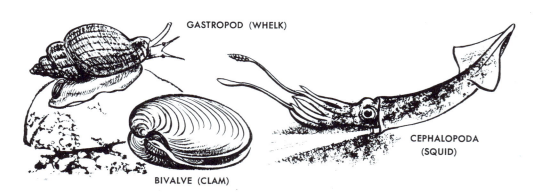

GASTROPOD (WHELK)

CEPHALOPODA (SQUID)

BIVALVE (CLAM)

them are very well known to everybody. The first of these common groups is called "Gastropoda," which means "stomach feet." Among the gastropods are snails, slugs, and periwinkles, all of which have one large "foot" on their stomachs. All gastropods have a head on which are eyes and feelers, and many of them carry single spiral shells on their backs.

The second common group of mollusks is the bivalve group. In this group you will find oysters, clams, mussels, scallops, and many others. All bivalves have shapeless bodies protected by double, hinged shells. All of them are water creatures.

The last common group of mollusks is called the "Cephalopoda," which means "head-footed." The members of this group have many arms, or tentacles, surrounding their mouths. This group includes the octopus, cuttlefish, squid, nautilus, and others. They are the aristocrats of the mollusk world, with a nervous system that raises them far above other mollusks.

All mollusks lay eggs, but some lay only a few and others, many. In some the young hatch out as larvae; in others, they are tiny reproductions of their parents.

The octopus belongs to a group of animals called "cephalopods." The name means "head-footed" because the foot is divided into long armlike tentacles that grow out around the head. The octopus has eight such tentacles.

HOW DOES AN OCTOPUS MOVE?

Even though the octopus belongs to that part of the animal kingdom known as mollusks, it is quite different from clams and oysters, which are mollusks, too. It is more closely related to the squids.

None of these has shells. They have only a soft mantle to enclose the body. The tentacles are long and flexible with rows of suckers on the underside. These enable the octopus to grab and hold very tightly to anything it catches.

In the back part of the body of the octopus is a funnel-siphon. Water comes into this siphon and the octopus extracts oxygen from it the way a fish does. The siphon is also the way it manages to move swiftly. The octopus can shoot a stream of water from this siphon with such force that it propels itself backward very rapidly. That is the

SIPHON

way it can get away from an enemy that comes too quickly to allow it the chance to crawl over the rocks or into crevices by means of its eight tentacles.

When an octopus lies quietly, the tentacles rest spread out over the floor of the shallow pool. Should an enemy approach, it will either escape or grab the enemy tightly. If things grow too serious, it can throw up a "smoke screen" and escape. From a sac in the lower back part of its body it can throw out a black inky fluid that clouds the surrounding water.

Also, an octopus can change color to match its surroundings. It can go from red to gray, yellow, brown, or blue-green.

174

Snails are mollusks, which means a kind of animal without backbones. There are two basic kinds of snails: the first includes the snails which have shells; the second, those which are covered merely by a thin mantle. Members of this second group are usually called "slugs."

DO SNAILS LAY EGGS?

All the members of this division of mollusks have one large foot on the underside. Therefore, they are called "gastropods," or stomach feet. This division also includes the large whelks of the ocean and the periwinkles. The ocean snail measures about 25 millimetres in the shell.

All these creatures are equipped with one or two pairs of feelers. They have a pair of eyes, which may be at the end of the feelers or at

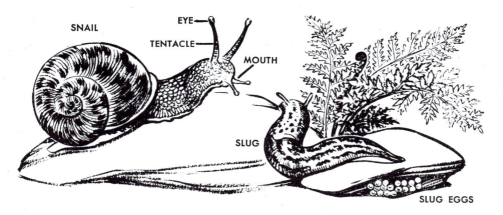

SNAIL
EYE
TENTACLE
MOUTH
SLUG
SLUG EGGS

their base, and a mouth. The mouth often extends into a trunk. At its end there are sharp teeth with which the snail can scrape off pieces of plants.

Some snails eat animal food. The oyster drill, for example, is a yellow-shelled sea snail which drills into oyster shells and feasts on their flesh.

Snails and slugs breathe either by means of single lungs or by gills. Their shells, which are often beautifully formed, are secreted, or given off, by the mantle. They are usually built up coil after coil, as the animal grows.

Most snails lay eggs. Some lay many small ones; others lay few but very large eggs. In a few species, however, the young are born alive! So you can see that this little creature is quite an interesting one to study. By the way, have you ever eaten snails? In many countries, the flesh of garden snails, of whelks, and periwinkles is considered a delicious food.

In the days when Columbus sailed the seas there were stories told of long-armed monsters that reached out of the water to scuttle ships and pull the sailors down to the depths of the ocean. Such stories were exaggerations. There never were such monsters, and what the sailors probably saw were giant octopuses or giant squid.

WHAT IS A SQUID?

Both of these creatures are mollusks, or shellfish. They belong to the class called "Cephalopoda." This name means "head-footed," because the foot is divided into long armlike tentacles that grow out around the head.

A typical squid has a long, slender body edged by triangular fins, a short square head with well-developed eyes, and ten arms. On the undersurface of the arms or tentacles, are arranged rows of suckers which are strengthened with tough horny rings. Two of these tentacles are longer and more flexible than the others. The suckers are concentrated at the extremity of the tentacles as a sort of "hand."

The two long tentacles are used by the squid to capture its prey. The other eight are used to transfer the food to the mouth of the squid. or for holding it while it is being crunched by the horny jaws, which are situated around the mouth in the center of the circle of arms.

Deep under the mantle, or skin, lies a horny growth which is something like a shell. This has replaced the true shell which the squid probably had at one time. There are many different kinds of squids, and one of them, the giant squid, is the largest invertebrate on earth, which means the largest animal without a backbone. Some giant squids found in the North Atlantic have been measured to be a length of 16 metres (including the outstretched tentacles). Another group of giant squid measure 2 metres.

The squid, like the octopus and the cuttlefish, can discharge an inklike fluid into the water to hide its whereabouts. One interesting group of squid is phosphorescent, which means it gives off light. The light organs are on the mantle, arms, inside the mantle cavity, and around the eyes. When seen at night, they appear quite beautiful. Other squid, called "flying squid," are able to leap across the surface of the water.

A catfish might say to you: "why do you call them 'whiskers?' They're not whiskers at all!" And, of course, it's only because those things on the fish's mouth resemble a cat's whiskers that we call them that. Actu-

WHY DO CATFISH HAVE WHISKERS?

ally they are barbels, or feelers, and help the catfish know what's going on all about him.

There's another way a catfish is supposed to resemble a cat: it makes a buzzing or croaking sound when caught that suggests a cat's purring. It's for these two reasons that this kind of fish got its name, "catfish."

Young boys are especially well acquainted with the catfish because it's one of the easiest fish to catch. It will bite at almost any bait, from a piece of red string to a worm. And because the catfish does such a good job of caring for its young and protecting its nest, there always seems to be a lot of catfish around.

Actually, the catfish family has about 2,000 different species. The European catfish is known to grow to a length of 3 metres and a weight of 180 kilograms. Some specimens of the Mississippi catfish and the Great Lakes catfish have been found to weigh 68 kilograms.

Many catfish are good eating, especially the white cat, found in the waters of the Chesapeake Bay and the Potomac River; the blue cat, found in Southern streams; and the bullheads, bull pouts, or horned pouts.

Some catfish have strange habits. One South American species is said to travel overland from pond to pond, and another builds a nest of blades of grass for its young. There is even an electric catfish in Africa which can give a painful electric shock. In the river Nile is a species which avoids the notice of its enemies by swimming with its black belly up and its white back down!

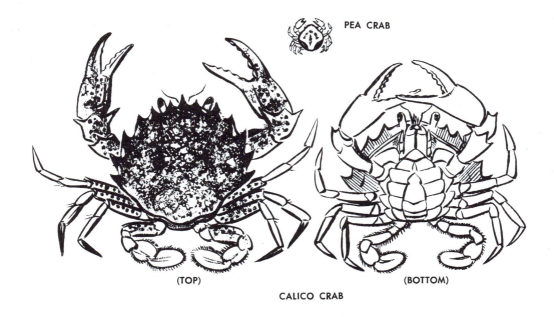

PEA CRAB

(TOP)

(BOTTOM)

CALICO CRAB

Whoever was the first man to eat a crab (or a lobster!), was probably very brave, or very hungry—or both. If you've never seen one before in your life, the last thing you'd think of doing is eating one!

WHEN WERE CRABS FIRST EATEN?

Crabs are so widely scattered all over the world, and have been known to man for such a long time, that we can never find out who was the first to eat crabs and when. Crabs were probably eaten by people who lived near the sea thousands of years ago. There are crabs off the coasts of Europe, North America, South America, India, Japan, and most of the Pacific Islands, Alaska, and so on.

The crab has a hard shell to protect its back, and is equipped with claws for weapons. But there are more than 1,000 kinds of crabs, so they vary quite a bit. The delicious pea crab is less than 25 centimetres and is often found inside the shells of living oysters. The Japanese giant crab, at the other extreme, may have a body that measures 30 centimetres across, and if you include the legs, it may measure 3.5 metres across.

Most crabs live in salt water, although there are several fresh-water species. Though there are crabs that live on land, these crabs always return to the water to lay their eggs.

The crab's small abdomen is folded under the body. The eyes are on the end of stalks which it can stick out or draw in at will. Crabs have six pairs of jaws, which are kept busy most of the time, since crabs are scavengers, eating whatever they can find. Many of them eat other crabs and small fish; some are vegetarians. The famous robber crabs of the tropics even go so far as to climb coconut trees for the nuts!

All crabs have five pairs of legs. The foremost pair are generally equipped with claws. The rearmost pair are frequently flattened at the ends into paddles for swimming. On land, crabs generally travel sidewise and can go quite rapidly.

By the way, "soft-shell crabs," which people like to eat, are not crabs with a special kind of soft shell, but crabs whose old shell has been shed and whose new shell has not yet hardened.

BLUE CRAB

SPIDER CRAB

When we look at an opened oyster lying in its shell, it's hard to believe that this is a creature capable of performing many complicated functions. Let's examine the oyster and see how it manages to get along in life.

CAN OYSTERS LIVE OUT OF WATER?

There are more than 100 species of living oysters, and their shape, size, and shell vary with their environment. The body of the American oyster rests on the left, cuplike side of the shell; the right, or upper side, is usually flat. The narrow part of the shell is the front end of the oyster; the broad and rounded part is the back.

The two shells, or valves, are held together by an elastic ligament. Underneath the shell is a soft membrane called the "mantle." The oyster has two rows of tentacles growing out of the mantle, which are used for protection. These tentacles can detect any disturbance, or change in light, or any irritating substance. They send a message through the nerves of the mantle to the muscle which closes the shell.

The oyster cannot attack other animals, so it can protect itself only by closing the shell tightly and keeping it sealed. This is done by the action of a special muscle. All edible oysters can live after being taken out of the water, due to this muscle. In fact, certain oysters can remain in good condition for about four months if they are kept at a temperature a few degrees above freezing. But when warmed, shaken, or handled roughly, the muscle relaxes, the valves gap open, the water inside the shell is lost, and the oyster soon dies.

The oyster breathes by means of gills, and pumps water into itself to obtain the oxygen. The oyster feeds on micro-organisms that exist in the water. These are living things so tiny that they can only be seen through a microscope. Yet the oyster is sensitive enough to select only the organisms for food that are the right size and shape and suitable in other ways.

The oyster has a narrow "throat" which opens into its stomach, and an intestine. It has a structure where the food is ground and digested by an enzyme. It also has blood cells which surround the food and digest it. The oyster has a heart, arteries, veins, and sinuses, and a complete circulatory system. The heart beats from 15 to 24 beats per minute. The blood of the oyster is colorless.

This brief description gives you an idea that there's more to an oyster than you suspected!

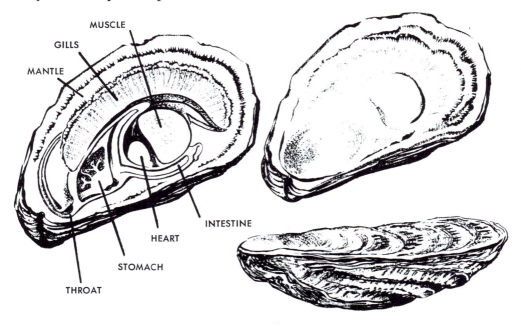

MUSCLE

GILLS

MANTLE

INTESTINE

HEART

STOMACH

THROAT

Anybody who owns a canary probably knows about "cuttlebone," which comes from the cuttlefish. The cuttlebone is given to canaries and other cage birds so they can sharpen their beaks on it.

WHAT IS A CUTTLEFISH?

But, except for this, the cuttlefish is quite unknown to most of us. The cuttlefish is not a fish, but a mollusk. It belongs to the class of mollusks called "cephalopods," which means "head-footed animals." This is because of the arrangement of the arms, or feet, around the mouth. The octopus also belongs to this class of mollusk.

The cuttlefish is a rather remarkable creature. It travels smoothly and silently through the water by moving the row of fins which are fastened to its shield-shaped body. Sometimes when it moves, it erects the first pair of its tentacles, or feelers. When it comes within striking distance of its prey, it suddenly shoots out its two long tentacles from pockets which are located in its broad head behind its staring bulging eyes.

It grasps its victim with the suckers at the ends of these tentacles, and draws it within reach of four shorter pairs of arms, which also have suckers, and are arranged around its head. It also has a parrot-like beak, and if its victim happens to have a hard shell, it simply crushes it in this beak.

If the cuttlefish decides it wants to retreat suddenly from an enemy, it backs away quickly. It does this by forcing out water through a tube called the "siphon." Sometimes, when it wants to discourage the enemy from chasing it, it darkens the water with a cloud of inkline fluid called "sepia."

This inklike sepia is used by man, by the way; it makes a rich brown pigment, or coloring matter. The flesh of the cuttlefish can be eaten after it is dried, and the cuttlebone, which is a bonelike shell beneath the skin of the cuttlefish, is powdered and used in some toothpastes.

Chapter 3

ALL ABOUT HUMAN BEINGS

Dwarfs, or midgets, as people sometimes call them, have fascinated people since ancient times. Many royal courts kept dwarfs for the amusement of the royal family. And one of the most famous dwarfs of all time, General Tom Thumb, was seen by millions of people. His real name was Charles Stratton, and he was less than 100 centimetres tall and weighed 11 kilograms at the age of 25!

WHY ARE SOME PEOPLE MIDGETS?

People may be very tall or very short and still be of normal height. Too much or too little growth is usually caused by disease or by the way certain glands do, or do not, work.

Generally speaking, a person's height is due to heredity. In Africa, tribes such as the Watusi and Masai have many men 2 metres tall. This is normal height for them. At the same time, there are pygmy tribes in Africa whose people are only about 1.3 metres tall. This is normal for them.

The dwarf whose height is not normal usually has some disorder in the endocrine glands. The endocrine, pituitary, adrenal, thyroid, and male and female sex glands all can influence how tall a person will be.

There is a kind of dwarf whose head and trunk are normal in size, but whose arms and legs are short. This can be caused by a disease. A normal body skeleton increases in length during childhood and adolescence because cartilage changes into bone at the growing ends of the bones. Diseases of the cartilage could prevent the arms and legs from growing in a normal manner.

Dwarfism can be caused by a lack of hormones in the pituitary gland. The child grows during the first few years and then stops. His proportions remain childlike. Such a child can be helped by hormones.

We all know that there are Pygmies. But is there any group of people taller than the average, as the Pygmies are shorter?

The answer is no. Height varies throughout the world. Some peoples, such as the Eskimos, Lapps, and certain Indian tribes in South America, are short. Some of the native tribes of eastern Africa have an average height of 1.8 metres or more. But they are not giants.

IS THERE ANY GROUP OF PEOPLE WHO ARE GIANTS?

In fact, giants seem to have existed only in myths and folklore. In many parts of Europe and Asia, there are legends of giants who existed in ancient times. But there is no scientific evidence that such people ever actually existed.

Yet we all know of giants who appear in circuses and side shows. How did they get to be so tall? Unfortunately, these are usually people who are suffering from an abnormal condition of their bodies. In most cases, it is a disturbance of one of the most important glands of the body, the pituitary.

The pituitary gland regulates the functioning and growth of many organs. Sometimes it develops a tumor which makes the gland larger. This larger gland then begins to produce too many of the hormones which are the secretion of this gland. One of these hormones is the growth hormone, which has an effect on the size of the organs and skeleton of the body.

When too much of this hormone is produced while the bones are still in the process of growing, they will continue to grow. Such a person might then reach 2.4 metres tall. This condition is known as giantism. But such a person is a giant only because something went wrong with his body.

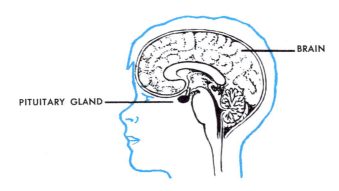

BRAIN

PITUITARY GLAND

Hormones are secreted by the endocrine glands. Endocrine means "the internal secretion of a gland." Another name for them is ductless glands, because they don't send their secretions into ducts but directly into the

WHAT IS A HORMONE?

bloodstream. Hormones are also produced by some organs such as the liver and the kidney, but most of the hormones in the body come from glands.

Each of the various hormones produces its own special effect in the body. In general, the job of the hormones is to regulate the internal activities of the body, such as growth and nutrition, the storage and use of food materials, and the reproductive processes. If the glands produce too much or not enough, a person may have an abnormal physical appearance.

Here are what some of the chief glands and hormones do in our bodies: The thyroid gland, located in the neck, produces a hormone which helps in the growth, development, and metabolic processes of the body.

The pituitary gland, located at the base of the skull, has two parts. As we know, one hormone produced by one part of this gland has the job of promoting growth.

Another part of the pituitary gland produces two hormones which help control our use of water, fat, our blood pressure, and the way we regulate the heat in our body.

There are two important glands located at the upper end of each kidney. They produce a hormone called adrenalin. This hormone is related to blood pressure and reactions to emotion and emergencies. When you become excited or frightened, you produce more of this hormone.

Other glands in the body produce hormones which have to do with making you act like a boy or a girl. So you see that hormones are responsible for a great deal about you and your health.

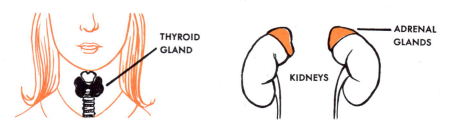

THYROID GLAND

ADRENAL GLANDS

KIDNEYS

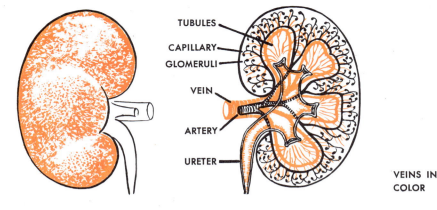

TUBULES
CAPILLARY
GLOMERULI
VEIN
ARTERY
URETER

VEINS IN COLOR

The kidneys, two flat, bean-shaped, solid organs, are among the most important in our body. About 10 centimetres, they lie on each side of the spine near the waistline.

HOW DO OUR KIDNEYS FUNCTION?

The kidneys remove unwanted substances from the body. It is just as important for the body to get rid of what it doesn't need and can't use as it is for it to take in what it needs. They also regulate the amount of water and other substances in the blood.

In the outer part of each kidney, the blood capillaries form tiny loops that make up a ball-like shape covered by a delicate membrane. In each kidney there are about 1,500,000 of these tiny balls called glomeruli. More blood flows through the kidneys every minute than through any other organ. The glomeruli allow some of the fluid of the blood which carries the finest dissolved materials to pass through their membranes.

The fluid that passes through is called urine. It is collected within the cuplike wall which covers each glomerulus. A very delicate tube called a tubule drains the urine from the cups.

As the urine flows through the tiny tubules, the lining cells are busy exchanging materials between the blood and urine. Substances that the body needs are taken back into the blood. In this way, sugar is not lost from the body.

Much of the water in the tubules also returns to the blood. In this way, the kidneys help to keep the body properly moist. If a person is perspiring or is not drinking enough water, the kidneys will return more fluid to the blood. Then less urine is formed, too. The kidney tubules also help regulate the acid in the blood.

All the small tubules collect in the inner part of each kidney and open into a delicate sac, the pelvis of the kidney. The urine then goes down two tubes called ureters that connect each kidney with the bladder.

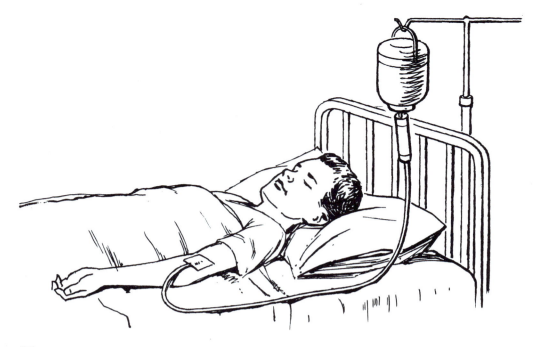

The average person has a little over six litres of blood in his body. This blood is composed of a fluid in which various types of cells are suspended. The fluid is called plasma.

WHAT IS PLASMA?

Of the total volume of the blood, about 55 per cent is made up of this plasma. It is a clear, slightly yellowish fluid. After you eat, small globules of fat become suspended in it and give it a milky appearance. This is why you are told not to eat before a blood sample is taken.

The plasma in your body is like a river which transports the articles vital to life. It transports the digested food materials from the walls of the small intestine to the body tissues. It also carries the waste materials from the tissues to the kidneys.

But that's only part of the job of the plasma. It carries the antibodies which give you immunity to disease, and the hormones which regulate various body activities. In addition, it transports most of the waste carbon dioxide from the tissues back to the lungs. So you see that the plasma actually contains several hundred different substances.

Aside from these substances, plasma is made up of about 91 per cent water, 7 per cent protein material, and 9/10 per cent mineral salts. The salts and proteins are very important in keeping the proper balance between the water in the tissues and in the blood. The mineral salts in the plasma also perform other vital functions in the body. The plasma obtains them from the food we eat.

In the body of an adult human being, there are about six litres of blood. Floating about in this liquid there are approximately 35 billion blood cells!

HOW DOES THE BODY MAKE BLOOD CELLS?

It is almost impossible for us to imagine such a tremendous quantity, but this might give you an idea. Each blood cell is so tiny that it can only be seen under a microscope. If you could make a string of these microscopic cells, that string would go four times around the earth!

Where do these cells come from? Obviously, the "factory" that turns out such an enormous quantity of cells must have amazing productive power — especially when you consider that sooner or later every one of these cells disintegrates and is replaced by a new one!

The birthplace of the blood cells is the bone marrow. If you look at an opened bone, you can see the reddish-grey, spongy marrow in the cavity of the bone. If you look at it under a microscope, you can see a whole network of blood vessels and connective-tissue fibers. Between these and blood vessels are countless marrow cells, and the blood cells are born in these marrow cells.

When the blood cell lives in the bone marrow, it is a genuine cell with a nucleus of its own. But before it leaves the bone marrow for the blood stream, it loses the nucleus. As a result, the ripe blood cell is no longer a complete cell. It is not really a living structure any longer, but a kind of mechanical apparatus.

The blood cell is like a balloon made of protoplasm, and filled with the blood pigment hemoglobin, which makes it red. The sole function of the blood cell is to combine with oxygen in the lungs, and to exchange the oxygen for carbon dioxide in the tissues.

The number and size of the blood cells in a living creature depend on its need for oxygen. Worms have no blood cells. Cold-blooded amphibians have large and relatively few cells in their blood. Animals that are small, warm-blooded, and live in mountainous regions have the most blood cells.

The human bone marrow adapts itself to our needs for oxygen. At high altitudes, it produces more cells; at low altitudes, less. People living on a mountain top may have almost twice as many blood cells as people living along the seacoast!

The blood which flows through the arteries, capillaries, and veins of your body contains many different materials and cells. Each part of the blood has its own special work and importance.

WHY IS OUR BLOOD RED? There is, first of all, the liquid part of the blood. This is called the plasma, and makes up a little more than half the blood. It is light yellow and a little thicker than water because many substances are dissolved in it.

What are some of these substances? — Proteins, antibodies that fight disease, fibrinogen that helps the blood to clot, carbohydrates, fats, salts, and so on, in addition to the blood cells.

The red cells (also called red blood corpuscles) give the blood its color. There are so many of them in the blood that it all looks red. There are about 35 billion of these tiny, round, flat discs moving around in your body all at once! And they stay in the blood vessels at all times.

As the young red cell grows and takes on adult form in the marrow, it loses its nucleus and builds up more and more hemoglobin. Hemoglobin is the red pigment, or color. It contains iron combined with protein.

As the blood passes through the lungs, oxygen joins the hemoglobin of the red cells. The red cells carry the oxygen through the arteries and capillaries to all cells of the body. Carbon dioxide from the body cells is returned to the lungs through the veins in the same way, combined mainly with hemoglobin.

Red cells live only about four months and then are broken up, mostly in the spleen. New red cells are always being formed to replace the cells that are worn out and destroyed.

In addition to the red blood cells, there are also several kinds of white blood cells.

You can see that blood, so necessary for life, is not a simple thing. Many different substances have their special work and importance.

WHAT DO WHITE BLOOD CELLS DO? Although the red cells are by far more numerous in the blood and give blood its color, the white blood cells have a critical role, too. The white blood cells are called leucocytes.

The most common leucocytes are granular cells. These cells pass in and out of the blood to the spot where germs or injured tissue have collected. Some of these cells, called neutrophiles, take bacteria into themselves and destroy them. They also give off substances which digest and soften dead tissue and form pus.

Other white cells in the blood are called lymphocytes. The lymphocytes often increase in numbers in a part of the body where infection has continued for more than a short time. This is a part of the body's process for fighting infections, so you can see their job is quite important.

Still other white blood cells are the monocytes. These cells, together with other cells in the tissues, have the ability to take up pieces of dead material. They can also surround material such as dirt, and keep it from coming in contact with healthy tissue cells.

By the way, even though white blood cells are so necessary to the body, too many of them are not good either. When too many white blood cells are formed, and they do not grow into the healthy, active cells that are needed, the condition is called leukemia, or cancer of the blood.

So the blood is like a chemical formula in which there has to be just the right amount of each substance — red cells, white cells, proteins, salts, carbohydrates, fats, and so on.

We can't afford to lose any blood. Even though a healthy person can lose as much as one third of all his blood and still live, a steady loss of blood, or loss of blood while we are sick, would be very dangerous.

WHAT MAKES BLOOD CLOT? Nature has protected us against this danger by giving blood the capacity to clot. If this clotting took place inside our circulatory system, it would be equally dangerous. So blood does not coagulate, or clot, when it is in contact with the smooth walls of the blood vessels. In fact, if blood is poured into a very smooth or lubricated glass vessel, it won't clot! If you dip a glass rod into blood, it won't clot either. Yet if you used a wooden rod, clotting would begin!

So it seems that it takes a rough surface, or an injury to the blood vessels, to start the clotting process. The first thing that happens is that very fine threads of a material called fibrin appear in the blood. These threads run every which way and form a kind of network. They entangle all the blood cells like flies in a spider's web. The blood stream stops moving at this point and is transformed into a kind of swamp of blood cells.

The fibrin threads are firm and very elastic and they hold the blood cells together in a clot. A clot of blood is like a piece of absorbent cotton which nature creates to protect us from loss of blood.

Everybody's blood clots at a slightly different rate. There are some people whose blood clots very slowly or not at all, and this condition is called hemophilia. It's a very curious disease because of the way it is transmitted. Hemophilia appears only in men, but it is never transmitted directly from father to son. It is transmitted from the father to the daughter, who remains healthy, but passes it on to her son. So it's the grandchild of the sick father who gets the disease!

Probably the most famous example in the history of this disease deals with Queen Victoria of England. Both she and her husband transmitted hemophilia from their ancestors. As a result, six of their great-grandchildren had the disease, and two of these were the Spanish Crown Prince and the son of the last Russian Czar!

There is no transportation system in any city that can compare in efficiency with the circulatory system of the body.

If you will imagine two systems of pipes, one large and one small,

HOW DO ARTERIES DIFFER FROM VEINS?

both meeting at a central pumping station, you'll have an idea of the circulatory system. The smaller system of pipes goes from the heart to the lungs and back. The larger one goes from the heart to the various other parts of the body.

These pipes are called arteries, veins, and capillaries. Arteries are blood vessels in which blood is going away from the heart. In veins, the blood is coming back to the heart. In general, arteries are carrying pure blood to various parts of the body; and the veins are bringing back blood loaded with waste products. The capillaries are tiny vessels for conducting blood from arteries to veins. The pumping station is the heart.

Arteries lie deep in the tissues, except at the wrist, over the instep, at the temple, and along the sides of the neck. At any of these places, the pulse can be felt, and a doctor can get an idea of the condition of the arteries.

The largest arteries have valves where they leave the heart. These vessels are made of many elastic muscles which can expand and contract. Arterial blood is bright red in color and moves through the arteries in spurts.

Veins lie closer to the surface of the skin; the blood in them is darker and flows more evenly; and they have valves at intervals all along their course.

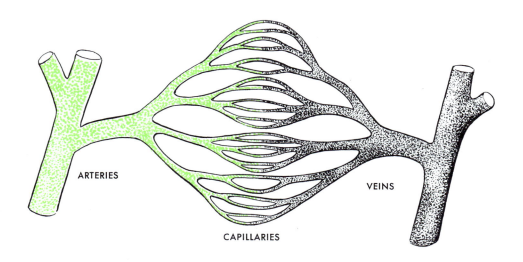

ARTERIES

VEINS

CAPILLARIES

Elderly people and people who spend a great deal of time on their feet sometimes develop varicose veins. You may have noticed them on people who have this condition; the veins are swollen, twisted, and quite blue.

WHAT ARE VARICOSE VEINS?

Varicose veins are veins that have lost their elasticity, a loss which causes them to swell and look twisted. The swelling occurs because the weakened walls of the veins can no longer withstand the pressure of the blood in the veins.

Imagine that the veins are simply continuous tubes running from the legs to the heart. When a person stands up, the weight of the column of blood in the veins presses out on the walls of the veins. Now, in normal veins, there are valves which prevent the full weight of the blood from causing pressure on the veins in the leg. But once a vein has lost its elasticity, it becomes distended or spread out. The walls of the vein don't hold "tightly" any more. When this happens, the valves can't close completely and so they can't function properly.

The result is that the weight of the blood in that vein presses out on the walls of the vein, and this causes them to swell out even more. Since our veins are distended a little bit anyway when we stand, the condition may not be noticed when it first appears.

Often, the change in the veins takes place over a long period of time. A person may first notice it when he has a sensation of heaviness or tiredness in the legs. He may develop cramps in his legs at night. He may have a dull ache in the feet and legs, and the ankles may swell up more than usual after a day's work. When this is accompanied by the appearance of enlarged and twisted veins, then it's a sign that a person probably has varicose veins.

There are many ways of treating varicose veins. In some cases, all that's needed is time spent keeping the legs above the heart level to permit the veins to empty more easily. In other cases, injections are given to "harden" the veins. And in severe cases, it may be necessary to remove portions of a vein.

There are all kinds of big roads and highways connecting big cities so that food and other necessary materials can reach them. But what about the small towns and little villages? They need food and supplies, too.

WHAT ARE CAPILLARIES?

The little roads and byways that reach the small towns and villages are like the capillaries in the human body. As we know, blood is pumped out of the heart to all parts of the body and the big vessels through which this blood flows are known as the arteries. But far from the heart, in all parts of the body, these big vessels become tiny hairlike branches called capillaries.

A capillary is 50 times thinner than the thinnest human hair! In fact, the average diameter of a capillary is about 0.008 millimetres. It is so thin that blood corpuscles pass through a capillary in single file, which means blood passes through the capillaries very slowly.

About 700 capillaries could be packed into the space occupied by a pin. Each capillary is about 0.5 millimetres long. Since the purpose of capillaries is to bring and take away needed substances to and from every part of the body, you can imagine how many millions upon millions of capillaries there are in the human body.

What happens when blood flows through a single capillary (which takes about a second)? The blood does not leave the capillary. But the wall of the capillary is very thin; it consists of only a single layer of cells. Through this wall, the blood gives up its oxygen to the surrounding tissues. In return, it receives the carbon dioxide which the tissues around the capillary have given up.

At the same time, other substances which supply nourishment to the tissues pass from the blood, and waste products enter the capillary. Eventually, the blood and the materials it has picked up are returned to the heart by way of the veins.

The heart, as we have learned, is a pump that sends the blood circulating through our body. The pumping action takes place when the left ventricle of the heart contracts. This forces the blood out into the arteries, which expand to receive the oncoming blood.

WHAT IS BLOOD PRESSURE?

But the arteries have a muscular lining which resists this pressure, and thus the blood is squeezed out of them into the smaller vessels of the body. Blood pressure is the amount of pressure on the blood as a result of the heart's pumping and the resistance of the arterial walls.

There are two kinds of pressure: maximum and minimum. The maximum pressure occurs when the left ventricle contracts; it is called the systolic pressure. The minimum pressure occurs just before the heartbeat which follows; it is called the diastolic pressure.

When your doctor measures your blood pressure, he uses an instrument which measures it in terms of a column of mercury, which rises and falls under the pressure. He reads it in millimetres rather than in inches. The average systolic pressure in a young man is about 120 millimetres (about 5 inches) of mercury. The diastolic pressure is about 80 millimetres of mercury. These figures are usually stated as 120/80, or 120 over 80.

When the blood pressure is in this range, it provides the body with a circulating supply of blood without unduly straining the walls of the blood vessels. But there are many variations from this range which may be quite normal.

With age, the blood pressure gradually rises until, at 60 years, it is about 140/87. There are many factors that affect the blood pressure. Overweight people often have a higher blood pressure than people of normal weight. Tension, exercise, and even posture may affect the blood pressure.

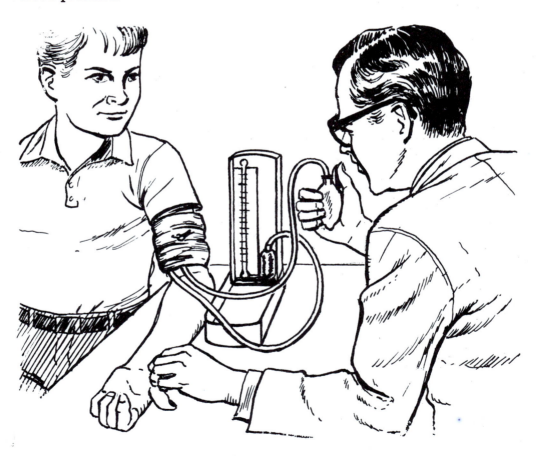

You have probably had your pulse taken hundreds of times. And it's quite a simple thing for you to take your own pulse or someone else's. When a nurse or doctor does it, the patient is sitting or lying down.

WHAT IS THE PULSE?

The arm is placed in a relaxed position with the thumb turned upward. With the index finger, the nurse finds the pulse beat on the wrist near the thumb side of the hand. The beats are counted for one minute.

Actually, the pulse can also be felt over the instep, at the temple, and along the sides of the neck. Now what is being felt and what is being measured? The pulse rate provides information about how fast the heart is beating and about the state of pressure in the circulatory system.

During the action of the heart there is a pause. During this pause, the wall of the aorta contracts. This contraction forces the excess blood (just received from the heart) to proceed along the circulatory system. This alternate expansion and shrinking, or pulsation, of the aorta produces a wave which passes along the entire system of arteries in the body. The pulsation of the arteries, which can be felt at any artery that can be felt through the skin, is called a pulse.

Since it depends on the contraction of the heart, the pulse tells us about the heart rate. The pulse rate depends on the blood requirements of the body. Small bodies lose more heat than large ones and need a more rapid circulation of the blood. So the pulse rate of small birds is almost 200! Cats have a pulse rate of 130; Man has about 75; the horse has 35; and an elephant has only 25.

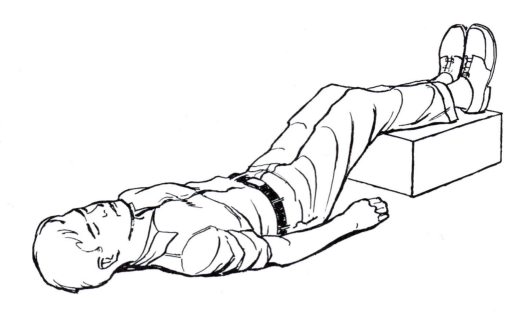

In a play or movie, a hero or heroine sometimes faints upon hearing bad news or when suddenly frightened. We usually associate fainting with an event of this kind. But the fact is that fainting can be the result of many situations.

WHAT CAUSES PEOPLE TO FAINT?

People may faint because of confinement in a close and poorly ventilated room, or because of hunger, fatigue, severe pain, emotional shock, or for many other reasons. The immediate cause of fainting is an insufficient supply of blood to the brain.

Because fainting happens so often, it is important to know what to do to help in such cases. A person who feels he is about to faint should be made to lie down immediately. If this is not possible, have him bend forward at the waist with his head between his knees. The idea is to try to get more blood to the brain.

When a person has fainted, keep him lying down and loosen any tight clothing. Lower the head or elevate the legs. Again, the object is to increase the supply of blood to the brain. When a person has regained consciousness, he may be given a stimulant such as coffee to drink, or spirits of ammonia to sniff.

Sometimes a person has become unconscious for reasons other

than fainting. For example, he may have suffered a blow on the head, shock, sunstroke, heat exhaustion, or even poisoning.

There are two types of unconsciousness and they should be treated differently. One is called "red" unconsciousness. The face is flushed and the pulse is strong. The patient should be made to lie down with the head and shoulders slightly elevated. Cold applications should be placed on the head. In "white" unconsciousness, the face is pale, the skin is clammy, and the pulse is weak. The patient should be kept lying down with the head lowered and should be covered to insure warmth.

WHAT IS SHOCK?

You may get a "shock" when you see your mark on a test, or you may say you're "shocked" if you see an accident. But medically speaking, this isn't shock. The word "shock" means a condition in which the essential activities of the body are affected. Usually, they are slowed up.

A person in a state of shock may have a sudden or gradual feeling of weakness or faintness. He may become very pale, and the skin may feel cold and clammy. Perspiration is increased, and the pupils of the eyes become enlarged.

Shock is also accompanied by changes in the mental state. It can begin with a feeling of restlessness, and it may develop to a state of unconsciousness.

All of these are symptoms of shock. They are produced because the volume of blood in effective circulation is lowered, along with the blood pressure. As in fainting, blood going to the brain may eventually lead to unconsciousness. This lack of blood in the capillaries also explains why the skin may feel cold.

Of course, if a person has been injured so that he is losing a great deal of blood, this in itself will produce a state of shock. But shock may also be caused by undergoing great stress, by strong emotion, by pain or sudden illness, or by some accident. The important thing is that for one reason or another, the blood doesn't circulate as it should, and as a result, the essential activities of the body are affected.

The best thing to do when a person is in a state of shock is to get a doctor. Do not move the patient, have him sit up, or use a pillow under his head. Lay the person on his back if he is unconscious, and keep him warm until help comes.

As human beings, we are subject not only to physical pain, but also to emotional pain. A situation may cause us great emotional distress. Sometimes we deal with this quite simply. For example, we may cry, or blush, or break out in a sweat.

WHY ARE SOME PEOPLE AFRAID OF HEIGHTS?

But sometimes, when the emotional stress is greater, or our power of resistance is weaker, we may develop other reactions for dealing with this pain. One such way is called a phobic reaction. What it means is that the emotional pain we feel, or the anxiety, as it is called, becomes attached to a specific object or situation. By avoiding this object or situation, we are able to avoid the emotional pain or anxiety that it symbolizes.

Some of the common phobias are fear of small, enclosed places, of large wide-open spaces, of public gatherings, of high places, of the dark, of animals, and of germs.

Of course, the person who has this phobia (fear of heights, for example) doesn't realize why he has it. He is not aware of the inner workings of his mind. All he knows is that he feels afraid in a certain

situation, and so he avoids it. He may even recognize that his fear is unreasonable.

To illustrate our point, let's take a child growing up in an average family; he loves his family but he is also sometimes afraid of some of them. He might be afraid of his father, for example, even though he loves him. He doesn't like to feel afraid of his father, so he unconsciously hides this feeling. He may transfer it to something high and may thus develop a fear of high places.

It is important to know that many, many people have emotional pain and that with medical help, these anxieties can be treated. We should show sympathy and understanding for people who have phobias.

There are many things that people sometimes claim they "see" that really aren't there. They may have visions of "ghosts" or strange creatures. Sometimes little children claim they "saw" things that no one else did. Sometimes these are fantasies or daydreams; sometimes they are illusions.

WHAT ARE HALLUCINATIONS?

There is a difference between an illusion and an hallucination. When a person has an illusion, there is something present that stimulates the eyes or senses. It can be verified, because other people see it, too. A mirage, for example, is a kind of illusion. But the main point is that something is there that causes the person to think he saw what he saw.

When a person has a hallucination, however, nothing is there! There is no outside stimulation to the eyes or the senses. The only stimulation comes from the person himself, from his own fantasy.

Hallucinations can be of various types, relating to the various senses. The most common have to do with hearing. A person imagines he hears voices, mutterings, laughter, cries, bells ringing, music playing or even shots ringing out! The second most common type of hallucination has to do with seeing. People imagine they see certain persons who aren't there, or they may see animals, objects, or whole scenes before them. Sometimes they "see" strange, horrible, and unearthly things that terrify them. And sometimes people even have hallucinations about tastes and smells, or things they feel on their skin!

There are many reasons why people have hallucinations. One of the most common is that a person is very troubled and disturbed by something. If someone has been aroused emotionally to a high pitch, perhaps very angry or frightened, he may have hallucinations.

In other words, persons who are hallucinating are usually in a state of great excitement, fear, ecstasy, or anticipation of something. Certain drugs also cause hallucinations. Cocaine, for example, gives the hallucination of insects crawling on the skin!

Every now and then, you read in the papers about a person who has "forgotten" who he is. He remembers nobody and nothing from his past, not even his name. We say this person is suffering from amnesia.

WHAT IS AMNESIA?

We all get emotionally upset from time to time. We feel hurt, angry, disappointed or frightened for one reason or another. When we feel such emotional pain, we want to do something about it. For example, a simple way of dealing with it is to cry, or blush, or break out in a cold sweat. In fact, these reactions happen without our control. They are considered normal reactions, since practically everyone has them.

But a person may react to emotional stress and pain in another way. Instead of facing the problems that caused him to be upset, he tries to act in such a way that he won't feel the anxiety. He "runs away" from it. He "protects" himself in this way from emotional pain.

One form of this reaction is amnesia. A person simply acts as if all those things which bothered and upset him so much didn't really happen to him but to someone else! He "forgets" his anxiety.

In forgetting this, he also forgets a great many other things that were linked to his anxiety — including who he was! He just can't remember anything about the past. But he may act quite normally about the present. He lives and works as another person, and may not attract any special attention.

Sometimes a person recovers from amnesia suddenly, of his own accord. In many cases, however, a person can be helped to recover by a psychiatrist. A curious thing is that people who recover from amnesia don't remember events which took place while they were suffering from amnesia.

Did you ever have the feeling that you knew something was going to happen just before it did? Or you could tell exactly what card was going to be turned up or what number called?

WHAT IS E. S. P.? There are many cases of people who seem to have this ability—not on rare occasions, but more frequently than the average person. How do they do it? It is believed by some that they are gifted with clairvoyance, or precognition, or that they have extra-sensory perception. This means that they can perceive things beyond the use of the ordinary senses.

At Duke University, for more than 25 years, Professor J. B. Rhine

has been carrying on experiments intended to prove that extra-sensory perception exists and to measure it in people. These experiments involved clairvoyance, telepathy, and precognition.

In the clairvoyance tests, a special deck of cards is used. This deck is made up of five cards, each with five different symbols: a cross, a circle, a star, wavy lines, and a square. The experiments consist of having people who are supposed to have extra-sensory perception identify cards in various ways without seeing them. When the number of correct guesses is higher than the average person achieves, this is considered proof that the person has extra-sensory perception.

In the telepathy experiments, a person tries to "read the mind" of the one conducting the experiment by guessing the cards.

In the precognition experiments, an attempt is made to predict a sequence of events before they occur, again using cards or dice.

There is a good deal of controversy as to whether these experiments have actually proved the existence of extra-sensory perception. But there is now considerable agreement that the results do indicate something that was not happening by chance alone.

Here's a sure way to win a bet! Challenge anybody you know to walk blindfolded straight down the sidewalk without going off the edge. He is sure to lose because he'll soon start walking in a circle!

WHY DO WE WALK IN CIRCLES WHEN WE'RE LOST?

People who have been lost in a fog or in a snowstorm, have often walked for hours imagining they were heading in a straight direction. After a while, they arrived right back where they started from.

Here's the reason why we can't walk in a straight line without our eyes to guide us. Our body is asymmetrical. This means there is not a

perfect balance between our right side and our left side. The heart for instance is on the left side, the liver on the right. The skeleton of our body is asymmetrical too. The spine is not perfectly straight. Our thighs and our feet are different on each side of our body. All of this means that the structure of the muscles in our body is asymmetrical, or not perfectly balanced.

Since our muscles differ from right side to left side, this affects the way we walk, our gait. When we close our eyes, the control of our gait depends on the muscles and structure of our body, and one side forces us to turn in a certain direction. We end up walking in a circle.

By the way, this is true not only of the muscles in our legs, but in our arms, too. Tests were made in which blindfolded people tried to drive a car in a straight line. In about 20 seconds, every person in the test began to drive off the road! It's a good reason for keeping your eyes wide open whether you're walking or driving!

Seasickness is related to the whole question of equilibrium and dizziness. Our organs of balance contain certain stiff hairs which are surrounded by liquid. When we move in any direction, the liquid moves the hairs.

WHY DO WE GET SEASICK?

These hairs send a message to the brain, which gives us the sensation of moving in that direction.

In our normal activities this liquid, called lymph, and the motion of the hairs are such that our bodies can adjust to changes easily and we manage to keep our balance. But what happens on a ship? As the position of the deck changes under our feet, the lymph is shaken back and forth. It actually rocks to and fro, and from side to side.

This makes the sensory hairs whip back and forth, too. So the messages they send to the brain are switched on and off. As soon as one "order" arrives at the brain, another "order" follows it with completely different instructions. The position of the ship changes so quickly that the brain receives messages which contradict each other!

The result is a state of confusion in that part of the nervous system. What we soon begin to feel, therefore, is dizziness, headache, spots in front of our eyes, flushes, cold sweats, gagging, and vomiting—all of which add up to what we know as seasickness.

Unfortunately, the only possible remedies for this can be to find some way of bringing the lymph in our organs of balance to a standstill, or to prevent the messages from influencing us. All the known remedies for seasickness act in the second way. There is no possible way yet known to make the lymph and the hairs in them stop their motion.

What a seasick remedy does, therefore, is one of the following: it paralyzes the part of the brain through which the messages travel; or it paralyzes the vomiting center in the brain, or it cuts down on the sensitivity of certain nerves.

Actually, one of the best remedies is to go to the steadiest part of the ship, the center, and to remain there as quietly as possible. Another important thing is to try not to be afraid, because fear and imagination always make seasickness worse!

In ancient times, people didn't understand diseases and what caused them. So they often behaved very cruelly to victims of certain diseases. People who had epilepsy in the Middle Ages were thought of as lunatics,

WHAT IS EPILEPSY?

or bewitched! Yet did you know that many great people and many geniuses were epileptic? Among them were the Duke of Wellington, Richard Wagner, Vincent van Gogh, and Louis Hector Berlioz.

Epilepsy is a disease of the nervous system. People with epilepsy have sudden spells during which they have spasms called convulsions, after which they may become unconscious or fall into a coma.

Doctors cannot yet explain exactly what happens and what causes the convulsions. It seems that the normal patterns of activity of the brain become disrupted for a short time. The brain tissue in these people is sensitive to chemical changes, and when some sort of change takes place, the brain responds by sending out discharges that cause the convulsions.

A person has to be predisposed to epilepsy to have such reactions, because other people may undergo the same chemical changes and not have convulsions. There is a possibility that it is hereditary.

An epileptic attack may be caused by a head injury, a high fever, tumors, or scars in the brain substance, disturbances in the blood supply, and so on. Injury to the brain may result in epilepsy.

Epilepsy, however, has nothing to do with mental development. A person who has epilepsy should be considered a normal individual, not an invalid or some sort of outcast. Epileptics can lead normal lives — go to school, work, marry, and raise families.

Medical science has developed drugs to prevent attacks, and to control them when they do occur. These medicines are usually given to people over a period of many years, or even for a lifetime, so that they lead normal, happy lives.

Of all the things that distinguish man from the rest of the animal kingdom, the most important is his brain. Many of the lower animals have no brain at all, or a tiny one, or one that is poorly developed. For

WHAT IS THE BRAIN?

instance, an earthworm has a brain about the size of a pinhead, a rabbit has a thimble-sized brain. The brain of a man weighs, on the average, about 1.3 kilograms.

By the way, the size of the brain is not the most important thing about it. An elephant has a bigger brain than man, but it is not as well developed.

The brain has three main divisions: the cerebrum, the cerebellum, and the medulla oblongata. The cerebrum is considered the most important part. It is from here that all our voluntary actions are controlled.

The cerebrum is also the biggest part of man's brain, filling most of the space in the upper and back part of the skull. The cerebrum is divided into two equal parts or hemispheres, and its surface is covered with wrinkles and folds. This surface is composed of gray matter, made up of cells. The higher the type of animal, the more numerous and deeper are the folds. Under this surface, called the cortex, there is white matter which is made up of nerve fibers. Through this part pass the messages to and from the cortex.

Certain sections of the cortex control certain body functions, so every part of the cortex is different. Science can point to certain parts as the controls over sight, or feeling, or hearing, or movement of certain muscles. That's why an injury to just one part of the brain (for instance, by a blood clot) can impair one's capacity to perform a certain function, such as speech.

The cerebellum is in the back of the skull, beneath the cerebrum. It controls the power of balancing and the co-ordination of the muscles. If it is injured, a man may not be able to walk in a straight line or stand erect.

The medulla oblongata is about the size of the end of the thumb and is found at the end of the spinal cord. It controls breathing, the beating of the heart, digestion, and many other activities that seem to go on by themselves. This is where the nerve fibers that go from the brain to the spinal cord cross. One side of the brain controls the other side of the body. The right half of the cerebrum, for example, controls the left leg, and so on.

A person's mental and physical growth usually correspond. Both types of growth stop at various ages, depending on the individual. For instance, one person may be 1.6 metres tall at the age of sixteen,

WHAT IS AN I.Q.? and never grow taller. But his brother may continue growing until he has reached 1.8 metres. at the age of nineteen. Mental growth for most people stops some time during the teens.

If you take all the children born on October 10, 1947, for example, and examine them today, they will be different in physical development. Some will be tall, some average, and some short. But they will also differ in mental development. Some will be bright and able to learn new things easily, some will be average, and some will be very slow in their ability to learn. This difference in mental development may be considered a difference in mental age.

While we can measure the height of a person, how do we measure mental development? A series of mental tests have been worked out for this purpose. Here is how it is done: First we find out which problems can be resolved by children of various ages. Six-year-olds can do certain problems; eight-year-olds can do others, and so on.

Now suppose we give the test for six-year-olds to various children. A few four- and five-year-old children can also do them. On the other hand, there may be children ten or twelve years old for whom they are too difficult. So now we have a way of measuring intelligence. If a six-year-old can do just the six-year-old test, he is average. If a child of four or five can do this test, he is superior. If a ten-year-old can't even do the six-year-old test, he is retarded.

The letters "I.Q." are an abbreviation for "intelligence quotient," which is a way of describing the results of these tests in mathematical terms. For example, a six-year-old child with a mental age of six has an I.Q. of 100. The mental age is divided by the chronological age (age in years) and then multiplied by 100. If a five-year-old has a mental age of six, his I.Q. is 120 (six divided by five, times 100). I.Q.'s between 90 and 100 are average; those above 110 are considered superior.

Every now and then we hear about someone in school who is considered a genius. Or we may read in the papers about someone who has done something so exceptional that he is described as a genius. And, of course, in studying history, we have learned about many famous men whom we recognize as geniuses.

WHAT IS A GENIUS?

Exactly what is a genius, and what does it take to be one? The word "genius" is used to describe someone who possesses extraordinary intelligence. The way the world can recognize a genius is by knowing what he has accomplished. There may be geniuses who have never accomplished anything extraordinary and who never became famous, but their I.Q.'s are, nevertheless, on a par with those who have. It may be too, that an unrecognized genius' accomplishments are unrecognized by average standards. Many recognized as geniuses today died in poverty, believing they had failed because their work was not acknowledged during their lifetimes.

Genius is not the same as talent. To have talent, a person has to be able to do some special type of work especially well. It means he is able to acquire a certain skill very quickly and easily. For instance, a person may have a talent for playing the piano, or ice-skating, or painting.

But genius is more than talent. A genius usually contributes something to the world which we would not have had without him.

Now, it's true that men of genius have usually specialized in some field such as chemistry, literature, music, or art. But unless the general intelligence of such a person is exceptional, too, he would merely have talent.

It is now believed that a person is born a genius. Training and opportunity bring out genius, but a true genius usually has tremendous drive which enables him to work hard and long and to overcome obstacles that would stop ordinary people.

EINSTEIN

$E = mc^2$

Can you recite the alphabet easily and quickly? Can you write your name easily? Can you play the scale on a musical instrument?

You would probably say that you memorized all this. But what

WHAT IS MEMORY?

you actually did was to learn them. And the way you learned them was by forming a habit! In other words, what was once quite difficult for you, such as reciting the alphabet or playing the scale, became easy and almost automatic when you formed a habit of doing it. So memory can be described as learning by means of forming habits.

A human being has a tremendous number of such habits that enable him to do most of the ordinary things in life, such as fastening a button or washing the hands. But suppose you read a book and someone asked you what the book was about, or to describe the plot. Surely, this cannot be called a habit.

But if you examine the situation carefully, you will see that something very much like habit does play a part. For example, in ordinary habits, you learn how to put certain elements together in the proper order. Now, when you give the plot of a book, or tell what it's about, you are doing the same kind of thing. In fact, some psychologists say that all learning (and this also means memory) is made up of a vast combination of simple habits.

But this doesn't mean that in learning and remembering you simply form habits by mechanically going through the motions of practice, or repeating them. There are several other things that enter into the situation and make it possible for you to learn and remember better.

One of these is the will to learn, or the motive or incentive. Another important thing is understanding what one is learning. For example, you will learn (or memorize) a poem more quickly when you understand it. And you will remember it longer, too.

Still another important help in learning and remembering is the association of new ideas with ideas you have already stored away in your memory.

Most of us think that every action we take is voluntary — that we sit down and stand up because we want to, or shake hands because we want to, and so on.

WHAT IS INSTINCT? But the actions of people and all living things are really not so easily explained. For example, as you ride a bicycle, you may make dozens of motions without even thinking about them as you do them. These actions are the result of learning and experience.

Now, suppose you touch something hot and instantly draw your finger away. You didn't even think of taking your finger away — you just did it. This action is a reflex action.

Now we come to a third kind of action that takes place without thinking on your part. You are hungry. You don't always tell yourself, "I am hungry, I will look for food." You just go about getting food. This kind of action might be described as an instinct.

Whether or not human beings really have instincts (such as seeking food, caring for one's young, etc.) is something psychologists are still not agreed upon. But we know that other animals act by instinct. An instinct is an action that accomplishes a certain objective without thinking on the part of the doer.

For example, a bird building a nest gathers sticks, grass, fibers, or down. It then arranges them upon a branch or ledge in such a way that the nest has a certain height and stability, and is like the nest of other birds of the same species. The only thing that can explain such behavior is instinct.

An instinctive action is always carried on because there is some natural stimulation inside the creature (such as hunger, fear, the desire to mate). In fact, it is quite probable that the secretions of certain glands in the body cause the bird or animal to perform what we call an instinctive act. Seeking food, mating, maternal care, migration, and hibernation are all related to the actions of the glands in a bird.

Almost all living animals have some instinctive behavior to satisfy some vital need of the body.

When you go to the doctor, does he ask you to cross your legs and then hit your knee with a small rubber hammer?

What the doctor is testing is the reflex action. In this case, it is a
WHAT CAUSES A REFLEX? special reflex called the patellar reflex, because the hammer struck a ligament called the patellar ligament.

What actually happens when the hammer strikes the ligament? A stimulus passes from a sensory cell in the ligament to the spinal cord. There it is transferred to a motor cell, and this sends an action current to the muscles of the leg. The leg twitches, just as if it were about to kick an enemy in self-defense.

This action is a reflex action. In other words, it is automatic. We have no control over it because it is not an action that is started in the brain. For instance, when you go to bed and close your eyes, you are performing a voluntary act. But if a speck of dust flies into your eye, you close it immediately whether you want to or not. This automatic movement is a reflex.

So we can define a reflex as an automatic response by the body to an external stimulus, without the influence of the will.

How does this happen?—The spinal cord is the transfer point for our reflexes. When sensory cells bring in the stimulus from the skin, they go to the spinal cord and are transferred there to motor cells. These motor cells send out currents to certain muscles and make them act. The nerve impulses do not pass through the brain.

More than 90 per cent of all the actions performed by man's nervous system are reflex actions!

The human nervous system is like a network of wires that lead from the brain, establishing contact with every portion of the body. The brain is the center of this system. From the brain, orders go forth over the

WHY DO WE HAVE TWO NERVOUS SYSTEMS?

nerve wires and make us move, laugh, eat, and otherwise behave like human beings.

The nerves also serve the brain as messengers. Through a special part of the nervous system, the brain is informed of everything that happens to the body. The main line of communication connecting brain and body is the spinal cord. It is enclosed within the backbone. The spinal cord is really a grouping together of the nerve trunks, similar to the grouping together of wires to form a cable.

Each trunk is composed of two sections called the dorsal (back) and ventral (front) roots. The dorsal roots are the ones that carry messages to the spinal cord, and from there to the brain. The ventral roots transmit the messages from the brain to the various parts of the body. The dorsal roots control sensation; the ventral roots control action. When someone touches us, we feel it through the dorsal nerve roots. If we move, the stimulus passes from the brain through the ventral roots.

This nervous system is called the cerebrospinal nervous system. It takes care of all our voluntary actions and our responses to external stimuli. Without this nervous system, there would be no thought, action, or sensation.

But as you know, the body also carries on involuntary actions. Vital organs have certain duties to perform which are done without conscious thought on our part. For example, digestion and breathing are carried on automatically and independently. Heart action is also automatic.

These involuntary actions, and many others, are carried on automatically by another nervous system called the automatic system. It does not require conscious control, though it does respond to stimuli from the cerebrospinal system. It forms a separate network within the body without which life would cease. So we need both systems to live and to function as human beings.

Alcohol is present in our body at all times. After every meal we eat, the carbohydrates, starch and sugar, form alcohol and enter the bloodstream. So there is always about a gram of alcohol circulating in our body.

WHY DOES ALCOHOL CAUSE DRUNKENNESS?

But what happens if we take in additional alcohol? Alcohol is a narcotic, which is how we describe a substance which enters the nerve cells quickly and tends to paralyze them. But before any narcotic paralyzes, it stimulates nerve cells, putting them in a state of excitement. So alcohol first acts as a stimulant. And in order for alcohol to continue to act as a stimulant rather than as a narcotic, it must be taken into the body in weak solutions.

The first thing alcohol does to the system is stimulate the gastric and salivary glands to produce their juices. That's why many European people take aperitifs made of spicy wines to stimulate the appetite.

The body absorbs warm alcohol solutions very quickly, and sugar and carbon dioxide speed up absorption, too. Champagne, for instance, contains both sugar and carbon dioxide, which is why it acts so quickly and produces such a stimulating effect.

How does alcohol affect the brain?—The first effect is a feeling of stimulation. Action and speech seem to be speeded up. The skin gets redder, blood pressure rises, the heart beats faster, and breathing is quickened.

But alcohol soon exerts a depressing effect on the brain. Our ability to observe, think, and pay attention is affected. As the higher functions of the brain are paralyzed, the power to control moods is lost.

Another serious effect is that inhibitions are relaxed. In our body, there are nerve fibers called inhibitory fibers which act as brakes in the nervous system. They are developed as the result of education and training, and make us disciplined, restrained people.

Under the influence of alcohol, these inhibitory fibers are paralyzed, our controls are relaxed, our judgment is unclear, and we are ready to say and do things we would never do if our minds were normal. Alcohol has produced a state of drunkenness!

Since ancient times, the disease we call leprosy has terrorized man. Aside from what it did to a person's body, a person with leprosy was forced to live away from other people. No one wanted to come near him or have him around; a leper had to spend the rest of his life alone.

WHAT IS LEPROSY?

Today we know much more about leprosy and treat this disease differently. Leprosy is an infectious or contagious disease which affects the skin or the nerves, or both. The bacteria that cause the infection were discovered by a Norwegian named Hansen, so leprosy is also known as Hansen's Disease.

Despite what was believed for hundreds of years, the leprosy germs are not highly contagious. Just how infection takes place, we don't know. But the germs most often enter and remain (at first) in the skin. If the body resistance is high, hard nodules or lumps form slowly. The skin nodules often become very heavy around the forehead, nose, ears, and lips, and this is what gives a person with leprosy a coarse appearance.

When his nerves are infected, a person loses the sensation of feeling. This is why a leper can injure himself very easily, even burn and cut himself without knowing it. The muscles become almost useless, which may cause the hands and feet to look like claws. In time, the bones of the hands and feet disappear.

Leprosy is found all over the world, but it is most common in the tropics, northern Africa, China, and India. Strangely enough, it may be found in the United States, too, chiefly in the South.

Now that doctors have found that leprosy is not highly contagious, many people with this disease are treated in their own homes, instead of being sent away. Some of the antibiotic drugs that have been developed stop the progress of the disease, and some people have been completely cured by them.

In our bodies there are certain cells which make up connective tissue—tissue that joins the various parts of the body together. All the cells in connective tissue can contract, or tighten up. In some parts of the body, these cells can contract to a special degree, so they transform themselves into muscle cells.

HOW DO OUR MUSCLES WORK?

At those points in the body where muscle cells are used frequently, they multiply and join together to form a single smooth muscle com-

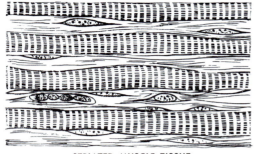
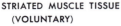

STRIATED MUSCLE TISSUE
(VOLUNTARY)

SMOOTH MUSCLE TISSUE
(INVOLUNTARY)

posed of many fibers. Smooth muscles are found in many parts of the body and help many organs to function. For instance, smooth muscles contract and dilate our eyes, regulate our breathing, make our intestines function.

The fiber of smooth muscles is strong, but it is slow. So whenever rapid motion is necessary, the body has developed the smooth muscles a step further. The fibers of the smooth muscles have developed into a higher form called striated muscle. All the muscles which make our limbs move are striated.

There are 639 muscles in the human body. The muscles are really the flesh of the body, just as the red meat bought at the butcher shop is really muscle. Muscles are all sizes and have many shapes. A medium-sized muscle contains about ten million muscle cells, and the whole body contains about six billion muscle cells!

Each of these six billion muscle cells is like a motor containing ten cylinders arranged in a row. The cylinders are tiny boxes that contain fluid. A muscle contracts when the brain sends a message to these tiny boxes. For a fraction of a second, the fluid in the tiny box congeals; then it becomes a fluid again. It is this action that causes the muscle to move.

The only muscles in our bodies that we can move are the striated muscles. The smooth muscles (for instance, those that control digestion) act independently of our will. When a muscle is stimulated into action, it reacts quickly. It may contract in less than one tenth of a second. But before it has time to relax, another message comes along. It contracts again and again. All these contractions take place so quickly that they become fused into one action with the result that the muscle performs a smooth, continuous action!

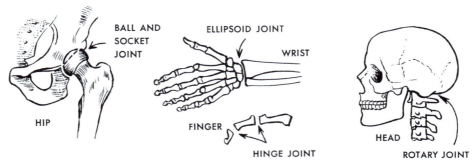

BALL AND SOCKET JOINT

ELLIPSOID JOINT

WRIST

HIP

FINGER

HINGE JOINT

HEAD

ROTARY JOINT

If our bodies didn't have joints, it would be impossible for us to live as we do. We would have to lie absolutely still always, unable to move our heads, walk, raise our arms, or move a single finger! Our ability to move is possible because of the existence of joints.

HOW DO OUR JOINTS WORK?

Wherever two bones glide over one another, a joint exists. A joint allows the bones to glide smoothly with very little friction. This is because the ends of the bones are covered by cartilage so that they don't really rub against each other. In addition, a whitish fluid which has the consistency of raw egg white is secreted by the joint. This is called the synovial fluid, and it acts like oil in a machine to reduce friction. When the joint is at rest, very little synovial fluid is produced and the joint actually becomes creaky.

In the human body, there are four important types of joints. One of these is a ball-and-socket joint such as is found at the shoulder. This shoulder joint has the greatest range of motion of any joint in the body. That's why you can move your arm in any direction in space. The hip joint is the largest ball-and-socket joint in the body, but because it is fitted more tightly, it doesn't permit as much range of motion.

The second kind of joint is an ellipsoid joint. In such a joint, an egg-shaped surface fits into an elliptical cavity. The wrist joint is an example of this kind. It enables us to make elliptical rather than circular movements. A variation of this kind of joint is the saddle joint, in which the bones can move in only two directions, like a rider in a saddle. We have this kind of joint in our backbone, which can be bent in only two directions, backward and forward, and from side to side.

A third type of joint is the hinge joint. Here the bones can be moved only to and fro in one plane, like doors or pocketknives. The joints between the bones of our fingers are hinge joints.

The last kind of joint is the rotary joint. This enables the bones to turn like a corkscrew. We have a rotary joint at the base of our skulls so we can turn our heads, and we have others in our elbows which enable us, for example, to turn a key in a lock.

The strength of normal, healthy human bones is amazing. The saying that our bones are "twice as strong as oak" is not far from wrong.

WHAT ARE OUR BONES MADE OF?

Bone needs to be strong because it forms the framework, or skeleton, that supports the whole body. Bones vary in shape and size according to the type of animal to which they belong. Fish and small birds have tiny bones. Elephants have bones that weigh several hundred pounds!

All bones have similar composition. Bone is a hard, grayish-white substance, of which about two thirds are inorganic, or mineral matter, especially phosphate of lime. This gives the bone hardness, but at the same time, it makes the bone more brittle.

The remaining third of the bone is organic, or animal matter. This gives the bones the toughness which helps them resist breakage. In certain types of bones, there is a fatty substance called marrow, which is organic matter with a very high food value.

There is also a small amount of water in bone, which seems to dry out as the body grows older. As this drying takes place and as the mineral matter in the bone increases, the bones become more breakable and slower to knit and heal.

When you break a bone in your arm, for example, it must be set. This means it must be fastened firmly in its natural place so that the ends cannot move. The bone must knit before you can use your arm again.

The knitting is done by tiny cells known as osteoblasts. They secrete a limey substance that makes the bones hard and firm again. These cells also help in the natural growth of bones. Other cells called osteoclasts tear down old tissue so that growth is possible. This double process of building up and tearing down is going on in the bones all the time.

OSTEOBLAST

OSTEOCLAST

The average body of a human being contains about three pounds of calcium. Most of this is found in the bones. Calcium is an essential part of the structure of the bone.

WHAT IS CALCIUM?

We might, in fact, compare the structure of a bone to reinforced concrete. The bone has certain fibers called collagen fibers which are like the flexible iron wires often embedded in concrete. Calcium forms the bed in which these bone fibers are fixed.

The calcium content of our bones changes as we grow older. During the first year, a child's bones have little calcium and great flexibility. A child can perform all kinds of contortions without breaking any bones. By the time a man is eighty, his bones may be 80 per cent calcium and break easily.

One of the reasons young children are urged to drink a great deal of milk is that milk is the ideal calcium containing food, and, of course, young bodies need plenty of calcium for their bones. One quart of cow's milk contains almost two grams of calcium. Cheese, buttermilk, and yogurt also supply great quantities of calcium.

In those parts of the country where calcium is hard to obtain, people have trouble with their teeth and often suffer from bone fractures. A frequent cause of calcium deficiency is the practice of making hard water soft by removing the calcium from it.

Hard water interferes with the lathering of soap. The calcium in hard water combines with acids and salts in the soap and produces compounds which don't dissolve.

The practice of removing calcium from hard water also has a bad effect on the foods cooked in the water. If the water has a low calcium content, foods cooked in it actually lose part of their own calcium to the water. But foods will gain in calcium content when cooked in hard water with a high calcium content.

Do you brush your teeth at least twice a day? If you do, and you brush hard, have you ever wondered why you don't wear your teeth down? The fact is that our teeth are pretty tough — about as hard as rocks.

WHAT ARE OUR TEETH MADE OF?

Every tooth is made up of the same two parts: a root, or roots, to anchor it in the jawbone, and a crown, the part that can be seen in the mouth.

Teeth are composed mostly of mineral salts, of which calcium and phosphorus are the most prominent. The enamel is hard and shiny, and covers the crown. The cementum is a bonelike material that covers the root. The dentine is an ivorylike material that forms the bulk or body of the tooth. And the dental pulp is in a hollow space called the pulp chamber inside the tooth. The dental pulp is made up of tissue that contains nerves, arteries, and veins. These enter the tooth through an opening at or near the root end.

As you've probably noticed when you look at your teeth in the mirror, they are different in size, and in shape. In a full set of teeth, there are four types, each having a special duty. The incisors, in the center of the mouth, cut or incise food. The cuspids, which tear food, are on either side of the incisors at the corners of the mouth. They have long, heavy roots and sharp, pointed crowns.

The bicuspids, just back of the cuspids, have two points, or cusps, and one or two roots. They tear and crush food. The molars, in the back of the mouth, have several cusps and two or three roots. They grind food.

When a scientist who has been digging for fossils or other remains of ancient life turns up with some teeth, he is very happy. Teeth are an important clue as to the kind of creature it was that lived there.

ARE OUR TEETH THE SAME AS ANIMAL TEETH?

For example, beasts of prey have tearing teeth, rodents have gnawing teeth, and cattle have grinding teeth. Every animal — whether horse, cow, mouse, cat, or dog — has teeth suitable for its way of life, its food, and even its general nature.

A beaver, for example, has great cutting teeth. The canine teeth of dogs and cats are sharp and long so that it is easy for them to seize and hold their prey. Their sharp back teeth cut up and break the flesh and bones.

A squirrel has teeth that can easily gnaw through the hard shell of a nut. Even fish have teeth that help them with their food. Some sharks have cutting teeth for eating fish, while other sharks have blunt teeth for crushing shellfish. The pike has teeth that lean backward as the prey is swallowed and then straighten up again. The teeth of snakes are set inward at an angle so that their prey cannot escape.

Man has what is known as a "collective" dentition, which means that he has many different kinds of teeth, one alongside another.

According to scientists, the structure of the human teeth is evidence that the human body is adapted to a mixed plant-and-animal diet.

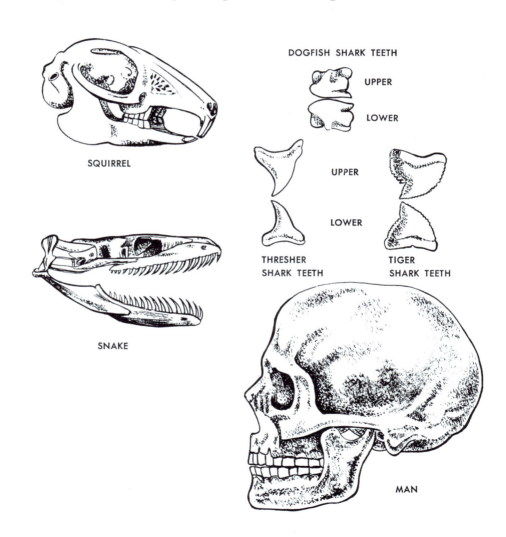

SQUIRREL

DOGFISH SHARK TEETH

UPPER

LOWER

UPPER

LOWER

THRESHER
SHARK TEETH

TIGER
SHARK TEETH

SNAKE

MAN

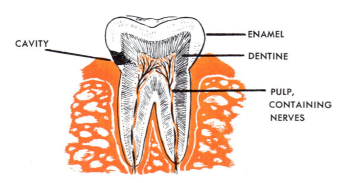

CAVITY

ENAMEL

DENTINE

PULP,
CONTAINING
NERVES

Among the lower animals, there is a whole succession of teeth through-out their lives. As teeth are fully developed and used up, they fall out and new ones take their place.

WHY DO OUR TEETH DECAY?

Man, however, has only a single replacement of his teeth. By the time a baby is about two years old, it has a total of 20 teeth, called the milk teeth. Beneath these milk teeth, there is a second series of teeth which begin to appear after the age of six. The milk teeth are replaced by about the age of twelve and then more teeth appear until the adult finally has his full set of 32 permanent teeth. Since we don't get another chance at new teeth, it is important to keep them healthy and free from decay.

The enamel is where decay usually begins. Let us say that some defect appears in the enamel. It can be an almost invisible opening, but since we always have bacteria in our mouth, they soon find this break in the surface and settle under the enamel.

They cannot eat the enamel, but they can feed on the juicy dentine and the lymph which is in the dentine canals. Soon they erode the walls of the canals, and a cavity is created beneath the enamel.

This may go unnoticed for some time, but if the wall of the tooth becomes thin as a result of the work of the bacteria, then we notice it very quickly. This is because heat and cold can now penetrate more strongly to the pulp cavity. The pulp occupies a hollow space in the center of the tooth and contains nerves. These nerves are stimulated by the heat or cold. When a tooth feels sensitive to heat or cold, you can be pretty sure it's a danger signal that decay is taking place.

When the bacteria penetrate through the dentine canals into the pulp cavity, they find a perfect feeding and breeding ground. Now we get a toothache. The decay of the tooth continues, the network of vessels that supply food to the tooth wither away, and the tooth, no longer nourished, becomes a dead shell.

Moral: Have your teeth examined regularly by your dentist!

Concentrate right now and imagine that you are about to eat a lemon. Think of yourself biting into this lemon. Do you feel the saliva beginning to flow?

WHAT IS SALIVA?

This is one of the interesting things about our salivary glands. They don't function mechanically, but are subject to the control of the brain. There are three pairs of salivary glands. One is in front of the ear, one under the tongue, and one under the lower jaw.

The salivary glands automatically adapt the amount and nature of the saliva to the immediate task. Animals that eat moist foods have little saliva. Fish have no salivary glands, but in grain-eating birds, they are very developed. When a cow receives fresh feed, its salivary glands secrete about fifty quarts. When it receives dry hay, the quantity of saliva rises to about 190 litres. The largest human salivary gland secretes about 23,600 litres of saliva in a lifetime!

Each of the salivary glands has its own special job. The largest one, the parotid gland in front of the ear, secretes large quantities of watery saliva. The chief purpose of this saliva is to dilute and to moisten the food well.

The glands near the lower jaw secrete a different kind of saliva; it makes the food "slippery."

Which of the salivary glands will produce the most saliva depends on the food we take in. If we bite into a juicy apple that doesn't have to be moistened, the lower glands will function. But if we eat a dry cracker, the parotid gland goes to work and produces large quantities of watery saliva.

Human saliva contains an enzyme known as amylase. This works on starch, splitting the molecules into dextrin and then into malt sugar.

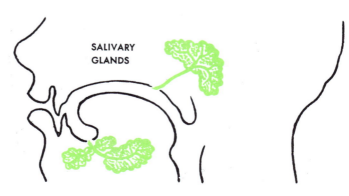

SALIVARY GLANDS

If we didn't eat, we couldn't keep our bodies alive, we couldn't grow, we wouldn't have energy, and various parts of our bodies couldn't function as they must. Modern scientists have been able to find out which sub-

WHY DO WE HAVE TO EAT?

stances in food our bodies need, and how much of these substances we need to be healthy. In other words, it isn't enough to just eat; we must take in enough of each type of food substance for a specific purpose.

Protein foods such as milk, eggs, cheese, meat and fish contain large quantities of the kind of material the body needs to build cells. The body cannot make new cells without protein.

Carbohydrates are foods which have a large quantity of starch or sugar, such as potatoes, flour, rice, and sugar. They are important to the body because they keep it warm and give it energy. Almost all foods also have some fat, and fat is the most concentrated energy-giving food the body uses.

But the body needs more than protein, carbohydrates, and fats. It must also have certain substances known as minerals. There are eighteen such necessary minerals. As you know, some of them, such as calcium and phosphorous, are needed by the bones and teeth to grow strong and healthy. Iron helps the cells work properly. With copper, the body grows and makes hemoglobin. Iodine helps the body work, too.

So, now we have proteins, carbohydrates, fats, and minerals that are all necessary to the body for it to function and grow. Is that all?— No. Science has discovered that vitamins also are necessary to control certain processes in the body. They are absolutely essential to health. Each vitamin serves the body in a special way, and no one vitamin can replace another. All of them together promote growth and keep people feeling well and strong.

By the way, water can be considered a food, too, and serves the body in a number of ways. From all this, you can see that eating isn't just a matter of satisfying hunger or pleasing appetite. A good, balanced diet is vital to health.

225

The feeling of hunger is a message sent to your brain by your body. The message is that nutritive materials are missing from the blood. Let's see how this happens.

WHAT MAKES US FEEL HUNGRY?

Our bodies and those of all living things must maintain a state of metabolic equilibrium. This means there has to be a certain balance and control over our intake of fuel and its use. To regulate our body weight we have thirst, hunger, and appetite.

In the brain we have a hunger center. It acts like a brake on the activities of the stomach and intestines. When the blood has sufficient nutritive materials, the hunger center stops the activities of the stomach and intestines. But when there is a lack of nutrition, the intestines and stomach become active. That's why you can hear your stomach rumbling when you're hungry.

But hunger itself has nothing to do with an empty stomach. For example, a person who is feverish may have an empty stomach but not feel hungry. His body uses up its protein supplies and feeds itself from within.

When you feel hungry, your body is crying out for fuel—any kind of fuel. A really hungry person will eat any kind of food. It is your appetite that sees to it that you choose the mixed diet that your body requires. For example, when a man sits down to dinner, one bowl of soup may be all the soup he wants. Then he goes on to meat and vegetables. When he's had enough of these, he may go on to dessert, cake, coffee. But it would be pretty hard for him to eat this same quantity of food if it all consisted of potatoes!

How long a living creature can go without food depends on its metabolism. Warm-blooded animals have a more active metabolism, and so use up their store of fuel more rapidly. The smaller and more active the animal, the more rapidly it uses up its food supplies.

SHREW (WARM-BLOODED)   BOX TURTLE (COLD-BLOODED)

VERY ACTIVE, EATS ALMOST CONSTANTLY   SLOW, EATS NOW AND THEN

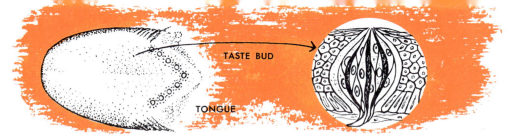

TASTE BUD

TONGUE

Taste depends on the impact of the atoms given off by a substance on certain specially sensitive organs in our bodies. If the atoms of a substance can't move about freely, we can't taste it. That's why we can only taste things that are in a state of solution.

HOW DO WE TASTE OUR FOOD?

Animals that live in water have taste buds all over their bodies. For instance, fish can taste with their tail fins! Animals that live on land have their taste buds concentrated in their mouths, and in man they exist only on the tongue.

If you examine your tongue in a mirror, you will see that it is covered with tiny, wartlike bumps, which are called papillae. The taste buds are situated in the walls of these papillae.

The number of taste buds found in animals depends on the needs of the particular species. For instance, a whale swallows whole schools of fish without chewing them; it has few taste buds, or none at all. A pig has 5,500 taste buds, a cow has 35,000, and an antelope, 50,000. Man is not by any means the most sensitive taster; he has only 3,000 taste buds!

The taste buds on the human tongue are distributed in different zones, and each zone is sensitive to a different kind of taste. The back of the tongue is more sensitive to bitter, the sides are sensitive to sour and salt, and the tip of the tongue picks up sweet tastes. In the center of the tongue, there is a zone without any taste buds, and it can taste nothing!

Smells are an important part of our tasting process. At least half of what we think of as taste is not taste at all, but really smell! This is true when we "taste" such things as coffee, tea, tobacco, wine, apples, oranges, and lemons. For instance, when we drink coffee, we first sense the warmth, then the bitterness that comes from the acid and the roasting, and then the sweetness, if it has been added. But not until the warm vapor released by the coffee hits our throat and nose and sends its messages to the brain, do we really "taste" the coffee! The proof is that if you close your nose with a clothespin, not only won't you be able to "taste" the coffee, but you'll find you can't tell the difference between two completely different things you are eating or drinking!

SMELLING
CELLS

RUBBING
ALCOHOL

Everybody likes pleasant odors—the perfume of flowers, or the aroma of a cake baking. But a disagreeable odor can be quite unpleasant. The strange thing is that the amount of odor in both pleasant and unpleasant

WHAT IS AN ODOR?

cases can be very, very tiny! Did you know that we can detect the odor of certain substances if only $\frac{1}{30,000,000,000}$ part by weight is present in a given weight of air? And this is true of man—whose sense of smell is a fraction as good as that of a dog!

What is it that produces what we call an odor? We detect an odor when a chemical substance comes in contact with certain nerve endings. This substance must be in the form of a gas or it couldn't travel through the air. This is why we can smell things at a distance.

The cells for smelling are in the hairs that grow in the mucous membrane in the nose. These endings cover a small area in the upper part of the nasal cavities. They are so arranged that when we breathe we draw the air over them. But if we deliberately want to smell something, such as a flower, we have to sniff. This directs the air right to the area.

In order for anything to produce an odor, it has to be either volatile, that is, in motion, or brought to us in some substance that is in motion. When it reaches the smelling area in the nose, it produces a nerve current that travels to the brain, where we interpret the smell.

There are five types of odors that we can detect: flowery (rose, violet, etc.); spicy (lemon, apple, etc.); burnt (coffee, etc.); rotten (rotten eggs, cheese, etc.); and ethereal (alcohol, benzine, etc.).

We often confuse smell with taste because the gaseous particles of many of the foods we eat reach the receptors for smell as we eat. For example, if you couldn't smell the coffee you drink, it wouldn't have the familiar taste. This is also why food often seems to lose its taste when you have a cold. Your sense of smell is blocked up during a cold, and this has an effect on the taste!

The food we take into our bodies supplies us with many important substances such as proteins, fats, carbohydrates, water, and mineral substances. But these alone are not enough. In order to maintain life we need still other substances known as vitamins.

WHY DO WE NEED VITAMIN C?

Vitamins are substances formed by plants or animals. They must be supplied to the body in minute quantities so that vital processes can continue undisturbed. When there is a lack of vitamins in our body, diseases will occur. For instance, lack of vitamin A affects our vision; lack of vitamin B produces a disease called beriberi, and so on.

Long before man knew about vitamins, it had been observed that when people couldn't get certain types of foods, diseases would develop. Sailors, for instance, who went on long trips and couldn't get fresh vegetables would get a disease called scurvy. In the seventeenth century British sailors were given lemons and limes to prevent this disease. And this, by the way, is why British sailors got the nickname, "limeys!"

The vitamin that prevents scurvy is vitamin C. It is also called ascorbic acid. Some vitamins are found in the embryos of plants. For example, vitamin B_1 is found in the germ of the wheat. Vitamin C is found in the fresh green leaves, the roots, the stems, the buds and the pods of fully developed plants.

A curious thing about vitamin C is that almost all mammals produce their own vitamin C in the liver and so never suffer from a lack of it. But man, the apes, and guinea pigs are the only mammals which cannot produce their own vitamin C in the liver!

What happens when there is a lack of this vitamin in the body? The blood vessels become fragile and bleed easily. Black-and-blue marks appear on the skin and near the eyes. The gums bleed easily. Our hormones and enzymes don't function well, our resistance to infection by bacteria is lowered, and we may develop inflammations in the throat.

Wherever you may go in the world—whatever the local customs, language, dress, or taste in food—you will find some form of bread! Of course, there are almost as many varieties of bread as there are nations.

WHY IS BREAD CALLED "THE STAFF OF LIFE ?"

In China, bread is made from rice flour. In India, they use millet. In Germany and in the Scandinavian countries, bread is made from rye and barley. There are countries that use beans, potatoes, and even acorns in the making of bread!

But bread as we usually think of it is made from cereal grains of various types. It is the most important single food to the largest number of people. The reason is simply that bread contains the largest share of the food substances we need for health for the least amount of money. Without bread, it would be necessary for people to eat larger quantities of more expensive foods such as eggs, milk, and fruits to maintain their health. With bread, even the poorest peoples are able to sustain life. That's why bread is called "the staff of life."

In earliest times, man used to chew grain seeds to obtain the energy he knew they provided. More than 3,000 years before Christ, the Egyptians learned to crush the grain to a flour between stones. They added water to form a dough, shaped it into flat cakes, and baked it.

There are two kinds of bread, leavened and unleavened. Leavened bread contains some substance which makes bubbles of carbon dioxide gas and makes the loaf rise. Unleavened bread is always dry and hard. Most ordinary bread is leavened with yeast. But biscuits, muffins, cakes, and pastries are leavened with baking powder or sour milk and soda.

Though bread can be made from many plants, the best and finest bread is made from wheat. This is because wheat contains a substance called gluten, which holds the gas bubbles better, and this produces a lighter loaf of bread.

By the way, the expression "to break bread" dates back to the ancient Hebrews. They used to bake their bread in thin sheets which they broke instead of cutting.

LEAVENED — UNLEAVENED

MATZOS

Everybody has a kind of instinctive feeling that being in the sunshine is good for us. But did you know that there are specific scientific reasons

WHY IS SUNSHINE HEALTHFUL?

why this is so? Let's consider some of the things that happen when we expose our bodies to the rays of the sun.

Sunlight actually destroys certain fungi and bacteria that may have settled on the skin. It acts as a pretty strong medicine in this way! Another way in which it acts as a medicine is by causing the white blood cells, or phagocytes, to become more active. These are the cells which attack disease germs in our body and help keep us healthy.

When sunlight strikes the skin, it causes it to send substances into the blood which gives the muscles new tone. The muscles become more tense and thus can work better. In fact, our nervous system gets a kind of "charge" from sunlight so that we feel stimulated and want to move about. This is one of the reasons why we're always so active on our vacations. We want to play ball and do exercises and go swimming. We want to move about more because the sun has helped wake up our nervous system.

The sun also has the very specific effect in that it creates a vitamin in our body. The ultraviolet light transforms a substance called ergosterol in the skin into vitamin D, which is called "the sunshine vitamin."

These are some of the reasons why we can say that exposing ourselves to the sun's rays is like swallowing a teaspoonful of medicine every five minutes. But it's important to remember that this medicine is by no means harmless! We have to be just as careful about sun bathing as we would have to be about taking medicine.

Sun bathing raises the blood pressure, so people who have heart trouble or certain lung diseases can be injured quite seriously by exposure to sunlight. In fact, everyone should expose himself to sunlight only in stages. In taking sun baths, for instance, it's a good idea to start by exposing only one fifth of the body for five minutes. The next day, expose another fifth of the body for an extra five minutes, and so on. Your doctor can give you the best advice on how to get all the benefits of sunlight without taking unnecessary risks.

The body of every living animal and plant is a chemical factory. In fact, if all kinds of chemical changes weren't constantly taking place, life would be impossible. You are able to use food, breathe, grow, and move

WHAT IS AN ENZYME?

because of the chemical changes which take place in the cells, tissues, and organs of your body.

Here is an example of this chemical life process. You eat a piece of bread, or a cereal, or a potato. The starch in this food is changed into sugars which go into the blood. There they are burned by the oxygen which is in the air you breathe, and your body obtains energy.

Chemists discovered that a process like this—in fact, every chemical process like this that goes on in a living body—can take place because it is helped by a very small amount of a protein which is produced by living cells. This is called an enzyme. An enzyme is said to be specific, which means it is fit to do only one special job. Each enzyme initiates only one chemical process.

Chemical changes, as we have said, take place in all living things. So when grains of wheat, barley, or some other cereal begin to grow, they make enzymes which change their starches into sugars. This change is called malting, and in each case, the enzyme which does it is called diastase.

Even though we know what enzymes do, we still don't know too much about them. They are organic compounds; that is, they are substances which always contain the elements carbon and hydrogen, and often oxygen and nitrogen, too.

There are a very great many different enzymes, but only a few have been isolated from the juices of plants or animals where they are found.

A curious thing about enzymes is that while only living cells can produce enzymes, they can produce chemical changes even without living tissue.

Everybody today is so weight-conscious, and so many people are on diets, that you could probably say fat is something nobody wants.

WHAT IS FAT?

Yet fat, of course, is very necessary to the body. It accumulates in this way: At certain points, the connective-tissue cells become filled with fat. First, tiny droplets appear inside the cells. They increase in size, run together into a large drop, and finally fill the cell and swell it out like a balloon. Eventually, the cell is changed into a large drop of fat surrounded by a thin envelope of tissue.

This takes place only in certain parts of the body. The ears, nose, forehead, and joints of the body normally have no fat tissue. Usually, the female body stores more fat than the male body. For example, the normal male body contains about 10 per cent fat, but a normal female has about 25 per cent. This means that a young man may have about 6 kilograms of fat in his body and a woman about 16 kilograms.

The chief reason the body stores fat is to have it as a food reserve. It is especially suited for this because fat is the best and most concentrated fuel that we know. The normal daily fuel of the body is sugar, which we obtain from starches. We burn up sugar very easily; it is a more difficult process to burn fat. But fat produces more heat than an equal amount of sugar. In fact, fat has about twice the energy value of sugar. Because of this, and the difficulty with which it burns, fat is especially suitable as a reserve to be stored in the body. When you take in too little food for your body's needs, the fat reserves begin to be used up.

Another reason the body needs fat is as a padding material. It acts like a water cushion. It can't be compressed, because it is resilient. These water cushions of fat are found in the buttocks so we can sit comfortably, under the arch of the foot, under the skin of the palm, in each cheek of the face, and in the cushions on which our eyeballs rest.

The third use of fat for the body is as an insulating material that keeps the body from losing heat.

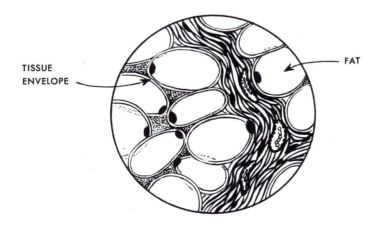

TISSUE ENVELOPE

FAT

Wouldn't it be wonderful if people who lost an arm or a leg or even a finger in an accident could simply grow another one in its place? Human beings can't do this, but there are living creatures who can! The process by which such organisms can replace structures or organs is called regeneration.

WHAT IS REGENERATION?

Regeneration varies quite a bit among these creatures. For example, in certain types of worms and in starfish, a tiny part of the body can restore the whole organism. If only a small piece is left, a whole new body will grow!

At the other extreme, we have a kind of regeneration that takes place in our own bodies. The top layer of our skin is constantly being worn off in small bits and replaced by other cells. Our hair and nails are replaced all the time. Even our second set of teeth is a kind of regeneration. And, of course, there is the shedding of feathers and fur and scales among animals, all of which are replaced by a process of regeneration.

The more complicated the organism (and man is a very complicated organism), the less it is able to regenerate. Man, and all mammals, cannot restore an entire organ. But creatures such as salamanders and insects can regenerate a whole limb. What we can regenerate really amounts to repairing damages such as bone fractures, skin and muscle injuries, and some kinds of nerves.

Regeneration takes place in two ways. In one case, new tissue grows from the surface of the wound. In the other, the remaining parts are transformed and reorganized, but new material does not grow.

When new material is grown (such as a limb), it takes place in this way. A regeneration "bud" is formed at the surface of the wound. It is usually cone-shaped and contains an embryonic type of cell, or cells, of the type that were present at the birth of the creature. These cells develop into specialized cells to form the new organ, and as they grow, a new organ is gradually formed!

STARFISH, GROWING NEW ARM

ARM, GROWING NEW STARFISH

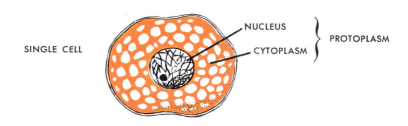

SINGLE CELL   NUCLEUS   CYTOPLASM   PROTOPLASM

The mystery of protoplasm is the mystery of life itself. We still do not know what makes protoplasm alive.

Protoplasm is the living part of all plants and animals. All organisms, plant or animal, are composed of cells. There may be many millions of cells, as in the human body, or there may be one as in the protozoa.

WHAT IS PROTOPLASM?

But the cell walls of all living things enclose the same life substance —protoplasm. In each cell, the protoplasm consists chiefly of two parts: the more solid central part called the nucleus, and the softer, more liquid part, the cytoplasm.

Each type of living thing has its own kind of protoplasm and the different types of cells within an organism have their own special forms of protoplasm. While protoplasm varies, 99 per cent of its bulk is made of carbon, hydrogen, oxygen, and nitrogen, with traces of many other elements.

When food is taken into a living body, it is first digested; that is, turned into liquid form. Then the digested food must be taken into and made a part of the protoplasm, a process known as assimilation. We still don't know exactly what takes place during assimilation.

It is known that assimilation results in replacing worn-out protoplasm and making more protoplasm. In doing this, protoplasm builds up dead matter into living material and changes foreign material into substances like itself. Protoplasm also stores and releases all the energy that plants and animals have.

Protoplasm is sensitive to shocks from the outside. A strong light, or heat, will kill it. Chemicals attract or repel protoplasm; electric currents cause it to behave in various ways.

If science will someday solve the mystery of what makes protoplasm do what it does, we will understand more about the mystery of life itself.

CHROMOSOME

Before a child is born, we can predict many of the biological characteristics of the child by observing the parents. This is because we know the laws of heredity.

WHAT ARE GENES?

For example, if one parent has brown eyes and the other has blue eyes, the child will be brown-eyed. If neither parent has any brown pigment in the ring around the pupil, the child also will have pure blue eyes. If one of the parents has curly hair, then the child will have an even chance of having curly hair.

However, the laws of human inheritance are sometimes quite complex. If a certain characteristic in the father is different from that in the mother, then the two contrary tendencies work themselves out. What happens is that one will appear in the child, and the other will not.

The trait that dominates the struggle is called dominant. The other trait is called recessive; it recedes from view. For example, brown eyes are a dominant trait, blue eyes, a recessive trait. That's why the child described above would have brown eyes.

How are the characteristics of the parents passed on to the child? They are passed on in the nucleus of the egg cell and in the nucleus of the sperm cell. These nuclei consist of a large number, perhaps several thousand, of particles called genes. These are not loosely scattered in the nuclei, but are strung along threads like a necklace of beads.

The ripe egg has 23 of these strings of genes and so has the ripe sperm. When egg and sperm unite, there are 23 pairs of these strings, called chromosomes.

The genes, even in the same chromosome, are not alike in the control that they have over development. Some are particularly effective in producing one organ; others, another organ or characteristic of the body. However, they all work together in the development of the body as a whole. The characteristics which belong to the genes of one thread are inherited together, though sometimes the threads may break up and interchange particles with other threads.

236

There are many different kinds of baldness, but in most cases, it's a condition over which a man has absolutely no control and for which there simply is no cure.

WHAT CAUSES BALDNESS?

People say all kinds of things about baldness: It means a man is getting old; or it means he's unusually intelligent; or he's unusually dull. But all baldness really means is that a man is losing his hair!

The kind of baldness we see most often is called pattern baldness. The hair begins to go at the temples, or there's a bald spot at the top of the head, or the baldness appears in some other pattern. This is the most difficult type of baldness to do anything about because it's inherited! The inheritance of pattern baldness is influenced by sex. It appears more in men than in women. Very often the woman carries the gene for this baldness and passes it on to her children. Once this type of baldness appears, about the best thing a man can do is get used to it!

Premature baldness may appear in men as early as the age of twenty-five or even earlier. One cause of this kind of baldness may be a failure to take proper care of the scalp, keep it clean, etc. Sometimes an imbalance of the sex hormones may bring on premature baldness. If proper scalp care is started at once, it may slow up the progress of this type of baldness.

Symptomatic baldness sometimes appears as a sign of infections or other conditions. When health is restored, the hair may grow back again in such cases. Sudden loss of hair can result from typhoid fever, scarlet fever, pneumonia, influenza, and other serious infections.

When there is a gradual loss or thinning of hair, it may sometimes be due to poor nutrition or a disturbance in the glands, especially the pituitary and thyroid glands. And, of course, baldness may come from disorders in the scalp itself, such as scalp injuries or disease.

Just as feathers are characteristic of birds, so hair is characteristic of mammals. Why do mammals have hair?— There is a variety of reasons. Let's consider some of them.

WHY DON'T WOMEN HAVE BEARDS?

The chief value of hair is that it conserves the heat of the body. In the tropics, it may serve an opposite function. Certain tropical animals are protected from direct sunlight by their hair.

Very long hair on certain parts of the body usually serves some special purpose. For instance, a mane may protect an animal's neck from the teeth of its enemies. Tails may act as flyswatters. Crests may attract the opposite sex. In the case of the porcupine, its stiff quills formed of bunched-up hair help it to attack its enemies. Hair may also serve as organs of touch. The whiskers of cats have special nerves that respond quickly to touch.

So you see that hair can serve a different purpose with different mammals. How about human beings? We know that beautiful hair in a woman can be very attractive to men. But we must assume that hair on human beings formerly played a more practical role than it does now.

When an infant is born, he is covered with a fine down. This is soon replaced by the delicate hair which we notice in all children. Then comes the age of puberty, and this coat of hair is transformed into the final coat of hair which the person will have as an adult.

The development of this adult hair coat is regulated by the sex glands. The male sex hormone works in such a way that the beard and the body hair are developed, while the growth of the hair on the head is inhibited, or slowed down in development.

The action of the female sex hormone is exactly the opposite! The growth of the hair on the head is developed, while the growth of the beard and body hair is inhibited. So women don't have beards because various glands and hormones in their bodies deliberately act to prevent this growth.

To explain why this is so, and why men's glands and hormones act to promote growth of beards, we probably have to go back to the early history of man. At one time, the function of the beard was probably to make it easy to tell men and women apart at a distance. It also probably served to give the male an appearance of power and dignity, and so make him more attractive to the female. Nature was helping man to attract the opposite sex, just as she does with other creatures.

For men who are becoming a little bald, hair doesn't grow fast enough! But in the case of a young boy, the hair seems to grow too fast!

HOW FAST DOES HAIR GROW?

The rate at which hair grows has actually been measured and found to be about 12 millimetres a month. The hair doesn't grow at the same rate throughout the day but seems to follow a kind of rhythm.

At night, the hair grows slowly, but as day begins, this is speeded up. Between 10 and 11 AM, the speed of growth is at its greatest. Then the hair grows slowly again. It picks up speed between 4 and 6 PM, and then the growing slows up again. Of course, these variations in the speed of growth are so tiny that you cannot possibly notice them. So don't expect to stand in front of the mirror at 10 AM and be able to watch your hair sprouting up!

If all the hair that grows on the body were to grow in a sort of hair cable, instead of as individual hairs, you would get some idea of the total amount of hair the body produces. This hair cable would grow at the rate of 3 centimetres per minute, and by the end of the year, the tip would be 37 miles (59 kilometres) away.

Not all people have the same amount of hair. Blond people have finer hair and more hair than dark persons. Red-haired people have the coarsest and the fewest hairs.

Most of us think of plastic surgery as the kind of operation people have when they want to straighten a nose, or otherwise change the appearance of their faces in some way.

WHAT IS PLASTIC SURGERY?

This is really cosmetic surgery and is only a branch of plastic surgery. Today, plastic surgery includes such things as correcting some deformity that a person may have been born with; or repairing the skin after a tumor has been removed or after a person has suffered severe burns.

Plastic surgery has been practiced for thousands of years in India. People who committed certain crimes there used to be punished by having their noses sliced off! Plastic surgeons in India used to take skin from the cheeks and reconstruct a nose.

In plastic surgery, the skin of the body is involved. The skin may be molded or rearranged on a certain part of the body, excessive tissue may be removed, or new skin tissue may be added. Or the surgery may involve a combination of all three of these techniques.

When the skin is removed from one part of the body and grafted onto another part, usually only the top two layers are used. This is because the skin then has a better chance to "live" in its new location. New blood vessels form and circulation keeps the skin alive. When thicker layers of skin are grafted, as when someone has had a bad accident or severe burns, the chances for the new skin to "live" are not as good, but when it does, it is likely to look more natural and normal.

Plastic surgery can help a person who has been injured regain a presentable and normal appearance and so continue to live and work happily.

Very often, however, people will undergo plastic surgery purely to improve their appearances. They may want to change the shapes of their ears, or noses. In some cases, they may want to remove wrinkles from the face, or have their faces "lifted." In such cases, the change is only temporary. In time, signs of age appear again.

PALM OF
HAND,
DRAWN
FROM
BURN

PLASTIC
SURGERY
REPAIRS
PALM
OF HAND

Do you know that in ancient Rome the average person could expect to live only 23 years? About a hundred years ago in the United States, one's life expectancy was 40 years.

WHY DOES EVERYONE GROW OLD?

Most people would like to live a long time; nobody wants to grow old. But growing old is a process that begins with birth itself and continues throughout life.

We all know what happens as a person grows older and older. All the functions and reactions of the body slow down. Some of a person's strength is lost, and the senses become duller. There is usually also a loss in weight and height. Along with this may come a failing of eyesight, partial deafness, gray hair, and flabby and less elastic skin.

Not all people age at the same rate, but certain changes that come with age cannot be escaped. This is because changes take place in the tissues of the body and in all its organs. For example, the tissue cells of the kidney, liver, pancreas, and spleen begin to waste away. This is because the blood vessels become aged and don't supply blood and nourishment as they used to. The thyroid and other glands deteriorate similarly.

The whole circulatory system of the body begins to change with age and doesn't function as actively as it used to. We don't even breathe in the same way because of these changes. The eyes, the ears, the bones and the joints, the blood, the skin, the hair, the nails and the teeth all begin to degenerate, or waste away.

In our digestive tracts, there is a cutting down of gastric juices. The stomach and intestines lose some of their muscle tone, and the blood supply is disturbed. This is why older people often have to change their diets.

These changes are biological and cannot be prevented, simply because older tissues and organs cannot do the job they once used to. But they don't happen uniformly. A man of sixty may have certain organs and tissues in his body that are like those of a man of eighty, while other parts of him may be in as good condition as those of men of forty, thirty, or even twenty.

Most of us have a vague idea that somewhere inside of us there are coils and coils of intestines, amazing passageways through which food passes in the process of digestion. But few people have a clear understanding of just how they work.

HOW LONG ARE OUR INTESTINES?

The length of the large intestine in animals depends on the kind of food they eat. Meat-eating animals have shorter intestines because there is less digestive work to do. The food they live on has already done part of the job of digestion. People who live on vegetables are supposed to have longer intestines than meat-eating people.

The human intestines are 3 metres long. But when a person dies, the intestines lose their elasticity and stretch to about 8.5 metres.

Most of the wall of the intestines consists of muscle fibres, so that the intestines can work on the food that goes through them. The intestines mix the food with certain secretions and then pass it along. In order to do this, the small intestine consists of countless loops. Each loop holds a bit of food and works on it, churning it and digesting it for about 30 minutes. Then it passes the food on to the next loop.

To help in this process of digestion, the wall of the small intestine contains about 20,000,000 small glands. These glands send about 5 to 10 litres of digestive juice into the intestine! This soaks and softens the food so that by the time it goes to the large intestine it's in a semi-liquid state.

If you were to look at the wall of the intestine with a magnifying lens, you would see that it isn't smooth, but resembles velvet. It is covered with millions of tiny tentacle-like villi. The villi tell the glands when to pour out the digestive juice, and also help in the process of digestion themselves.

Food that cannot be digested by juices is digested in the large intestine by bacteria that live there. This is known as putrefaction. Billions of bacteria break down the coarser parts of the food we eat, such as the skins of fruit, and extract valuable materials the body needs.

This is only a rough idea of the way our intestines work. They are among the most amazing organs in our bodies, beautifully organized to do hundreds of things to the food we take in to keep alive.

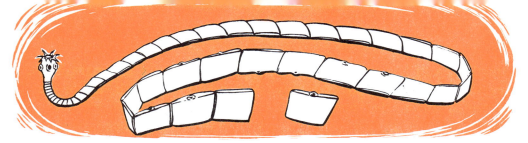

This certainly isn't a pleasant subject, but many people suffer from tapeworm and so there is great curiosity about it. A kind of flatworm, the tapeworm is an intestinal parasite.

WHAT IS A TAPEWORM?

This means that it lives in the digestive tract of another animal, called the host, and is fed by food which the host has partly digested. The host of the tapeworm is nearly always a backboned animal such as a fish, a dog, or a man. The tapeworm has sucking discs on its head, by means of which it attaches itself to the inside of the intestines. It has no sense organs such as eyes or ears.

The muscles of a tapeworm are almost useless, and its nervous system is primitive. It has no mouth or digestive tract; it absorbs dissolved food through the walls of its body.

There are many species of tapeworms, ranging in length from about 0.1 millimetres to 9 metres. They are of many shapes. They may be unsegmented (undivided), or composed of a chain of segment-like parts. These grow one after the other, always forming behind the head. Each adult is both male and female.

How can a human being get a tapeworm inside his digestive tract? It could happen in the following way: The fertilized eggs of a tapeworm are passed out by the worm. Then a hog eats the eggs. Then the larvae hatch in the hog's intestine.

Inside the hog, these small larvae burrow through the wall of the intestine and go to other parts of the hog's body. When they settle, they form a hard cyst.

Now suppose a human being eats pork that has been improperly cooked. (Proper cooking would kill the larvae in the cyst.) The human digestive juices free the larvae. They then attach themselves to the human intestines and there develop into adults—and a human being finds he has a tapeworm!

The harm a tapeworm does is taking part of the nourishment of the host's food and secreting poisonous substances. Tapeworms do not cause death to man except in rare cases. There are now drugs which can remove a tapeworm from the intestines.

Sometimes you hear people say they don't want to live like parasites; they want to make their own way. A parasite lives with, in, or on another organism, the "host."

WHAT IS A PARASITE?

All living things depend on one another. But the parasite lives with another organism in a very special way. The parasite takes from the host and gives it nothing in return!

A parasite may be either a plant or an animal, and it may live off either a plant or an animal. Occasionally, a parasite can live with many types of hosts, but usually there is only one kind of host it can live with. Sometimes, the parasite kills its host by taking too much of the nourishment the host needs, or it may give off substances which poison the host.

Nearly all forms of parasites produce large numbers of young and are very tough. If this were not true, the destruction they cause would destroy them, too!

Let us consider some organisms that are parasites. The smallest of these are bacterial germs. Such bacteria, as you know, can cause disease in man and in plants.

A little higher up are found fungus parasites. Ringworm in man is caused by one of these plant parasites, and other types can cause rust, mildew, and blights in plants.

There are many parasites in the animal kingdom. Here, too, the smallest are the most important ones. These are the microscopic, single-celled animals called Protozoa. These parasites cause African sleeping sickness, malaria, and other diseases among humans.

Certain worms are another group of animal parasites. A round worm called the trichina, causes trichinosis in pigs and in human beings. The hookworm and the tapeworm are other parasites. Still higher up on the scale are such parasites as fleas, ticks, and lice.

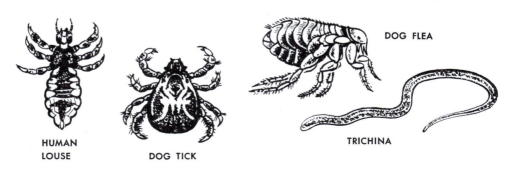

HUMAN
LOUSE

DOG TICK

DOG FLEA

TRICHINA

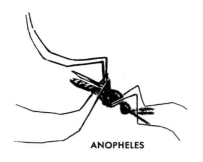

ANOPHELES

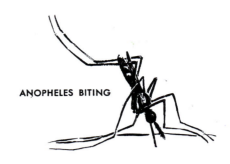

ANOPHELES BITING

It may be hard for us to believe, but every year more than 2,000,000 people die of malaria! It's one of the most common diseases in the world, especially near tropical rivers and coasts. The reason it's com-

WHAT IS MALARIA?

mon in such regions is that they are the habitats of the anopheles, the mosquito which carries the germ.

The malaria germ destroys red blood cells. Each germ soon divides into several parts. These are released from the red blood cell to attack new blood cells, causing chills and fever.

Chills followed by fever are a common sign of malaria. Attacks come usually every three or four days. In the most serious cases, the destroyed red blood cells may clog the blood vessels (usually of the brain) and cause death.

The germs live in the stomach of the female anopheles mosquito. These germs travel from the mosquito's stomach to the salivary glands in its mouth. When the mosquito bites a human being, the germs enter the blood stream.

While malaria is such a common disease, health officials believe it is possible to wipe it out someday. This is because if the anopheles mosquito were controlled, the germ would not spread. But in order to do this, all kinds of international groups and many governments would have to get together on a planned program. So far, the best hope for accomplishing this is to spray every dwelling in the regions where malaria exists with DDT.

Another way to control the anopheles mosquito is to clean out its breeding grounds. This involves draining swamps, stagnant pools, rain barrels—every possible place in which the mosquito might lay its eggs.

Before the cause of malaria was discovered, it was believed that damp "poisonous" swamp air was the cause. And that's how the disease got its name—the word "malaria" comes from Italian words meaning "bad air!"

As man learns how to keep himself more clean and sanitary practices spread through the world, some of our worst diseases are gradually eliminated. One of these is typhoid fever. Just 60 years ago, thousands

WHAT IS TYPHOID FEVER?

upon thousands of people were dying from it every year. Now deaths from typhoid average only a fraction of what they were, and are now confined mainly to the more backward regions.

Typhoid fever is caused by a bacillus called *Salmonella typhosa*. It lives in the products of excretion. After it leaves the body, the bacilli can continue to exist, but they do not multiply.

Some people who have had the disease become cured but continue to be typhoid carriers. This means their body still gives off the bacilli that cause the disease, even though they themselves are now healthy. This is because one attack of typhoid fever usually makes the infected person immune for life.

So a person who spreads the typhoid bacilli may spread it into sewage. The sewage may contaminate water that people drink or shellfish that are in the water. Quite often, uncooked foods are contaminated by the soiled hands of a typhoid carrier. Flies may also carry the baccili to food.

When a person gets typhoid, he begins to feel generally ill and feverish. He will have headaches, chills, and sweats, as well as periods of delirium. A blank, staring expression is a common sign. The fever reaches a high level where it remains for a week or two and then begins to go down. In about 30 days, the temperature is normal. A rash also appears during the disease.

Today typhoid can be prevented by sanitary handling of water and sewage in a community. Also, people who might be typhoid carriers should not be allowed to handle food. There is a vaccine for typhoid fever which usually lasts for at least a year and may last for a number of years.

SALMONELLA TYPHOSA

Rabies is one of the oldest diseases known to man. Once the disease appears in man or animals, death is almost certain. Just what is this terrible disease?

WHAT IS RABIES?

Rabies is a disease that infects the brain and spinal cord, which is why it is so harmful to the life of the body. The infection is caused by a virus, which means a germ too small to be seen with the ordinary microscope.

The rabies virus can infect all warm-blooded animals, but man receives it most often when bitten by a dog infected with the virus. This is why when a human being is bitten by a dog, an effort is always made to find the dog and examine it to see if it might have rabies. It just doesn't pay to take chances!

It isn't too easy to tell when a dog has been infected with rabies because it takes such a long time for the disease to show up—usually four to six weeks. At first the dog is quiet, has a fever, and isn't interested in food. Then it becomes excited. Saliva froths from the mouth. It growls and barks, and is likely to bite. After these symptoms appear, it's pretty hopeless. The dog will die in about three to five days.

In human beings, the disease begins much as it does in the dog. A man who is infected by rabies will be quiet at first. He will have fever and feel strange. Soon he feels his muscles draw strongly together. When he tries to drink, the muscles of his mouth and throat tighten, as if he were in a spasm. The muscle spasms are due to changes in the nervous system. But it was believed that they were due to an actual fear of the water, so rabies was given another name—"hydrophobia." This means "fear of water," and is not a true description of the disease.

Death comes from rabies usually when the breathing muscles go into spasm. As you can see, with this disease prevention is of the utmost importance. The bite area must be cleaned thoroughly, and a serum is given within three days of the bite. This acts against the virus before it has a chance to increase and attack the brain. Injections are given each day for a period of two or three weeks. All of this is to prevent the virus from taking hold in the body.

A virus is the smallest organism that produces disease. It cannot be seen directly by the ordinary microscope.

CAN A VIRUS BE SEEN?

But this doesn't mean that science hasn't been able to study the structure of a virus. Today there are ultramicroscopes that enable these tiny organisms to become visible. And science is able to know quite a bit about the sizes and shapes of various types of viruses by means of the electron microscope.

The electron microscope uses beams of electrons instead of rays of light. The electrons pass through the specimen being observed and strike a photographic plate on which a picture is obtained. In this way, it is possible to magnify an object about 100,000 times.

By using the electron microscope, it has been shown that viruses range in size from about 300 millimicrons to 10 millimicrons. What is a millimicron? It is one thousandth of a micron. And a micron is about 0.00004 millimetres.

Nobody is quite sure yet exactly what viruses are. Some scientists think they are closely related to bacteria. Other investigators believe they are like elementary particles, similar to "genes." Still others believe viruses are possibly midway between living and nonliving matter.

As far as we know, viruses can grow and reproduce only within living tissue. This means it's impossible to cultivate them away from living tissue, and it makes it difficult to study their growth habits. That's why they are classified by their ability to infect living cells and by the reactions they produce in the body of animals or humans.

Does the virus produce a poison or toxin? It is now believed that they do produce toxins, but the toxin and the virus particle cannot be separated. And we still don't know how these toxins produce disease if they do!

Bacteria are the most widespread creatures in the world. Everything we touch, every breath of air contains millions of them. About 80 per cent of all bacteria are harmless. A small percentage is actually useful to us, and a small group of them are harmful to human beings.

WHAT IS AN ANTIBODY?

Since man is constantly taking in bacteria of all kinds, it is obvious that our body and these bacteria form a kind of "working" relationship. Our body supports colonies of bacteria and in turn these bacteria may perform useful functions, such as helping to decompose food.

But what about harmful bacteria which enter our body? For example, the bacteria that cause diphtheria produce a powerful poison called "diphtheria toxin," which spreads through the blood system. Other bacteria, not so deadly, also produce poisons in our blood.

When this happens, our body produces substances to fight these poisons or toxins. These substances are called antibodies. Certain specific antibodies which are produced to fight bacterial toxins are known as antitoxins.

They have the power to nullify any harmful effect produced by the toxin by combining with it. Each antibody is specific for the substance or toxin which causes it to be produced. It's as if the body had a big police force. As soon as a dangerous stranger enters, a policeman meets him and goes along with him to be sure he'll do no harm.

But the body doesn't produce enough antibodies to handle each kind of harmful bacteria that enters our body. Doctors then inject serum containing antitoxin to combat many diseases.

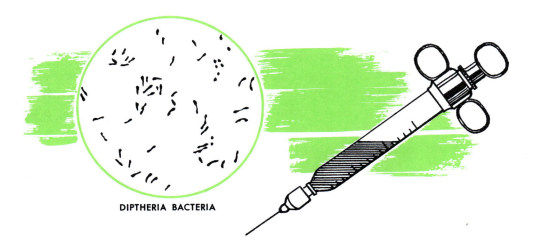

DIPTHERIA BACTERIA

All around us there are invisible forms of life which we call germs. They are in the air, in the soil, in the water we drink and the food we eat. Many of them are harmless or even beneficial to man, but others may cause diseases.

WHAT IS IMMUNITY?

The human body has many natural weapons to fight off the attack of the harmful germs. For instance, the digestive juices and the blood itself kill off many kinds of germs. But certain ones enter the body and start an infection. Then the anti-germ "soldiers" in the body spring into action. These are the white corpuscles in the blood. They can pass right through the thin walls of blood vessels and they can wander all over the body. The white blood corpuscles gather at the point of attack and destroy the germs by feeding on them.

But disease isn't always caused by a direct attack of germs. Germs throw off a chemical substance called a "toxin" which acts as a poison in the body. Once again, the body has a built-in defense. The toxin causes certain cells in the body to go to work to produce a substance that destroys the toxin. This is called an "antitoxin." If the antitoxin is produced quickly enough and in enough quantity, the germ poison is neutralized. The body gets well.

This antitoxin is always a very special one that works only against the toxin for which it was produced. It remains in the blood for some time after the toxin has disappeared. Now suppose the same germ attacks the body and produces new toxin. Instead of becoming sick, we show no symptoms of the disease at all! The reason is that our body already has a resistance to the disease; it has the antitoxin all ready. We call this condition "acquired" immunity. It is "acquired" because our resistance came after the original attack of the germs.

Now let us suppose there is an attack of germs upon the body, spreading toxins through our system, and yet we don't get that specific disease. This means our blood had enough antitoxin in it to begin with to prevent the specific poison from doing any harm. We call this a "natural" immunity. It is a quality of our blood that we inherited.

If we introduce a little toxin in our blood so it can produce anti-toxin to prevent disease, we call it artificial immunity. This is exactly what happens when we are vaccinated against diphtheria and typhoid.

There are few diseases that have caused as much discussion and as much fear as polio. In fact, the fear of polio is all out of proportion to the damage it causes.

WHAT IS POLIO? Polio is the nickname for infantile paralysis, or acute anterior poliomyelitis. It occurs in epidemics, but some is present all the time. Though it most often attacks children, anybody can catch it. Of the great numbers of people who catch polio, few are seriously affected.

The most common type of polio gives a day or two of illness, headache, fever, sore throat, and upset stomach, but no paralysis. There are at least 100 of these cases to every 1 that the doctor can diagnose as serious polio. Among diagnosed cases of polio half of the patients recover completely, 30 per cent have mild after-effects, 14 per cent have more severe paralysis, and 6 per cent may die. There is only one chance in 156 of a child contracting polio in the first 20 years of his life.

Polio is caused by three different viruses. A virus is a disease-causing organism so small that it can pass through a filter which stops bacteria. A virus must live in a living cell. When polio virus enters the body, it travels along nerves and in the blood to the spinal cord and brain. There it grows in cells in the gray matter of the spinal cord.

When these nerve cells are swollen and sick, the muscles they control cannot operate. They are paralyzed. If the nerves recover, the muscles can move again. But if the nerve cells are killed by the virus, the muscle cells connected to these nerves are paralyzed forever.

There are several kinds of polio, depending on what part of the body is infected. Spinal polio affects the nerves in the spinal cord. Bulbar polio affects a part of the brain and may paralyze the breathing muscles. Many lives have been saved by the "iron lung," which mechanically performs the act of breathing for such a victim.

Today there is every hope that the menace of polio can be wiped out. Dr. Jonas Salk has developed an anti-polio vaccine which millions of people have used to protect them against polio infection. This has been one of the greatest medical advances in many years, and has brought new hope of health and safety to the world.

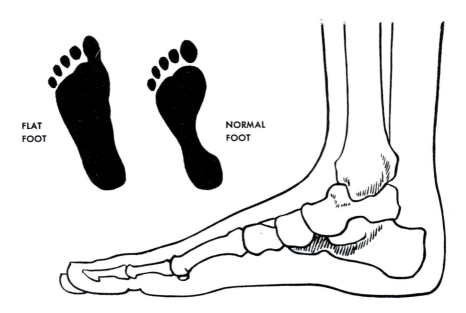

FLAT
FOOT

NORMAL
FOOT

The next time you step out of the bath tub or shower, notice the tracks made by your wet feet. If the tracks are kidney-shaped, your foot is normal. If the prints your feet make have the shape of a sole, because the entire sole touches the floor, you have flat feet.

WHAT CAUSES FLAT FEET?

The foot is a tripod, because it stands on three points. One is the heel in back. The other two are the two supporting points in the ball of the foot. Over these three points the foot forms an arch. This arch is not firm, but is elastic and springy. This is due to the arrangement of the bones, cartilage, ligaments, tendons, and muscles of the foot.

Actually, from an "engineering" point of view, a springy arch is the best type of construction for a structure that has to support weight. The space beneath the arch in the foot is filled with fat. Through this fat go the blood-vessels, nerves, and tendons of the toes, without being squeezed during walking.

When man went about barefoot outdoors, he probably never had any trouble with his feet. The reason is that the irregular and "springy" nature of the earth forces the foot to take a new position with every step. In this way, the entire foot, including the delicate muscles and ligaments of the arch, are always active. This gives all parts of the foot plenty of exercise.

When we walk on smooth city streets and hard floors, only a few points of the foot are constantly stimulated. So the foot adapts itself in a special way to this uniform stimulation. It actually remains in a state known as "spastic tension." This spastic state of the foot disurbs the process whereby all parts of the foot are fed and exercised as they should be. Certain tissues, where the blood circulates poorly, become tired, anemic, and weak. Then the arch of the foot becomes unable to bear the weight of the body and it drops down. The result is flat feet!

Of course, some cases of flat feet are due to the fact that certain people are born with naturally weak tissues. They are just born with weak arches.

When we look out across a field, how do we know one distant object is bigger than another, or that one is behind another? Why do we see everything in three dimensions, in proper relation to each other, instead of seeing everything "flat?"

HOW DO WE SEE IN THREE DIMENSIONS?

The fact is that when we "see" things, we see them not only with our eyes, but with our minds as well. We see things in the light of experience. Our mind, based on certain experiences, helps us interpret what we see. And unless the mind can use the cues it has learned to interpret what we see, we can become very confused indeed.

For instance, experience has given us an idea about the size of things. A man in a boat some distance from shore looks much smaller than a man on shore. But you don't say one is a very large man and the other a very small man. What you say to yourself is that one man is nearby and the other is farther away.

What are some of the other "cues" your mind uses? One of them is perspective. You know that when you look down the railroad tracks they seem to come together. So you consider the width of the tracks and get an idea about distance. Experience tells you that close objects look sharply defined and distant objects seem hazy.

From experience, you have also learned how to "read" shadows. They give you cues to the shape and relationship of objects. Close objects often cover up parts of things that are farther away. In this way you have learned to tell that one distant tree or house is nearer than another.

Moving the head will help you decide whether a tree or pole is farther away. Close one eye and move your head. The object farther away will seem to move with you, while nearer objects go the other way. Even focusing the eyes helps you in judging the distance of objects. You are conscious of more strain as you fix your eyes on objects nearby than on those farther away.

Finally, the combined action of both eyes working together gives you important cues. As objects move nearer to you and you try to keep them in focus, your eyes converge and there is a strain on the eye muscles. This strain becomes a cue to distance. The other cue comes from the fact that each eye picks up a slightly different image. The difference in the image helps you get a good impression of distance. All of this explains why seeing in three dimensions depends so much on past experience which the mind has to interpret.

Just imagine what life was like for millions of people before eyeglasses were invented! If you were near-sighted and you looked up at night you couldn't see the stars. You couldn't see clouds or distant mountains, or birds flying through the air.

HOW DO EYEGLASSES CORRECT VISION?

Today near-sighted people can see as much as people with normal eyes, because eyeglasses can correct their vision. To begin very simply, we can see because light enters our eye and falls on the retina in the eye, which is like the sensitized plate of a camera. Obviously, if the light falls in back of the retina or in front of it, we won't be able to see. So the eye has a lens to focus the light and make it fall in the right place.

When normal eyes look at distant objects, the image falls on the retina without any problem. But when the same eye looks at a close

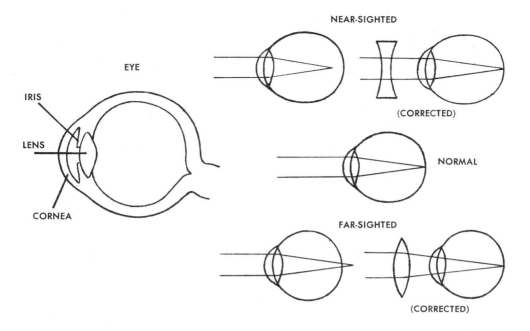

NEAR-SIGHTED

EYE

(CORRECTED)

IRIS

LENS

NORMAL

CORNEA

FAR-SIGHTED

(CORRECTED)

object (say less than 5 metres away), the image falls behind the retina. So the lens of the eye "accommodates." It means that a certain muscle contracts and changes the shape of the lens. This makes the image fall on the retina and the eye sees the object clearly.

Now two things can happen to make this accommodation impossible. First, as people get older the lenses in the eyes lose their elasticity. They can't change shape to focus images correctly. The second thing is that some people are born with eyes that are too short or too long.

People with too short eyes are far-sighted. They can see distant objects well, but they must accommodate very strongly to see close objects. Sometimes it is impossible to do this enough to focus the image on the retina. So they wear glasses. The glasses do the job that their own eye lens cannot do. They focus the image on the retina and don't have to accommodate at all.

A near-sighted person has eyes that are too long. The image is focused in front of the retina and looks blurred. But the near-sighted person can do nothing about it. If he accommodates (makes the muscle contract the eye), it will only make the image move farther forward. So he wears glasses that focus the image farther back and on the retina, and then he can see clearly.

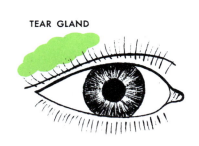

TEAR GLAND

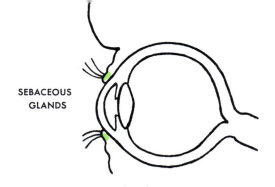

SEBACEOUS
GLANDS

When we drive a motor-vehicle in bad weather, it is very important to have the windscreen wiper working efficiently. Yet the best windscreen wiper ever made for any car can't compare with the "windscreen wiper" nature has given us for our eyes!

WHY DO WE BLINK OUR EYES?

The lids of our eyes, which move up and down when we blink, are our built-in windscreen wipers. The lids are made up of folds of skin, and they can be raised and lowered by certain muscles. But they move so rapidly that they don't disturb our vision in any way.

A curious thing about our lids is that they work automatically, just as windscreen wipers do on motor-cars when they're turned on. We blink our eyes every six seconds! This means that in the course of a lifetime, we pull them back and forth about 250 million times!

Why is blinking important to us? How does it protect our eyes? One reason has to do with our eyelashes. These are the short curved hairs which are attached to each lid. Their job is to catch dust which might go into our eyes. When you walk through rain or a sandstorm, the lids automatically drop down and the eyelashes keep out foreign matter. The eyebrows, by the way, carry off rain or perspiration to a side, so that the drops won't run into the eyes.

But the chief benefit of blinking is that this provides automatic lubrication and irrigation of the eyes. Along the edge of each lid there are twenty or thirty tiny sebaceous glands. These glands have their opening between the lashes. Every time our lids close, these glands go to work and a secretion comes out. This secretion lubricates the edge of the eye lid and the lashes, so that they won't become dry.

Here is how blinking provides "irrigation" for the eye. In each eye we have a tear gland, where the liquid that makes tears is stored. Every time we blink, the eyelid applies suction to the opening of the tear gland and takes out some of the fluid. This prevents the eye from drying out. We might say that we "cry" every time we blink our eyes!

256

You know what a "cataract" is in nature. It's a great waterfall or down-pouring of water. Now why should a certain kind of eye trouble also be called a "cataract?"

WHAT IS A CATARACT OF THE EYE?

This is because in ancient times it was believed that this particular eye trouble was caused by an opaque film that came down like a cataract over the lens of the eye. A cataract of the eye is simply a cloudy or opaque discoloration within the lens of the eye. It may or may not interfere with vision. In fact, many people may have cataracts without knowing it.

The way people find out they have cataracts is when parts of the field of vision become blurred or cloudy. Another sign is when such a person can see better in the twilight than when the light is good. When there is less light the pupil is larger and this enables more light to enter the eye.

A cataract causes the pupil of the eye to appear gray or white instead of black. Among old people with cataracts, the pupils may become very small or contracted. When a person has total cataract, the entire lens of the eye becomes milky.

A cataract is generally regarded as a disease of old age. But a baby may have a cataract at birth, or in early childhood. Sometimes people get a cataract of the eye as a result of injury or from circulatory diseases.

When children have cataracts, it is possible to restore useful vision to the eyes by means of a surgical operation without removing the lenses of the eye. But usually when a cataract begins to impair the vision so that a person can't carry on his normal activities, an operation is neces-sary that will remove the lenses. This is done on one eye at a time to avoid a long period of total blindness.

A great many people who must have such an operation naturally worry about it quite a bit. But the fact is that a good eye surgeon can perform such an operation with very little risk of failure. Afterwards the eyes may be fitted with glasses which enable the patient to see almost as well as with the lenses of the eyes.

We know pretty well what happens during sleep. Our body is inactive, we lose consciousness, and we fail to respond to things that are happening around us.

HOW DO WE FALL ASLEEP?

We also know a great deal of what takes place in our body during sleep. We know how the muscles relax, how certain vital functions continue, what happens to our circulation, our temperature, and so on.

But how do we go to sleep? What actually takes place that enables us to fall asleep? Strangely enough, the most we can say is that there are a great many theories about this. And so far, it has been impossible to prove whether these theories are right or wrong!

For example, it was once believed that we fell asleep when the blood in our body shifted out of or into an important organ. Well, this theory at least is no longer believed because we now know that no such shift of blood takes place.

Another theory no longer believed is that the chain of nerve cells in our body, which act as pathways in our nervous system, were actually broken, and we then fell asleep.

One possibility was that the impulses to the brain were shut off by our body, and that as a result we were no longer in a "wakeful state." There are even theories about falling asleep which claim that it is a positive instinct. This means that it's not just a matter of stopping wakefulness, but a positive process by which the body instinctively puts itself to sleep.

There is a whole group of chemical theories about falling asleep too. These claim that some substance that the body needs to stay awake is used up, and so we go to sleep, and during sleep this substance is replenished. Or that certain toxic substances are accumulated when we are awake and these produce sleep.

So here we still have a mystery about one of the most common and important things we do. It's as if our body knows that we need sleep to restore our tired organs and tissues and in one way or another sees to it that we get this sleep.

Every night we close our eyes and go off to another world—the world of sleep. When we awaken, it's as if we have come back from a journey, except that we don't know what really happened to us.

WHAT HAPPENS TO US WHEN WE SLEEP?

We may know we dreamed, or were cold or hot. But what else did we do? What was happening to our body while we slept?

One important thing that happened, of course, was that the muscles of our body relaxed. If someone were to raise our arm gently while we slept, it would be quite limp and we wouldn't resist. One of the reasons we take a horizontal position when we go to sleep is to allow this muscle relaxation. A set of muscles that doesn't relax during sleep, however, is around the eyes and the eyelids. These muscles are contracted to keep our eyes closed.

During a night's sleep, our body does a lot of moving. We may move just one part of the body or another, or turn over completely to change our position. Some people move more, some less, and it also depends on how tired we are, the temperature, what we ate before we went to bed, and so on. The average person moves about 20 to 40 times a night, but we move only about 30 seconds in each hour, or a few minutes in a whole night.

When we are awake, each one of us reacts differently to external events. But when we are asleep, we all react almost in the same way to whatever messages our sense organs pick up. Noise, light, heat, smells— produce practically the same reactions in all sleeping persons!

What happens inside our body during sleep? The blood continues to circulate of course, but the heart beat is slower. We breathe more slowly, too, and not as deeply as when awake. Digestion goes on at its usual rate. The liver and kidneys continue working, but at a slightly decreased rate. Our body temperature drops as much as one degree. Perspiring in general may increase, but is less active in the palms of the hands and soles of the feet during sleep than when we are awake.

It is not true, as some people think, that we sleep more deeply at certain times during the night. In any one night, we may go from shallow sleep to deep sleep, over and over again!

Sleeping sickness is a very serious disease that attacks men and animals in Africa.

It is an infection caused by parasites called "trypanosomes." These parasites, or germs, are carried by the tsetse fly which is common in many parts of central Africa.

WHAT IS SLEEPING SICKNESS?

The tsetse fly may pick up the parasites when it bites a sick man or animal. The trypanosomes enter the fly's stomach and begin to multiply. They then pass through the salivary glands which supply juice to the fly's mouth. Here they develop into forms which can infect man.

When the fly bites a man, the parasites are injected beneath the skin. A tiny sore spot appears. During the next three weeks trypanosomes begin to circulate in the blood. About this time the infected man begins to have fever that comes and goes. Often, the skin breaks out in a rash. The brain becomes slightly swollen. In some parts of Africa the infection sometimes stops here and the sick man usually recovers.

But in Zimbabwe and Malawi, the disease takes a more serious form. Within a year, the patient begins to show signs that his brain has become affected. He develops severe headaches. He becomes excited very easily. He begins to act in an uncontrollable way.

Then comes the next stage. He becomes very quiet. And finally, he goes to sleep—and stays asleep. He is in a coma, which means he is unconscious. He still has fever. Finally, he becomes paralyzed, his body wastes away, and he dies.

The reason the person becomes unconscious is that an infection takes place in a very important part of the body—the brain and meninges, which is the covering of the brain. There are many things that may cause an infection, or inflammation, of the brain. Such a condition is called "encephalitis." African sleeping sickness is really a severe form of encephalitis.

By the way, the tsetse fly does not pass on the germ of this disease to its offspring. So sleeping sickness would die out—if there were no sick animals or men for the fly to bite!

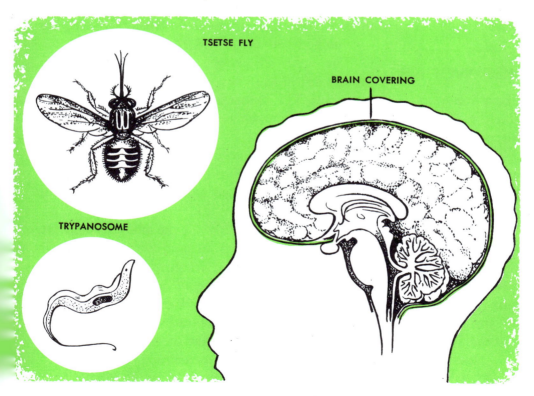

TSETSE FLY

BRAIN COVERING

TRYPANOSOME

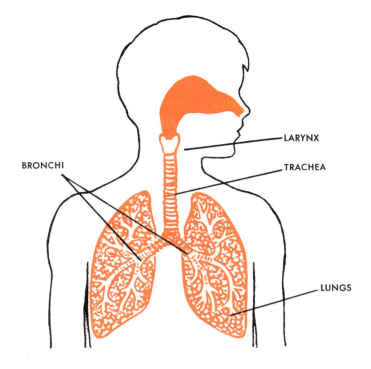

BRONCHI

LARYNX

TRACHEA

LUNGS

Man breathes by drawing air into his lungs (inhaling) and letting it out again (exhaling). In breathing, a fresh supply of air is brought into contact in the lung with tissue very rich in blood. In the lung, gases are exchanged between blood and the air.

HOW DO OUR LUNGS WORK?

The lungs are large, soft organs, which fill both sides of the chest cavity. The lung tissue is like a fine sponge in some ways. The spaces, or air sacs, are the pockets where the air is received, the proper gases used, and the unwanted gases forced out.

The air sacs are separated from each other by very thin walls filled with very delicate blood vessels, the capillaries. Only a few cells separate the blood from the air, so gases can pass easily through these thin walls.

The lungs are elastic (stretchable), and fill the chest. When we breathe in, the chest enlarges and the lungs expand with it. Then air rushes in through the nose, pharynx, larynx, trachea (the tube going down), and bronchi (two smaller tubes, one of which enters each lung), and finally into the air sacs of the lungs. When we breathe out, the space inside the chest becomes smaller, the lungs snap partly closed, and the air is forced out again through the upper tubes.

How much air can the lungs hold? To measure this, we have to consider the usual breath, plus the extra air it is possible to inhale if we try, and the amount that can be forced out. This is called the "vital capacity," or the amount of air the lungs will hold. An adult man has a vital capacity of a little over seven pints of air; a woman's vital capacity is about five pints.

The lung is never empty, even when the greatest effort has been made to force air out. The amount of air remaining after exhaling with great force is called "residual air," and when we inhale we mix fresh air with this residual air.

Breathing is both voluntary and involuntary. It goes on regularly even when we don't think about it, or are asleep. But we can stop breathing for a short time if we wish—as when we hold our breath when we are under water.

Asthma is not a disease itself, but a symptom of some other condition. When a person has asthma, he finds it hard to breathe because there is an obstruction to the flow of air into and out of the lungs.

WHAT IS ASTHMA?

This barrier or obstruction may be caused by a swelling of the mucous membranes, or by a constriction of the tubes leading from the windpipe to the lungs. When a person has an attack of asthma, he develops shortness or breath, wheezing, and coughing. The attack may come on gradually or develop suddenly.

The only way to get rid of asthma is to find out the cause and eliminate it. The cause may be an allergy, an emotional disturbance, or atmospheric conditions. If a person develops asthma before he is 30 years old, it is usually the result of an allergy. He may be sensitive to pollens, dust, animals, or certain foods or medicines.

There are many dusts and pollens which cause asthma. Children,

263

especially, tend to develop asthma from food allergies which may be caused by eggs, milk, or wheat products.

Doctors have also observed that an attack of asthma may be caused by emotional disturbance. For example, if a person has family troubles or financial worries asthma may develop. In many cases the emotional disturbance consists of a feeling of being unwanted or unloved. This produces a state which sets off a chain reaction ending in an attack of asthma.

This is why in cases of asthma the diagnosis by the physician is very important. He will take a complete and careful medical history of the patient. He will ask all kinds of questions about the patient's eating habits, health habits, and environment. If there has been even the slightest change in the person's routine, he will investigate to see if it has anything to do with the attack of asthma. It may have come after a visit to relatives who keep certain animals, or a visit to the beach, or after eating certain new foods. People who have asthma are often put on special diets by the doctor.

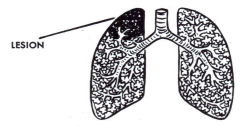

LESION

TB, or tuberculosis, is a disease caused by infection by a germ known as the "tubercle bacillus." It is, unfortunately, a common infection in all parts of the world, and is most common where people live in crowded, unsanitary conditions and have poor nutrition.

WHAT IS TB?

Luckily, man has strong resistance to the infection. Less than 10 per cent of people infected with TB die of it. Chest X-rays and testing to detect the disease, pasteurising milk (it can be contracted from cows through their milk), isolating victims and treating it with various drugs have all helped to control TB in many countries.

There are three types of tubercle bacillus—human, bovine (cow), and avian (bird). Man can be infected by both the human and bovine types. The germs most often enter the body by being breathed into the lungs. The infection they cause first is called the "primary lesion." This is an inflammation and breakdown of the tissues.

After the primary lesion, the germs are usually carried to the region of the chest. Here they set up an even greater inflammation. By this time the body has had time to develop some resistance or immunity to the infection. In most cases the lesions heal with thick scar tissue. However, some germs may remain without causing further trouble.

Sometimes a tuberculosis infection appears again in the body when a person reaches his later years. It may be a new infection or the old one becoming active. The germs may spread through the lungs.

Tuberculosis germs may also enter the blood stream and be carried to other organs and thus infect the kidneys or joints. When tuberculosis spreads through the body it is a wasting disease, which means it uses up the body. In fact, it used to be called "consumption," because it "consumed," or ate up, the body. The patient has fever, perspires heavily, loses his appetite, and becomes thin and weak.

Since a person may have a small spot of infection without knowing it, it is a good idea to have regular physical check-ups by a doctor.

SINUSES

Every now and then you meet somebody whose nose seems all stuffed up, or he complains of pains in the eyes and cheeks, and headaches. When you ask him if he has a cold, he may answer: "No, I have sinus trouble."

WHAT ARE THE SINUSES?

What is a sinus, and why do people get "sinus trouble?" Strictly speaking, a sinus is a space filled with blood or with air. But for most people, the expression "sinus trouble" means an infection of one of the cavities connected with the nose.

There are eight or more of these small cavities in the bones of the forehead and face. There are two sinuses in the frontal bones in the forehead. The largest sinuses are in the cheek bones. And there are smaller ones that open into the back and sides of the nose.

All these cavities are lined with mucuous membranes. These membranes are continuations of those in the nose, and the secretions from the sinuses drain through the nose. There are many theories about why we have these sinuses. It may be that they help to warm the nasal passages and to keep them moist. Or, they may give more resonance to the voice, or play some part in the sense of smell. It may be that we have them simply to provide vacant spaces in the skull so it won't be so heavy!

Sinuses may become infected after a severe cold, or influenza, or some other infectious disease. When sinuses are infected, we feel pain in the face, in the forehead, or behind the eyes, which usually comes on about the same time every day. There is sometimes a discharge from the nose.

The pain is caused by the discharge which collects in the sinus and cannot get out because the mucuous membrane which is connected with the nose is swollen. Sometimes the sinus in the cheek bone, called the "antrum," is infected as the result of a dental disease.

An operation for sinus trouble is rarely required. When it is done, the purpose is to enlarge the opening into the nose so that better drainage will take place. The best thing to do about sinus trouble is to prevent it. Great care should be taken to avoid colds. A doctor should be allowed to treat any obstruction in the nose during the early stages, and the dentist should have a chance to treat any dental disease before it becomes serious. Also, it is probably a good idea not to live in hot stuffy rooms, which may help bring on sinus trouble.

During the "hay fever season," newspapers in many cities publish the day's pollen count. What is pollen, what does it have to do with hay fever, and what is a pollen count?

WHAT IS A POLLEN COUNT?

A person is said to have hay fever when he is sensitive to pollen and some other substances that are present in the air. Pollen is the reproductive element of plants and is contained in the flowers of most plants. Usually, it occurs as a fine dust or grains.

While insects spread pollen, it is the wind that spreads most of the pollen that causes hay fever. There are three chief groups of plants whose pollen causes hay fever, and each of these groups has a different season. For example, trees produce the pollen that causes hay fever during April and May, various grasses are responsible for hay fever that comes from May to July, and weeds produce the pollen that causes hay fever from August to October.

Since some weeds can produce more than 100,000 pollen grains from a single plant, you can see that at certain times there can be quite a bit of pollen in the air. Naturally, the more pollen there is about, the more the hay fever victims suffer.

This is why a pollen count is taken. People who must leave the area during the heavy pollen season know when to come back. The way a pollen count is taken is quite simple. A glass slide, one side of which is coated with oil, is placed in a horizontal position in the atmosphere to be tested. The slide is usually left for 24 hours. Then the pollen grains collected on it are counted with the aid of a microscope.

Wind and weather have a great deal to do with the amount of pollen in the air. Heavy rains during the summer months cause plants to flourish and produce large quantities of pollen. If the summer months are dry, much smaller amounts of pollen will be produced. Sunshine helps the pollen mature, while damp weather retards it. If it rains in the early part of the day, the spreading of pollen will be held down somewhat.

The reason we call it "hay fever," by the way, is that the symptoms of the disease appeared during the haying season in England. A doctor in 1812 wrote a report on it and called it "hay fever," and the name has remained.

ROSE

RAGWEED

CATKINS OF POPLAR TREE

When coffee was first introduced in Europe during the second part of the seventeenth century, there was a great deal of controversy about it. Many "learned doctors" announced that coffee was a strong poison

WHY ARE PEOPLE AFFECTED BY COFFEE?

and should be prohibited. Others insisted it was a good thing to drink coffee, and "coffee-houses" sprang up everywhere.

Coffee can actually act as a poison when it is given in large doses to animals in laboratory tests. It can also produce toxic effects in small children. But for adults who drink it in moderation, it is definitely not a poison.

The coffee bean contains one per cent of a substance known as caffein, which is always combined with acids. Most people believe that it is the caffein which produces all the effects that coffee has on the body, but the other substances in the coffee bean are involved too.

Here are some of the things that happen when someone drinks coffee. The odor of the coffee itself produces stimulating effects in various parts of the body. The blood vessels in the brain are dilated so that circulation is improved, and this removes some of the fatigue toxins from the brain.

Coffee increases the pulse rate, which means it stimulates the heart. Coffee increases the tone of the muscles, so they can work harder. The intestine becomes more active because of coffee, which has a slight laxative effect. Coffee makes the gastric glands secrete more actively. For healthy people, this is desirable, especially after a heavy meal. But for others it may produce "heartburn." Coffee also helps the body remove salts from the blood.

Coffee actually produces different effects on the body at different times of the day! The morning coffee for instance, acts on the kidneys and helps the body get rid of waste products accumulated during the night. Coffee after lunch, however, acts on the gastric glands and helps digestion. Afternoon coffee acts on the muscles and helps us feel less tired. And coffee taken in the evening seems to stimulate the mind and the imagination!

Nowadays it is possible to buy "de-caffeinated" coffee, and millions of people drink this rather than "regular" coffee. What is caffein, and why do some people try to avoid it?

WHAT IS CAFFEIN?

The roasted coffee bean is so full of different substances that science has not yet detected all of them. But the best known substance in the bean is caffein. It is a stimulant and is chemically related to uric acid. Caffein is not found in a free state, but combined with acids. The coffee bean contains about one per cent caffein.

Since caffein is a stimulant, some people avoid drinking coffee at night—because that's the time when they want to relax. Other people seem quite able to sleep despite the caffein in their coffee.

As we mentioned above, the caffein in coffee acts differently at different times, and has a different effect on different people. But we can't think of caffein in coffee as if we were taking it in a pure state. The way it is combined with other substances in coffee and with food makes quite a difference. For example, if you take milk or cream in your coffee, the caffein of the coffee combines with the protein of the milk, and the action is thus weakened. You are partially "de-caffein-ating" your coffee.

De-caffeinated coffee is made by using steam, or by soaking green coffee in a benzene derivative (ether) before roasting. The product is still pure coffee, but a great deal of the caffein has been removed.

Do you know that when you use your voice, you are really acting like a musical virtuoso? You are performing on one of the most difficult and complicated musical instruments known to man. And the reason you can do it is that you learned when you were young and have been practicing it ever since!

WHY DO SOME PEOPLE HAVE BEAUTIFUL VOICES?

Consider just the vocal cords, which are only part of the apparatus which produces our voice. Controlling them is a matter of the utmost precision. Sixteen muscles, the most delicate muscles in the body, move our vocal cords. They can assume about 170 different positions! Just the right amount of air has to be blown upward to make them vibrate in a certain way. If the vocal cords are tensed in a certain way so they vibrate about 80 times per second, the vibration of the air which we hear as sound has deep tones. If the cords are tensed and vibrate as much as 1,000 times per second, we hear high tones. The general pitch of our voice is determined by the length of our vocal cords.

But the human vocal apparatus is a complicated mechanism, an instrument with walls consisting of bones, muscles, mucous membranes, and with resonating spaces which are like the wooden sounding board of the violin. Among these resonating spaces are the windpipe, the lungs, the oral and nasal cavities, the nasal sinuses, and the thorax.

The range and quality of a voice depend on the form and the size of the resonating spaces. Persons who have beautiful voices have resonating spaces that are shaped in such a way that they may be considered perfect musical instruments. But having these resonating spaces is not enough. They must know how to control them artistically. A singer uses the entire vocal apparatus when he sings—from the diaphragm to the frontal sinuses.

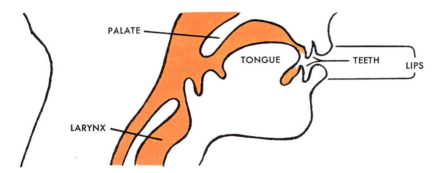

Probably the most complex and difficult musical instrument that can be imagined is the apparatus in human beings that produces speech! In order for sounds and letters to be formed, this entire apparatus must be

WHY DO PEOPLE STAMMER?

used. This includes the abdomen, chest, larynx, mouth, nose, diaphragm, various muscles, tongue, palate, lips, and teeth!

The most important ones used in making spoken sounds are the muscles of the mouth, the palate, lips, and tongue. The only reason we can "play" this instrument so well, is that we learned how to do it when we were most adaptable during early childhood, and because we have practiced it ever since!

Obviously, if we can't play this instrument (the vocal apparatus) with perfect coordination, then something happens to our speech. It comes out wrong and we stammer.

Stammering, or stuttering, occurs when there is a spasm in one or more of the organs that are involved in producing speech. Our production of words is suddenly checked; there is a pause, and this is often followed by a repetition in quick succession of the sound at which we stopped originally.

There are many grades of stammering. It can range from a slight inability to pronounce certain letters or syllables easily, to a condition in which muscles of the tongue, throat, and face are caught in a spasm.

Stammering rarely shows itself before the age of four or five. A child may begin to stammer because there is actually something wrong with one of the organs used in producing sounds. Very often, an emotional disturbance will cause stammering.

Usually, when a person stammers, it is the "explosive" consonants that give the most trouble . . . "b, p, d, t, k," and the hard "g." An explosive consonant is produced by checking the air on its way out, pressing the lips together, then suddenly stopping the interruption of the air by opening the lips. Try to see how you make the "b" sound. It's explosive!

Stuttering may often be corrected if a person gets instruction in reading and speaking slowly and deliberately, carefully pronouncing each syllable. Of course, if an emotional disturbance is the cause for stammering, special treatment is necessary.

Many people think of the word "drug" as meaning a habit-forming substance that is taken to relieve pain or to produce sleep. Actually, a drug is any substance or mixture of substances used as a medicine.

WHAT ARE DRUGS?

The mixing of such substances, the art of healing with "drugs," is a very ancient one. In fact, the first step forward in the treatment of diseases came about through the knowledge that priests and teachers had of plant products and their healing power. The ancient Greeks used plant products as drugs thousands of years ago.

Today, many of our important drugs still come from plants. Morphine and opium are made from the juice of the poppy. Cocaine, which is used to deaden the nerves for operations, comes from the coca plant. Quinine is extracted from a bark called "cinchona." Castor oil comes from castor beans.

Many of the important drugs we use today come from minerals, and these include salts, bromides, and phosphorus. Did you know that the organs of animals also provide useful drugs for man? The thyroid gland, the adrenal glands, and the pancreas produce substances that are made into medicine.

Still another kind of drug are the vaccines, toxoids, and antitoxins. A vaccine contains dead or weakened disease germs. When put into the body, antibodies are created which circulate in the blood stream and protect against that specific disease. A toxoid works in the same way, except that it contains inactive poisons made by disease germs. An antitoxin contains large amounts of antibodies, and it is used to help the body fight infections.

With the development of science, we have been able to make synthetic drugs. These originate, not in plants or animals, but in the laboratories of the research chemist. More and more of our drugs are synthetic, since they can be produced cheaply and in great quantities. Probably the best known synthetic drug is aspirin.

Recently science has made another discovery in the field of drugs —antibiotics. These are chemicals which are produced by molds. The chemicals have the power to stop the growth of many disease-causing bacteria. Penicillin and streptomycin are two important antibiotics.

Today, unfortunately, we often read and hear about "dope" addicts, and their addiction problem is of great concern to our society.

"Dope" is a slang term for "narcotics." Narcotics are habit-forming

WHAT IS "DOPE"? drugs which lessen pain and cause drowsiness. They give a temporary feeling of well-being which is called "narcosis." Some narcotics are very useful, but they must all be used only when given by a physician!

The reason for this is that if they are used often, they are habit-forming. The person becomes an "addict." This means he must take the drug regularly, or he suffers greatly when he is without it. Once addiction is started, it is difficult to overcome. Addicts often will pay large sums to buy illegal drugs and they will steal and commit crimes, if necessary, to pay for them.

Five of the best known narcotic drugs are: morphine, codeine, heroin, cocaine, and marijuana. Morphine is one of the most useful drugs for the relief of pain and to prevent the harmful effects of severe pain. It is obtained from opium. Morphine affects the brain more than it does other organs of the body. Worries disappear, and the patient becomes relaxed, quiet, and often drowsy. However, the senses of hearing, sight, and touch do not change.

Codeine relieves pain but it has very little effect on the mind. So it is not often used by "dope addicts." Heroin, however, does give this feeling of well being, but it is a poor relief for severe pain. Since it is habit-forming but without much medical value, it is against the law in the United States to manufacture it.

Cocaine is a narcotic made from the leaves of the coca shrub. It affects the mind most seriously. Marijuana comes from certain plants, especially hemp. It has no medical use, and it is used by addicts in the form of cigarettes (the dried leaves and flowers are used instead of tobacco).

No person—of any age—should ever take any narcotic drugs without the care and guidance of a doctor!

Every now and then you read of someone being arrested for using or possessing marijuana. The law prohibits its use in many countries.

Marijuana is obtained from the hemp plant. It is a drug but, unlike

WHAT IS MARIJUANA?

many other drugs, it is not recognized as a medicine. It acts as a narcotic, which means it can produce a stupor. As a narcotic it is either smoked or eaten, and it has been used by people since ancient times. In India it is known as *bhang, charas,* or *ghanga;* in Egypt it is known as *hashish;* in North Africa it is known as *kif;* and in the Western Hemisphere it is called "marijuana."

Marijuana affects the central nervous system. Many people who are emotionally unstable and have been involved in crimes of all sorts prove to be marijuana users.

When a person takes marijuana it can produce all kinds of strange results. A person may feel thirsty, hungry, and crave sweet foods. It may make him nauseous, dizzy, or sleepy. It may make him very irritable, give him delusions of grandeur, or the feeling that he is being persecuted. Sometimes it makes people very talkative and unable to control their laughter, or it may cause fear, depression, mental confusion, and even delirium.

Some people who have smoked just one marijuana cigarette have suffered very disagreeable effects a short time afterward. Young people who make the mistake of wanting to "try it" are often led into the terrible practice of using heroin or morphine afterward, and they become addicts.

Marijuana itself is a complex kind of drug and much study remains to be done about it by scientists. But there is no question that it should be avoided by everyone who wants to lead a healthy, happy life.

MARIJUANA

Nobody ever needs an antidote unless he has been poisoned. An antidote by itself has no meaning. It is a substance which prevents the action of a poison. And a poison is any substance which produces harmful or deadly effects on living tissue.

WHAT IS AN ANTIDOTE?

There are basically four kinds of poisons, divided according to the way they affect the body. Corrosive poisons (like strong acids) destroy tissues locally. Irritant poisons produce congestion of the organ with which they come in contact. The next kind of poison, neurotoxins, affect the nerves within the cell. And finally, the hemotoxins combine with the blood and prevent oxygen from forming hemoglobin. Carbon monoxide (such as comes from the exhaust of an automobile) is a hemotoxin. It causes death because the blood is deprived of oxygen that nourishes the tissues and brain.

In treating cases of poisoning, three things are usually done immediately. The first is to dilute the poison. This is done by having the patient drink as much water as possible. The next step is to empty the stomach, and this is done by inducing vomiting. Then a specific antidote is given against the particular poison.

Antidotes act in several different ways in preventing the action of a poison. One way is by combining chemically with the poisonous substance, thus making it harmless. For example, soda combines with an acid, vinegar combines with lye.

An antidote may also act physically by coating the mucous membranes with a protective layer. Olive oil and milk act as antidotes in this way. A third way antidotes may work is by absorbing the poisonous substances on the surface of finely divided particles. Charcoal acts in this way. Some antidotes actually produce the opposite effect from the original poison in the body, and so they counteract the action of the poison. Of course, one of the chief things a doctor tries to do in a case of poisoning is to eliminate the poison from the body, and there are many ways to accomplish this.

The best rule to follow is prevention. Poisonous substances should be kept where children cannot get at them, and products that contain poison should be clearly marked and carefully stored.

Chapter 4

HOW IT BEGAN

What does the word "superstition" mean to you? When you try to define it, don't you find it's quite hard to do so?

Suppose, for example, you said it was a belief in something that wasn't really so. Well, there are many things all of us believe in that can't be proved. Besides, at certain times in man's history, everyone believed in certain things that we now regard as superstitions. And the people who believed in them at that time weren't superstitious at all!

HOW DID SUPERSTITIONS BEGIN?

For example, they believed that the shadow or reflection of a person was a part of the soul. So they considered that you would harm the soul if you broke anything on which this shadow or reflection appeared. Therefore, they considered it harmful or "unlucky" to break a mirror. But remember, at that time this was a belief held by most people.

Today, if someone considers it "unlucky" to break a mirror he is superstitious, because today we no longer believe that a shadow or reflection is part of the soul. So a superstition is actually a belief or practice that people cling to after new knowledge or facts have appeared to disprove them. That's why it's impossible to say when superstition began.

In ancient times man tried to explain events in the world as best he could with the knowledge at hand. He didn't know much about the sun, stars, moon, comets, and so on. So he made up explanations about them and followed certain practices to protect himself from their "influence." That is why astrology was an accepted belief at one time. But with the development of science, the heavenly bodies came to be known and understood. The old beliefs should have died out. When they didn't and when people still believed, for example, that seeing a shooting star brought good luck, then these beliefs became superstitions.

Man has always had superstitions about numbers and about days. Some were supposed to be lucky; some, unlucky. Why the number 13 came to be considered unlucky no one really knows, though there are some

WHY IS FRIDAY THE 13th CONSIDERED UNLUCKY?

theories about it. One explanation has to do with Scandinavian mythology. There were 12 demigods, according to this legend, and then Loki appeared, making the 13th. Since Loki was evil and cruel and caused human misfortunes, and since he was the 13th demigod, the number 13 came to be a sign of bad luck.

Some people think the superstition goes back to the fact that there were 13 persons at the Last Supper, and that Judas was the 13th guest! Whatever its origin, the superstition about the number 13 is found in practically every country in Europe and America.

Superstitions about lucky and unlucky days are just as common as those about numbers, and Friday probably has more than any of them centering about it.

In ancient Rome, the sixth day of the week was dedicated to Venus. When the northern nations adopted the Roman method of designating days, they named the sixth day after Frigg or Freya, which was their nearest equivalent to Venus, and hence the name Friday.

The Norsemen actually considered Friday the luckiest day of the week, but the Christians regarded it as the unluckiest. One reason for this is that Christ was crucified on a Friday.

The Mohammedans say that Adam was created on a Friday, and according to legend, Adam and Eve ate the forbidden fruit on a Friday and they died on a Friday.

Superstitious people feel that when you combine the unlucky number 13 with the unlucky day Friday, you've really got an unlucky day!

It seems almost a shame to learn the true facts about Santa Claus. We almost hate to discover what's really behind some tradition we especially enjoy because that might spoil it for us.

HOW DID THE IDEA OF SANTA CLAUS ORIGINATE?

Well, knowing about Christmas and Santa Claus shouldn't spoil anything for you, but only make it more meaningful. Long before Christ was born, people used to celebrate the winter solstice as the birthday of the sun. This time of year was a holiday in many parts of the world before it became the Christmas celebration. That's why some of the customs and traditions of Christmas go back to pagan times.

The custom of giving presents, for example, goes back to the ancient Romans. In the Bible, as you know, the Wise Men brought gifts to Jesus on the 12th day after his birth. And so in some countries, the children receive their presents not on Christmas, but 12 days later.

In some of the northern countries of Europe, the gifts are exchanged almost three weeks before Christmas. The reason for this is that the gifts are supposed to be brought by Saint Nicholas on the eve of his feast day, December 6th.

Saint Nicholas was a bishop of the fourth century who came to be regarded as a special friend of the children. So, in countries like Holland, Belgium, Switzerland and Austria, and in parts of Germany, Saint Nicholas returns every year with gifts for good children.

When the Dutch went abroad, they carried the traditions of Saint Nicholas with them. They called him *San Nicolaas*, and this soon was changed to *Sankt Klaus*, and then Santa Claus. But in this country, we moved the date of his arrival to Christmas Eve, and gradually his red costume, the reindeer, and his home at the North Pole became part of the tradition.

If man didn't have a wonderful power of imagination, we'd probably have no superstitions at all. Also, if people didn't learn more and more about certain things that happen in nature, these superstitions would probably never die.

WHAT IS THE WILL-O'-THE-WISP?

The will-o'-the-wisp has been the subject of many amazing superstitions for hundreds of years. There are many tales told of travelers who lost their way in swamps and marshes by following a blue flame that seemed to dance ahead of them. This was the will-o'-the-wisp, or jack-o'-lantern, and it was supposed to be an evil spirit that lured men to their death.

Another name for the will-o'-the-wisp is corpse-candle. In fact, it had different names in different parts of England. Some called it Sylhiam Lamp, others, Joan-in-the-Wad, and still others, Friar's Lanthorn.

Now, there is such a thing as a pale bluish flame that can be seen floating above swamps and marshes. It is seen not only in England, but in Germany, in Scotland, in Ireland, and in Venezuela! Sometimes it shines steadily in one place, but often it travels rapidly. And sometimes it disappears and reappears from time to time.

The Latin name for it is *ignis fatuus,* which means "foolish fire." It is caused by the burning of some of the gases which are released by the decay of plant and animal remains found in bogs. One of these gases is a compound of phosporous and hydrogen. In dry air, this gas often bursts into flame, and thus we have our will-o'-the-wisp.

Why has it been the cause of so much superstition? The reason is probably that it is often seen in churchyards, where the soil and climate are right for producing it. When people attempted to follow it, they finally lost it, of course, since it was caused by the burning of gases.

In certain parts of Wales, the following explanation of the will-o'-the-wisp is still believed by the peasants. Long ago, St. David promised the Welshmen that no one would die without first having a light come from the churchyard to summon him. So now they believe that the will-o'-the-wisp is the spirit of a deceased relative come from the churchyard to fetch the spirit of a dying man or woman.

No matter how much we like our own country, and our way of government, and the people of our country, we know it isn't perfect. In fact, there never has been a place on earth where everyone who lived there felt it to be perfect.

WHAT IS UTOPIA?

But many people have often dreamed of living in a perfect place. What would it be like? Well, no one would be poor. But nobody would be rich either. There would be no need to be rich—since everyone would have all the things he needed. Everyone would be happy all the time. There would be very little need for a government, because the people would be considerate of everyone else.

The trouble with such a place is that no one ever really expects to find it. We know it's "too good to be true." Such a place therefore is "nowhere"—and that's exactly what the word "utopia" means. It's made up of two Greek words meaning "not a place"—or nowhere! But the way we use the word "utopia," we mean a perfect place to live.

The word "utopia" was first used by Sir Thomas More, an English writer who lived in the sixteenth century. He published a book in 1516 called *Utopia* in which he described a perfect island country. His book became very popular.

The idea of utopia, however, goes back long before this book. In fact, More got the idea for his book from the famous ancient Greek philosopher Plato, who wrote a book called "The Republic," in which he described what would be a perfect state.

There were also many legends among such people as the Norse, the Celts, and the Arabs, about a perfect place that was supposed to exist somewhere in the Atlantic Ocean. When the exploration of the Western world actually began, most of these legends were no longer believed. But with More's book, "Utopia," it became common for writers to tell of an imaginary place that was perfect. It existed only in their fantasy.

Today, when people describe certain changes they want to make in government or society, these ideas are sometimes called "utopian." This means they fail to recognize defects in human nature that make a perfect place to live practically impossible.

MARTIN LUTHER

Early in the sixteenth century a religious revolution called the Reformation began. Out of it grew the many Protestant religions. As both words, Reformation and Protestant, indicate, the basis of this religious revolution was a desire to change what was then happening in the Catholic Church.

HOW DID THE PROTESTANT RELIGION BEGIN?

What did these people want to change and why?—One thing they objected to was the kind of lives many of the clergy led. They felt that the clergy were not concentrating enough on spiritual matters and were too concerned with material things.

The reformers also objected to the sale of indulgences. These were statements releasing people from punishment for their sins. Many of the people were jealous, too, of the huge possessions held by the monasteries, even though many of them were good landlords.

There were other forces at work at this time, too. Many people followed the reformers largely for political and economic reasons. Nationalism was rising, and with the feeling of nationalism, there came the desire for a national church.

Another factor was that the authority of the Pope was being questioned as far as it concerned non-church affairs. And there was a great division when two or more popes disputed the right of the others.

In 1517 the sale of indulgences by dishonest agents became so widespread that Martin Luther, a German scholar of the order of St. Augustine, protested. He was excommunicated and condemned as a heretic, but his doctrines spread.

In 1530 he drew up the Augsburg Confession which contained twenty-one articles of the Protestant faith. This resulted in a complete break between the Lutherans and the Catholics. In time, the reformed doctrines, on which the Protestant churches are based, were accepted in various forms and in different countries.

ROMAN WEDDING

Marriage, as a custom, goes back to the very earliest history of man. It has passed through three stages. The first was marriage by capture. Primitive man simply stole the woman he wanted for his wife.

HOW DID WEDDINGS START?

Then came marriage by contract or purchase. A bride was bought by a man. Finally came the marriage based on mutual love. But even today we still have traces of the first two stages. "Giving the bride away" is a relic of the time when the bride was really sold. The "best man" at weddings today probably goes back to the strong-armed warrior who helped primitive man carry off his captured bride. And the honeymoon itself symbolizes the period during which the bridegroom was forced to hide his captured bride until her kinsmen grew tired of searching for her!

Today we have "weddings" without realizing that this very word goes back to one of the early stages of marriage. Among the Anglo-Saxons, the "wed" was the money, horses, or cattle which the groom gave as security and as a pledge to prove his purchase of the bride from her father.

Of course, when it comes to wedding customs, most of them can be traced back to ancient meanings which have long been forgotten. For example, the "something blue" which brides wear is borrowed from ancient Israel. In those times brides were told to wear a ribband of blue on the borders of their garments because blue was the color of purity, love, and fidelity.

When we ask, Who giveth this woman to this man? we are going back to the times when a bride was actually purchased. It is believed that the custom of having bridesmaids goes back to Roman times when there had to be ten witnesses at the solemn marriage ceremony.

Why do we tie shoes on the back of newlyweds' cars? It is believed that this goes back to the custom of exchanging or giving away of shoes to indicate that authority had been exchanged. So the shoe suggests that now the husband rather than the father has authority over the bride.

This custom is not only found all over the world, but it goes back to very ancient times.

WHY DO WE THROW RICE AT THE BRIDE AND GROOM?

The marriage ceremony, like so many other important events in life, is full of symbolism. (This means that we perform certain acts as symbols of things we wish to express, instead of expressing them directly.)

The use of rice is one of those symbols. It has played a part in marriage ceremonies for centuries. In certain primitive tribes, for instance, the act of eating rice together was the way people got married. This was probably because eating together symbolized living together, and rice happened to be the local food.

Among other peoples, the bride and groom first ate rice together to be married, and then rice was sprinkled over them.

In some cases, rice was used at weddings not to bring the bride and groom together, but to protect them from evil spirits. It was believed that these spirits always appeared at a marriage, and by throwing rice after the married couple, these evil spirits were fed and kept from doing harm to the newlyweds.

But for most ancient peoples, rice was a symbol of fruitfulness, and the custom of throwing rice at the bride and groom today goes back to that meaning. It means that we are saying, in symbolic form, "May you have many children and an abundance of good things in your future together!"

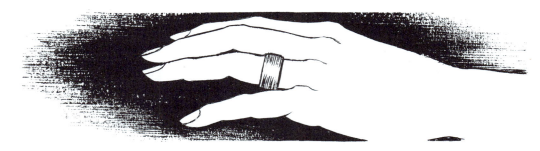

The wearing of a wedding ring is one of the oldest and most universal customs of mankind. The tradition goes back so far that no one can really tell how it first began.

WHEN WERE WEDDING RINGS FIRST WORN?

The fact that the ring is a circle may be one reason why it began to be used. The circle is a symbol of completeness. In connection with marriage, it represents the rounding out of the life of a person. We can see how a man without a wife, or a woman without a husband, could have been considered incomplete people. When they are married they make a complete unit, which the circle of the ring symbolizes.

Some people believe the wedding ring really started as a bracelet that was placed on women who were captured in primitive times. Gradually the circular bracelet on the arm or leg, which indicated that she was the property of one man in the tribe, was changed to a ring on the finger.

We know also that primitive man believed in magic. He used to weave a cord and tie it around the waist of the woman he wanted. He believed that with this ceremony her spirit entered his body and she was his forever. The wedding ring may have started this way.

The first people who actually used wedding rings in marriage were the Egyptians. In hieroglyphics, which is Egyptian picture-writing, a circle stands for eternity, and the wedding ring was a symbol of a marriage that would last forever. Christians began to use a ring in marriage around the year 900.

Why is the ring worn on the fourth finger of the left hand? The ancient Greeks believed that a certain vein passed from this finger directly to the heart. But probably the real reason is that we use this finger least of all the fingers, so it's more convenient to wear an ornament on it!

Years ago there used to a great many popular jokes that began: "Confucius say. . . ." It seems as if everybody knows that Confucius said many wise things.

WHO WAS CONFUCIUS?

Confucius was one of the greatest moral teachers of all time. He lived in China about five hundred years before Christ. Confucius studied ancient Chinese writings from which he took ideas that to him seemed important to the development of fine character. Then he taught these ideas to the princes and to the students of all classes who flocked to him for instruction. The rules he laid down 2,400 years ago are still held up as ideals.

Confucius' Chinese name was Kung-Fu-tse. At the age of 22, three years after his marriage, Confucius began to teach men how to live happily. His principle rule for happiness, "What you do not wish done to yourself, do not do to others," was much like the Golden Rule.

Confucius held office under many different princes whom he tried to interest in the right moral conduct, the conduct based on love, justice, reverence, wisdom, and sincerity.

One of his teachings, the reverence for parents, had a tremendous effect on China, because it teaches reverence not only while the parents are living but after they are dead. As a form of ancestor worship, it caused China for a long time to look to the past instead of moving forward.

Confucius did not consider himself a god. In fact, he taught nothing about a supreme being or a hereafter. He believed that man was natur-

ally good and could preserve this goodness by living harmoniously with his fellow men.

Within five hundred years after his death, his teachings became the philosophy of the state. But when Buddhism appeared, the teachings of Confucius were almost forgotten for a period. They were later revived, and even today his teachings influence the lives of millions of people.

Buddhism is one of the great religions of the world. Most of its followers live in Sri Lanka, China, Japan, Korea, and Thailand, but there are Buddhists everywhere.

WHO WAS BUDDHA?

The founder of this religion was Prince Gautama Siddhartha, born to luxury. One day, as he left his palace he saw three men, one very sick, one very old, and one dead. Very disturbed by this evidence of man's suffering, he began to wonder how man might find true and lasting happiness.

He fasted and meditated as he sought the answer. One day, as he sat under a fig tree, which became known as the Bò Tree, or tree of enlightenment, he suddenly saw clearly that the cure for all unhappiness lay in a mastery of one's self and one's selfish desires. He set out to teach his discovery to the world. As Buddha, "the Enlightened One," he wandered through India with his disciples for more than forty years, teaching the people how to find true happiness.

The followers of Buddha came to consider him a god and set up images of him and worshiped them. But Buddha himself didn't believe there was a supreme god. He believed and taught that the soul of man passes after death to a higher or lower organism, according to his good or bad deeds during life.

This transmigration of the soul into another body goes on through many cycles until all desire is overcome. Then the soul enters Nirvana, or a state of perfect peace. In order to reach this state, man must follow the Eight-Fold Path of Right Faith, by observing Right Intention, Right Speech, Right Conduct, Right Livelihood, Right Effort, Right Thinking, and Right Meditation.

In the early part of the seventh century, a young Arab felt himself divinely inspired to found a new religion and go forth as its prophet. This great man, whose name was Mohammed, sowed the seeds of a faith

WHO WAS MOHAMMED?
that has become one of the three foremost world religions.

Mohammed proclaimed the one God of the Jews and Christians to be the only true God. He placed himself beside Adam, Noah, Abraham, Moses, and Jesus. Mohammed called his religion Islam (which means submission to the will of God).

It is known by this name to its more than 550,000,000 followers. The true believers are called Moslems.

Islam is based largely on the Jewish and Christian religions. According to Mohammed, God revealed himself to man through his chosen prophets, among them Mohammed. God gave the Law to Moses, the Gospel to Jesus, and the Koran to Mohammed.

Mohammedans believe in the unity of God, unchangeable, all-powerful, all-knowing, all-merciful, and eternal. The creed of Islam is: "There is no God but Allah, and Mohammed is his Prophet." Allah is the Arabic word for God. God sits enthroned in the highest of the seven heavens. Around Him are the angels, pure and radiant.

The belief that the soul lives on after death forms a principal part of the Islamic religion. The Moslems hold that on judgment day the souls of the dead will rise, and together with the souls of the living, will appear before God's throne to answer for their deeds. Moslems also believe that the fate, or kismet, of each individual is settled before birth and written down in the great Book of God. A Moslem must practice five chief religious duties, one of which is a pilgrimage to Mecca, the birthplace of Mohammed and the holy city of the Moslems, at least once during his lifetime.

BRIGHAM YOUNG

A Mormon is a member of the Church of Jesus Christ of Latter-day Saints. The name Mormonism, which is commonly used in speaking of this religion, comes from the use of the Book of Mormon as one of the works of scripture in this church.

WHAT IS A MORMON?

The Church of Jesus Christ of Latter-day Saints was formally organized by Joseph Smith in Fayette, New York, on April 6, 1830. Because of the persecution to which Joseph Smith and his followers were subjected, some moved westward to Ohio, some to Missouri, and finally, to Nauvoo, Illinois where they established their first permanent settlement. In 1844, Joseph Smith and his brother Hyrum were killed by a mob even though they were in the Carthage, Illinois, jail for protection from the mob.

Brigham Young then became president of the church, and in 1846, about fifteen thousand of his followers started the pioneer movement to the Rocky Mountain territory. In July of 1847, the first advance company reached Salt Lake Valley, in what is now Utah, and began the cultivation of that territory. Utah has remained the headquarters of the Mormon Church.

The principle beliefs of the church are given briefly in its Articles of Faith. These include belief in a personal God; in Jesus Christ; in repentance; in baptism by immersion for the remission of sins; that men will be punished only for their own sins and not for Adam's; that through the atonement of Christ, all men may be saved by obedience to the Gospel.

According to its members, Mormonism gives man an exalted place in the universe. They believe man possesses unlimited possibilities, and "What God is, man may become." Members of the church support it by the principle of "tithing." This means members contribute one tenth of their income or earnings for the maintenance and operation of the church.

The church also has a missionary system maintained by members at their own expense. About two thousand young people are constantly engaged in this work.

When you go to sleep and have a dream, "you" are doing something in the dream. But at the same time, there is your body asleep in bed! Who or what, is that other "you" that does all those things in your dream?

WHAT IS REINCARNATION?

Primitive man, who didn't understand dreams as we do today, believed that a part of you actually left your body during sleep, and he considered that part your "soul." Now, if your "soul" could leave your body during sleep, then it could also leave your body when you died!

Based on this idea, there grew up a belief in reincarnation. It is also referred to as the transmigration of souls, and metempsychosis. It is the belief that at death the soul leaves the human body and enters the body of some other living thing, and thus is "born again," or reincarnated.

It wasn't only primitive man who held this belief. The ancient Egyptians made it a part of their religion. That's why they embalmed bodies—to prevent or delay reincarnation. Many great Greek philosophers such as Plato and Pythagoras believed this, too. It is part of the Buddhist belief, and certain sects of early Christians believed it, too.

The forms in which reincarnation is supposed to take place vary in different parts of the world. There are even many ways of picturing the soul that leaves the human body. In some parts of India, it is pictured as an insect. In many parts of Europe, it was pictured as a bird, usually a dove. It is also commonly shown as a butterfly.

Many people who believe in reincarnation hold that the soul enters the body of another human being. But there are those who think it enters the bodies of insects and animals, such as tigers, sharks, and alligators. And in some parts of the world, it is believed that the soul enters into flowers.

We think of our way of life as the only one, and when we learn about other civilizations, we are often shocked, or at least surprised. When we mourn somebody, we naturally wear black. What else could one wear?

WHY IS BLACK WORN FOR MOURNING?

Well, in Japan and China, they wear pure white when mourning! And in some sections of Africa, the natives apply red paint to their bodies as a sign of mourning.

The reason we wear black is simply that, according to our traditions, this is the best way to express grief. When we see people dressed in black mourning clothes they look somber and sad, so it seems natural to us that black is the color of mourning clothes.

But have you ever wondered why we wear mourning clothes at all? Of course, we now do it as a mark of love or respect for someone who has died. But in trying to trace mourning clothes back to their beginnings, scholars have come up with interesting answers.

When we put on mourning clothes, they are usually the reverse of the kind of clothes we wear every day. In other words, it's a kind of disguise. Some people think that ancient peoples put on this disguise because they were afraid that the spirit which had brought death would return and find them!

Now, this might seem pretty far-fetched, if there weren't some peoples who do exactly this even today. Among many primitive tribes in various parts of the world, as soon as someone dies, the widow and other relatives put on all sorts of disguises. Sometimes they cover the body with mud and put on a costume of grass. In other tribes, the women cover their bodies entirely with veils.

So perhaps our black mourning clothes go back to the idea of frightening away spirits or hiding from them! There are other mourning customs that are linked to this fear of spirits. For example, mourning is a period of retirement. We withdraw from normal activities and life.

There are countless examples of primitive and ancient peoples who retired from social life when a relative died. In some cases, the widow spent the rest of her life in a kind of retirement. And it may all have started from the fear of "contaminating" other people with the spirit of death!

The catacombs were underground tombs near Rome where the early Christians were buried. These tombs were cut in soft rock in a sacred area surrounding the city of Rome.

WHAT ARE THE CATACOMBS?

When Emperor Nero began his persecutions of the Christians, they gathered in the tombs to worship. This was because every citizen was safe from attack in the burial grounds. Later, in the middle of the third century, even the burial grounds were not safe. The Christians then blocked up the regular entrances and made secret ones. They extended for miles in the underground galleries. It is said that the catacombs would be longer than the peninsula of Italy if the passages were in a straight line!

When the persecutions of the Christians ended under Constantine, the catacombs were visited by many pilgrims. When the Goths conquered and sacked Rome in A.D. 410, the entrances of the catacombs were filled up in order to protect them. By the twelfth century, the existence of the catacombs was forgotten. They were so well hidden that it was not until 1578 that one was accidentally found.

Passages in the catacombs are usually straight and from 3 to 4 metres deep. They were dug just wide enough for two gravediggers, one behind another, to pass along them with a bier. The stairs that led down were often 12 metres underground. At the bottom, galleries branch off in all directions.

Some of the catacombs have two or more levels. One, the catacomb of St. Sebastian, has four. The walls of the galleries were cut into niches for the bodies of the dead. Originally, they were walled up with tiles or stone. Many of these partitions have given way, and present-day visitors to the tombs must walk between long rows of skeletons.

The Taj Mahal is a love story, a sad and beautiful one. If it didn't exist, we could easily imagine that the story of its construction was simply a fairy tale.

WHAT IS THE TAJ MAHAL? Three hundred years ago, there lived in India an emperor called Shah Jahan. His favorite wife was a beautiful and intelligent woman whom he loved greatly and made his counselor and constant companion. Her title was Mumtazi Mahal; its shortened form, Taj Mahal, means "pride of the palace."

In the year 1630 this beloved wife of the emperor died. He was so brokenhearted that he thought of giving up his throne. He decided, out of love for his wife, to build her the most beautiful tomb that had ever been seen.

He summoned the best artists and architects from India, Turkey, Persia, and Arabia, and finally, the design was completed. It took more than twenty thousand men working over a period of 18 years to build the Taj Mahal, one of the most beautiful buildings in the world.

The building itself stands on a marble platform 29 metres square and 6.7 metres high. Minarets, or towers, rise from each of the four corners. The Taj itself soars another 61 metres into the air. It is an eight-sided building made of white marble, and inlaid with twelve kinds of semi-precious stones in floral designs as well as with black marble inscriptions from the Koran. (The emperor was of the Moslem faith.) The building materials came from many countries, including Arabia, Egypt, Tibet, and various parts of India.

The emperor planned to build an identical tomb of black marble for himself on the other side of the river connected by a silver bridge. But his son imprisoned him in the palace before he could finish, and for the rest of his life, he could only gaze across the river at the shrine of his beloved.

No one knows exactly how old the pyramids are. A thousand years before Christ, they were already old and mysterious. The Great Pyramid at Giza has been attributed to King Cheops of the fourth dynasty (about 2900 B.C.).

HOW WERE THE EGYPTIAN PYRAMIDS BUILT?

The pyramids are tombs. The ancient Egyptian kings believed that their future lives depended upon the perfect preservation of their bodies. The dead were therefore embalmed, and the mummies were hidden below the level of the ground in the interior of these great masses of stone. Even the inner passages were blocked and concealed from possible robbers. Food and other necessities were put in the tombs for the kings to eat in their future lives.

The building of such a tremendous structure was a marvelous engineering feat. It is said that it took 100,000 men working for twenty years to build the Great Pyramid! Each block of stone is 7 metres high. Some are 5.5 metres wide. Let's see if we can trace the story of the building of this particular pyramid.

The blocks of limestone and granite used in building the pyramid were brought by boat from quarries across the Nile and to the south. This could be done for only three months each spring when the Nile

was flooded. So it took twenty years and some 500,000 trips to bring all the stone needed!

Boats unloaded at a landing space connected to the site of the pyramid by a stone road. The blocks, weighing about 2 tonnes each, were then pulled up the road on sledges by gangs of men. Stone blocks pulled up the road were laid out in neat rows and then pulled to the site by other gangs of men. The number of blocks in the Great Pyramid have been estimated at 2,300,000.

As the pyramid rose, a huge ramp was built to get the materials to higher levels. Gangs of men pulled the blocks up the ramp. Each layer of the pyramid was made of blocks of limestone set side by side. Mortar was used to slide the stones, rather than to cement them together. Blocks in the center were rough, but those on the outside were cut more carefully. The final surface was made of very smooth limestone with almost invisible joints. The pyramid has three inside chambers with connecting passages.

English is the native language of more than 400 million people. Chinese is the native language of more than 650 million people. Yet English is by far the most important language in the world today.

WHEN DID THE ENGLISH LANGUAGE BEGIN?

This is because it is spoken in more different parts of the world than any other language, it is the language of commerce, and it is the second language of many countries.

The English language is about five hundred years old. Like most of the languages of Europe, it can be traced back to a language described as Indo-European. This language was spoken about five thousand years ago on the steppes of southern Russia, probably by wandering tribes between the Rhine River and the Aral Sea.

Before recorded history, the people who spoke this ancient language had dispersed and their language had been broken up into different dialects. One of these dialects, known as Primitive Germanic, or Teutonic, began to split up into other dialects about the beginning of the Christian Era. It split up into two basic dialects: East Germanic, and West Germanic. The West Germanic dialect split up again into two dialects, High German and Low German.

From the High German came the modern German language. From

296

the Low German came Dutch and English. English, however, was derived from Low German after many, many changes and developments over the years.

What first developed from Low German in the direction of the English language was a dialect called Old English or Anglo-Saxon. It was introduced into Britain during the Anglo-Saxon conquest, which took place about the year 449. Of course, when Anglo-Saxon began to be mixed with the native language that the conquerors found (probably Celtic), a new language began to develop. This language, as it was spoken until about 1150, is called Old English. From 1150 to 1500, the language is called Middle English, and from the year 1500 onward came the language we know as Modern English.

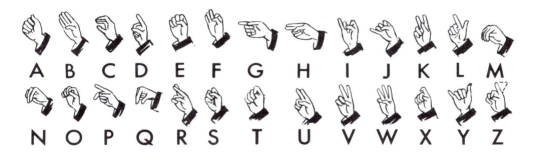

A B C D E F G H I J K L M
N O P Q R S T U V W X Y Z

The history of man is full of cruelty towards those whose sickness we have been unable to understand. For thousands of years, for example, deaf-mutes were treated as if they were dangerous to society. In many

WHO INVENTED SIGN LANGUAGE?

countries they were regarded as idiots and were locked up in asylums. Very often they were killed to get them out of the way.

In the sixteenth century a man came along who wanted to do something to help the deaf-mutes. He was an Italian doctor named Jerome Cardan who believed that deaf-mutes could be taught by using written characters. His work attracted great interest, and by the seventeenth century, a finger alphabet was worked out which was similar to the finger alphabet in use today. It took another hundred years, however, before the first public school for deaf-mutes was established at Leipzig, Germany. Today, every civilized country in the world has institutions for educating its deaf and hard-of-hearing.

Most people call a person who has lost any of his sense of hearing deaf. Actually, this term should be used only for those who were born without hearing or who lost their hearing before they learned to talk. Loss of hearing is caused in many ways. It may come about through some disease, or through severe injury to the head, or through something being wrong with the inner ear.

Why can't deaf people talk? Nearly always, it's because the deaf person never heard spoken words! It is a condition that can be remedied. In fact, nearly all deaf children with normal intelligence can learn to talk if they are given special instruction.

Up to about seventy-five years ago, the deaf were taught to communicate ideas almost entirely by means of signs, facial expression, and the finger alphabet. With the hand alphabet, some deaf-mutes can spell out words at the rate of 130 a minute! But they still depend mostly on sign language. For example, the forefinger rubbed across the lips means, "You are not telling me the truth." A tap on the chin with three fingers means, "My uncle."

Today, the deaf are taught to understand what is said to them and even to speak themselves. They learn to speak by watching the lips of the speaker, and by observing and feeling the lips and vocal organs of the teacher and then imitating the motions.

A	B	C	D	E	F	G	H	I	J
K	L	M	N	O	P	Q	R	S	T

If you were unfortunate enough to be blind, one of the greatest losses you would feel would be not being able to read. Just think how important the ability to read books is to you. Well, people realized this a long time ago and tried to find methods for enabling blind people to read.

WHAT IS THE BRAILLE SYSTEM?

For example, as far back as 1517 there was a system of engraving letters on blocks of wood so blind people could make them out with their fingers. A person's fingertips are very sensitive, and a blind person can "read" with his fingers. A great many other systems were worked out over the years, using raised lines for the letters. But they all presented one big problem: while blind people could learn to read in this way, they couldn't easily write this way because they couldn't see how to form the letters.

In 1829 a man called Louis Braille, who was blind himself and was a teacher of the blind, developed a system that could be read by the blind and written by them too with a simple instrument.

The Braille system consists of dots. Imagine an oblong block. This is called "the Braille cell." On this block are arranged raised dots, from one to six. The cell is 3 dots high and two dots wide. The Braille alphabet consists of different arrangements of the dots. Since 63 combinations are possible, there can be an entire alphabet plus signs for punctuation and contractions and so on. For example, "A" in the Braille system consists of one dot on the upper row at the left. "B" is two dots, in the two upper rows at the left. (Remember, there are three horizontal rows of two dots each.)

The Braille system is one of the most widely used alphabets for the blind, and has helped many blind people to enjoy the pleasures of reading and writing. In fact, today there are a great many Braille magazines and newspapers published. Another help for the blind today is the "Talking Book." This is a long-playing record of a book, and there are even special "Talking Books" for blind children.

The word "hieroglyphs" means "sacred carvings." Actually, it is not an accurate name for the ancient writing of the Egyptians. It came about because when the early Greeks first saw these writings, they believed they were made by priests for sacred purposes.

WHAT IS HIEROGLYPHIC WRITING?

But Egyptian hieroglyphics is really one of the oldest known systems of writing. Some of the inscriptions go back to before 3000 B.C., and hieroglyphics continued to be the written language of Egypt for more than 3000 years.

At first the Egyptians used a crude form of picture writing, such as has been used by primitive races throughout the world. The hieroglyphics were simply pictures, each one representing a natural object. The sun was represented by a disk, the moon by a crescent, water by wavy lines, a man by the figure of a man, and so on.

But these "picturegrams" could not represent the things that the eye could not see—such as thoughts, light, and day. So hieroglyphics in time became symbols of ideas rather than pictures of objects. A disk might suggest "day" instead of only the sun; another symbol meant "turn." These idea signs were called "ideograms."

The next step in the development of hieroglyphics was in the use of images to represent sounds instead of the actual objects. For example, the bee might mean, not an insect, but the syllable "bee." A leaf might represent the syllable "leaf." By putting these together, they would make the word "belief." (We are using English words to show how it was done.) Such hieroglyphics used as sound signs, are known as "phonograms."

Now the Egyptians could write down any words they knew, whether the word meant a thing of which they could draw a picture or not. From these phonograms there developed a series of signs, each representing only a letter. In writing, the Egyptians used only consonants. For example, "drink" would be written "drnk" (using Egyptian words, of course). The Egyptians also kept on using old signs in their writing—ideograms, phonograms, and picturegrams all combined. In time, it became so complicated that the common people couldn't understand it!

Can you write as fast as you can speak? Almost nobody can. But very often it is necessary to take down the words as someone speaks them in order to have a record. One way of doing this is writing in shorthand.

WHO INVENTED SHORTHAND?

Shorthand is the art of writing by means of signs that can be made quickly. These signs, which are not the same as words, can be read later by a person who knows the system. Today, the word shorthand is used to describe this method, but it has also been called stenography (which means little or narrow writing), and tachygraphy (which means swift writing), and brachygraphy (which means short writing).

You may think that the idea of shorthand is a modern invention, but it is actually about 2,000 years old! In ancient Roman times, men like Cicero and Seneca were making great speeches in the Roman senate. A man named Tiro, in 63 B.C., invented a system of shorthand for taking down these speeches.

His system was so good that it was taught in the Roman schools; it was learned by the emperors, and remained in use for hundreds of years. It was based on the use of initials, which made it a kind of abbreviation. In this system, a consonant could be written so it slanted in three different directions, and according to this direction it indicated the vowel which followed it.

Modern shorthand was born in England at the time of Queen Elizabeth. A system was invented that allowed each sign to slant in four different directions and the base of each sign could be made in twelve different ways. In 1837 Isaac Pitman introduced his system of shorthand which was based on sounds, so that all words are written as they sound, not as they are spelled. There are twenty-six signs for the twenty-four consonant sounds, and dots and dashes are used for the vowels. In 1888 Gregg introduced an improved system of shorthand which is the one most widely used today.

SHORTHAND INVENTED BY TIRO

STYLUS

IVORY TABLET

Suppose you and your friends wanted to set up a system of sending secret messages to each other. You might say, "Instead of using letters, let's use numbers." Each number will stand for a certain letter of the alphabet.

WHAT IS CRYPTOGRAPHY?

You would then have a code. Cryptography is writing using a secret code. Sometimes the word "cipher" is used instead of code. Did you know that Julius Caesar used a cipher to keep his message secret from enemy eyes? In modern times, ciphers and codes are used by both government and business for important and secret messages.

In general, there are two kinds of cipher. One kind is the substitution of a number, letter, or other symbol for each letter in a message. The other kind is the transposition or rearrangement of the order of the letters in a message.

There are endless ways in which these two types can be used. The first type is the simpler system and is the one boys and girls usually use in a homemade cipher. The word "code" is usually used for a message which can be translated by use of a codebook held by both the sender and the receiver of the message.

Codes and ciphers can be "broken," or solved, by direct methods of deciphering and decoding. To do this, the key to a cipher or codebook is necessary. These are sometimes hard to find.

A scientific method of reading cryptograms (secret messages) has been developed and is called crypto-analysis. A person reading cryptograms usually must determine what language the secret message uses. He must decide whether the message is in cipher or code. Tables of the frequency of the use of letters in a language, and many other things, are necessary in breaking ciphers and codes.

Wouldn't it be nice if you could just speak and write as you like, without having to learn the rules of grammar?

When you have something to express, you want to express it accu-

WHY DO WE HAVE GRAMMAR?

rately, don't you? You don't want to be misunderstood. If everybody spoke and wrote perfect English, and everything you heard and read was expressed in perfect, accurate English, you probably wouldn't have to study grammar! Grammar teaches you what corrections to make in your speech and writing and why the corrections should be made. And the study of grammar helps you improve the way you express yourself by using English which is accurate, clear, varied, and interesting.

Correct grammar differs, of course, according to the language. Even the basic principles of grammar are different for different languages. But it goes beyond that. Language is a living thing, changing with the years. When certain forms of speech are "worn out," they are thrown away and no longer used. When the needs of people change, the grammar changes.

In other words, grammar grows and changes, and there is no such thing as correct use of English for the past, the present, and the future. For example, in Shakespeare's play *Hamlet,* there is the line: "The door is broke." Today, only an uneducated person would say, "My arm is broke." Yet this would have been correct in Shakespeare's time!

All the words that man has invented are divided into eight classes, which are called parts of speech. These are: nouns, pronouns, verbs, adjectives, adverbs, prepositions, conjunctions, and interjections. By studying grammar, you learn how to use each of these correctly and effectively.

Grammar may seem like a nuisance to study, but it will help you to express yourself better and more accurately.

What is a dictionary as we know it today? It is a book that lists the words of a language and gives their meanings, usually in alphabetical order. Often there is also information regarding the pronunciation, the origin of the words, and how they are used.

HOW DID DICTIONARIES BEGIN?

Strangely enough, it took hundreds of years for even the idea of such a book to develop. The first time the word "dictionary" was used it appeared in its Latin form, *dictionarius,* which means "a collection of words." This was about the year 1225, and it was the title of a manuscript containing Latin words to be memorized. This *dictionarius* was used only in the classroom in the teaching of Latin.

In the fifteenth century, English words began to appear in dictionaries, but they were used only to help the study of Latin. In one of them, about twelve thousand English words appeared, each with its Latin equivalent.

What is considered to be the first real English dictionary was printed in 1552. This book still had a Latin title, and the study of Latin was part of its purpose, but it also was useful for those who wanted to learn to read English. What makes it the first English dictionary is that at last the English word was first defined in English and then came the Latin translation.

This dictionary was compiled by a man called Richard Huloet, and he had quite a sense of humor! For example, here is something from this first dictionary: "Black (or blewe) spotte in the face or bodye, made with a stroke, as when a wife hath a blewe eye, she sayth she hath stombled on hir good man his fyste."

Gradually, more and more books of this type appeared. Many of them contained only a few thousand words, especially chosen by the author for some specified purpose. One such dictionary, for instance, didn't have the words arranged by their initial letters but by the spelling of their final syllables. This was to help poets and it was a sort of rhyming dictionary.

In fact, the compilers of early dictionaries made no attempt to include all words. They were satisfied just to explain the hard words. From these beginnings came our modern dictionaries some of which include all the words in the English language.

Today we don't think of a cartoon as being associated with great art, but at one time it was. During the period of the Italian Renaissance, the term "cartoon" meant the first sketch in actual size of a large work of

WHO WROTE THE FIRST CARTOON STRIP?

art, such as a mural. When newspapers and magazines began to use drawings to illustrate news and editorial opinion and to provide amusement, these drawings became known as cartoons.

In the days before newspapers, artists like Hogarth, Daumier, and Rowlandson made series of drawings on a single theme. Sometimes such a series of drawings pictured the adventures of one character. They were the ancestors of present-day cartoons and comic strips.

In the nineteenth and early twentieth centuries there were a number of magazines which specialized in cartoons. In Paris there was one called *Charivari* and in London there was the famous *Punch*. It may be that newspapers and other magazines got the idea of including cartoons as a regular feature from these publications.

The first comic strips appeared in the early 1900's. Richard Outcault, the artist who created "Buster Brown," published this comic strip in 1902. It was so popular that children all over the country wanted to dress in "Buster Brown" clothes.

Another of the early comic strips was "Bringing Up Father." This came out in 1912. It has since been translated into at least thirty languages and published in more than seventy countries.

In an effort to make a continuous story out of some of the better-known comics, one publisher printed a series of them in a book. This idea spread very quickly and dozens of comic books began to appear in a new edition every month.

Now comic books are being used for educational purposes, and history, scientific subjects, and classical stories and novels have been put into comic book form.

The first newspapers were nothing like our papers today. They were more like letters containing news. In the fifth century B.C., there were men in Rome who wrote these newsletters and sent them to people who lived far away from the capital.

WHO PUBLISHED THE FIRST NEWSPAPER?

Something more like our papers was established by Julius Caesar in 60 B.C. He had the government publish a daily bulletin for posting in the Forum. Devoted chiefly to government announcements, it was called *Acta Diurna,* which meant "Daily Happenings."

One of the chief needs for getting news quickly in early days was for business purposes. Businessmen had to know what important things had happened. So one of the first newspapers, or newsletters, was started in the sixteenth century by the Fuggers, a famous German family of international bankers. They actually established a system for gathering the news so that it would be reliable.

In Venice, at about the same time, people paid a fee of one *gazeta* to read notices that were issued by the government every day. These were called *Notizie Scritte* ("Written News").

The first regular newspaper established in London was the *Intelligencer* in 1663. Most early papers that were established could be published only once a week, because both communication and production were slow.

The first American newspaper, *Publick Occurrences,* was started in Boston in 1690, but the governor of the colony quickly stopped it. Benjamin Franklin conducted the *Pennsylvania Gazette* from 1729 to 1765. The people were so eager to have newspapers that by the time of the American Revolution there were 37 of them being published in the Colonies!

One of the most influential newspapers ever published is *The Times* of London, which began to be published in 1785 as the *Daily Universal Register.*

Every year, when the Nobel Prizes are announced there is a great deal of publicity about the winners. They are interviewed and articles are written about them. This is because winning the Nobel Prize is considered by most people the highest honor that can be achieved in certain particular fields of work such as chemistry, physics, medicine, and literature. There is also a Nobel Peace Prize, awarded for efforts on behalf of peace.

WHAT IS THE NOBEL PRIZE?

The curious thing about these prizes is that they were started by a man who did a great deal to help the science of destruction! Alfred Nobel was born in Stockholm and lived from 1833 to 1896. Among the things which he invented and patented were dynamite, blasting gelatin (more powerful than dynamite), and a new kind of detonator for explosives.

It may be that having created such deadly explosives, Nobel felt a need to do something "noble" for the world. He was interested in establishing peace, and had a plan he thought would prevent war. By the way, besides being a brilliant scientist, Nobel was also a poet. He thought that literature and science were the most important factors in human progress.

When he died, Nobel left a fund of $9,000,000. The money was to be used in giving prizes to those who made outstanding contributions in physics, chemistry, medicine, literature, and the advancement of world

ALFRED NOBEL

peace. The prizes were first awarded on December 10, 1901, the anniversary of Nobel's death.

Since Nobel was a Swede, the Nobel Foundation of Sweden distributed the awards. The organizations selected to determine the winners were: for physics and chemistry, the Swedish Academy of Science; for medicine, the Caroline Institute of Stockholm; for literature, the Swedish Academy; for peace, a committee of five persons chosen by the Norwegian Parliament. A prize for economics was first awarded in 1969.

A library is an attempt to gather together man's writings, and this effort was first made long before the birth of Christ.

DID THEY HAVE LIBRARIES IN ANCIENT TIMES?

Scientists who dug up Ur, the city of the patriarch Abraham, discovered a clay signet. This was a cylinder of clay on which there were writings. It goes back to 800 B.C., and may have belonged to the first library.

As early as 600 B.C., the people of Mesopotamia had well-organized libraries in their temples and palaces. The "books" in these early libraries were clay tablets. Thousands of these tablets were arranged in subject order in the temples and palaces, and these collections were the first real libraries.

The Egyptians had libraries, too. They were in the temples under the care of priests. The books were in the form of rolls, made of papyrus. But the most famous library of ancient times was established at Alexandria, Egypt. It was started about 300 B.C., and it was the first attempt to collect the whole of Greek literature. It had at least 700,000 papyrus rolls and was completely catalogued and classified just as in our modern libraries.

The Romans at first were not very interested in libraries. But then they became inspired by the Greeks and established a system of public libraries. Wealthy citizens in Rome took an interest in founding libraries for the people, and in making large collections for themselves.

Many of these early Roman libraries were located in the forums and the public baths. In the fourth century, there were twenty-eight

BOOKS CHAINED IN 15TH CENTURY ENGLAND

public libraries in Rome! Most of these were destroyed by fire, pillage, dampness, or neglect when the Roman Empire was over-run by barbarians from the North.

Public libraries as they are known today began in the nineteenth century in England. An 1850 act of the English Parliament allowed public libraries to be started. Today, of course, we consider a public library a basic part of civilization.

When you read a fairy tale that you enjoy very much, you may imagine that the author of the book made it up. If the book was written in modern times, this may be so. But did you know that long ago people did not invent fairy tales?

HOW DID FAIRY TALES BEGIN?

The great storytellers used to simply report what they had heard, for the stories had existed for thousands of years. According to some people, many fairy tales are based on a memory of something that really happened. But, of course, one has to look beyond the mere incidents of the stories to find out what it was.

Human beings love the unknown and the mysterious. As a result, when stories are handed down from parent to child, happenings that once upon a time were quite ordinary are made to appear almost super-natural another day.

Whatever the actual beginning of fairy tales, there is no doubt that people once believed in fairies. Some of the fairies they believed in were just like human beings, except that they had all sorts of magical powers. They could make themselves invisible or change their forms, often appearing as animals or birds. They could pass through walls and other solid objects. They could foretell the future. Some were immortal; others lived hundreds of years.

Today, almost everyone thinks of fairies as those tiny beings with gauzy wings about whom the poets wrote. But the people themselves believed there were many different types of fairies. Some were measured by inches, some were a few feet high, and some were the size of humans. And not all had wings. In fact, they didn't seem to need wings. They could change stalks into horses, or had fairy horses on which to ride.

The names and types of fairies that were supposed to exist in various countries are familiar to most of us—pixies, elves, leprechauns, brownies, goblins, gnomes, and so on.

Was there actually a Mother Goose who wrote the delightful fairy tales and nursery jingles that all children love? Three different countries give three different answers as to who Mother Goose was.

WHO WROTE MOTHER GOOSE?

In England, it was believed that Mother Goose was an old woman who sold flowers on the streets of Oxford. In France, there are people who believe that Mother Goose was really Queen Bertha. She married her cousin, Robert the Pious. Because he already had a wife, Queen Bertha was punished by the pope. One of her feet became shaped like that of a goose. From then on, she was called Mother Goose.

In the United States, there are some who say that Mother Goose's name was Elizabeth Fergoose. She was the mother-in-law of a Boston printer who lived in the early part of the eighteenth century.

The first time the tales attributed to Mother Goose were set down was in 1696. For many centuries they had been handed down from generation to generation by word of mouth. But in that year, a Frenchman called Charles Perrault wrote them down. His collection included *Cinderella* and *Sleeping Beauty*.

Perrault sent the manuscript to a bookseller named Moetjens who lived at The Hague, in Holland. Moetjens published the tales in his magazine in 1696 and 1697. They immediately became popular. In 1697 a printer in Paris published eight of the tales in book form. The volume was called *Histories or Stories of Past Time*. On the cover was a little sign on which was written "Tales of My Mother Goose."

So you see these tales and nursery rhymes have been told and read to children for hundreds of years. The earliest translation of the Mother Goose tales into English was in 1729.

We still don't know who first wrote *Simple Simon, Little Miss Muffet,* and all the others which became part of Mother Goose. But in 1760 a collection of Mother Goose jingles was published in London, and about twenty-five years later it was reprinted and published in Worcester, Massachusetts.

EGYPTIAN
LEATHER BALL

MIDDLE AGES

WOODEN SOLDIERS

WOODEN BREAD KNEADER

What does a toy mean to you? Is it just anything you play with; for example, two pieces of wood, a rock or a piece of cloth? While these may serve as toys sometimes, we really mean something more than that by the word "toy."

DID CHILDREN HAVE TOYS IN ANCIENT TIMES?

A toy is usually something to amuse children that in some way mimics what grownups do. A gun, a car or wagon, a doll, or a little house are such toys. So are balls and tops. But since children, from the beginning of time, have liked to mimic grownups, we can assume that toys have probably existed since the earliest history of man.

Archaeologists have dug up in the ruins of ancient cities such toys as clappers, rattles, tiny pots, and miniature animals of clay, bronze, and lead. In the ruins of an ancient Persian city, they found a toy lion which stands on wheels. In the stand is a hole for a string with which to pull it, just as such a toy might be made today. And this toy is about 3,000 years old!

In ancient Egyptian ruins, they have found balls, tops, and dolls. In fact, they even found a little bread kneader which is worked with a string. We know that both Greek and Roman youngsters had clappers, wagons, and carts. In Cyprus, they have found toy wine carts, which children must have played with just as you might play with toy trucks today.

During the Middle Ages, children played with clay horses, armed knights, and bows and arrows. During Renaissance times, toys were often made by skilled workmen and were miniature copies of the weapons and household goods of that time.

One of the reasons we can't trace toys back to prehistoric times is that they were usually made of wood. Wood decays quickly in the ground and these toys from the earliest days of man can no longer be found.

Did you ever walk in a forest and suddenly come upon a little brook bubbling merrily along its path? Didn't it sound like music? When the rain pitter-patters against a roof, or a bird sings heartily—aren't these like music?

HOW DID MUSIC BEGIN?

When man first began to notice his surroundings, there was a kind of music already here. And then when he wanted to express great joy, when he wanted to jump and shout and somehow express what he felt, he felt music in his being, perhaps before he was able to express it.

Eventually, man learned to sing, and this was the first man-made music. What do you think would be the first thing man would want to express in song? Happiness? Yes, the happiness of love. The first songs ever sung were love songs. On the other hand, when man was face to face with death which brought him fear, he expressed this, too, in a different kind of song, a kind of dirge or chant. So love songs and dirges were the first music man ever made!

Another kind of music came with the development of the dance. Man needed some sort of accompaniment while he danced. So he clapped his hands, cracked his fingers, or stamped on the earth—or beat upon a drum!

The drum is probably one of the oldest instruments man invented to produce sound. It's so old that we can never trace its beginnings, but we find it among all ancient peoples everywhere in the world.

The earliest wind instruments created by man were the whistle and the reed pipe. The whistles were made of bone, wood, and clay. From them, the flute was developed. The flute is so ancient that the Egyptians had it more than 6,000 years ago!

Stringed instruments probably came soon afterward. Did you know that the ancient Egyptians had them, too?

The word "drama" comes from a Greek term meaning a thing done. A drama tells a story by means of action and speech.

We do not know exactly when drama began. It grew out of religious ceremonies in which the life of a god was portrayed by a man or a group of men. The drama that we know today goes back to the times of ancient Greece.

WHEN DID DRAMA BEGIN?

In Greece the art of the drama reached great heights. The two great classes of drama, tragedy and comedy, were invented by the Greeks. In general, tragedy deals with suffering and death and has an unhappy ending. Comedy treats the brighter side of life with humor and sentiment, and ends happily.

The plays of the Greeks, known as classical drama, were written in verse. This was also true of the plays of the most important dramatists until about a hundred years ago. Today, nearly all plays are written in prose.

The Greek drama began with the worship of Dionysus, the god of wine. The plays were performed only on holy occasions. The theatre was always as sacred as the temple. It was the early custom at the rites of Dionysus for a chorus of men to chant hymns in praise of the god.

There is an ancient tradition that one of the leaders of the chorus, Thespis, was the first one to impersonate Dionysus. He thus became the first actor. To this day, actors are sometimes called thespians.

Do you enjoy Westerns on TV? They're certainly popular with millions of people. Yet can you imagine anyone enjoying exactly the same Western year after year for dozens of years?

WHO WROTE THE FIRST OPERA?

But there is a form of entertainment that people enjoy in just that way! They know the plot, they even have most of the lines memorized, yet they love to see it performed year after year! That form of entertainment is the opera.

Perhaps opera is so popular because it is interesting to both the ear and the eye. An opera is a play in which the parts are sung instead of spoken.

In addition to the principal parts taken by soloists, there is usually a chorus. The orchestra plays at the beginning of the opera and before each act. It accompanies the singers and the action of the story.

The music at the beginning of an opera is called an overture, or prelude. There are two kinds of solos in an opera. The aria is like a long song. The recitative is almost like a recitation to music. The complete words of an opera are called the libretto. The complete music is known as the score. In many operas, a ballet is added to the story.

It is usually agreed that the beginning of opera dates from 1600. At that time, an Italian musical composer, Jacopo Peri, composed the opera *Eurydice*, and it was performed at the marriage of Henry IV of France. So you can see that opera has been a popular form of entertainment for almost four hundred years.

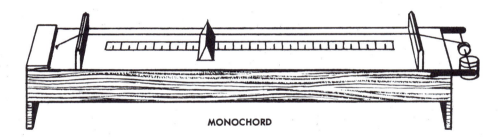

MONOCHORD

Except for the organ, the piano is the most complex of any musical instrument. In fact, its proper name is the pianoforte, which means "soft-strong." This is because the piano is capable of a variety of tones.

WHEN DID THE PIANO ORIGINATE?

Yet the piano grew from a very simple instrument called a monochord. This was a box with a single string which had the intervals of the scale marked off on it.

About the year 1000 A.D., a man named Guido d'Arezzo invented a movable bridge for the monochord and added keys and more strings. This new instrument he created was in use until the sixteenth century. Later on it took another form—the clavichord. The sound in the clavichord is produced by the vibration of strings through the pressure of a brass pin flattened on top.

A closely related instrument was the spinet. It was an oblong instrument with a compass of four octaves. Its strings were set in motion by picking or twanging.

A well-known instrument of the seventeenth century was the harpsichord. It is larger than either the clavichord or the spinet and generally has two keyboards. It is shaped like a grand piano. Its strings are twanged by tiny quills.

The really big difference which set the piano apart from such instruments was the hammer action. This was the creation of Bartolommeo Christofori in 1709. The hammer action did away forever with the scratching sound which could not be avoided in the more primitive instruments.

By the time of Mozart and Beethoven, the pianoforte had become the popular keyboard instrument we know today. Beethoven was the first composer to bring about greater use of the piano, his music often calling for the lower, richer tones of the piano.

Everybody loves to hear a band! A parade wouldn't be a parade without one, and can you imagine the circus without a band? Nowadays, a band has even become part of our sports activities, and school bands play at all the big games.

HOW DID BANDS ORIGINATE?

The first brass bands were nothing like our bands of today. A few traveling musicians would appear here and there, play for a while, and then move on. By the end of the thirteenth century, however, these bands had grown in size and had become so popular that they began to form special organizations. They established guilds just as did people who specialized in other kinds of work, and these guilds had rules and regulations and guarded the rights of the musicians who played in bands.

During those days, every church had its brass band, and no wedding or festival was complete without it. In time, practically every town in Europe had its own little brass band!

After these bands had developed to the point where they became so popular, they began to accompany armies on the march. This was in the sixteenth century, and the first bands that marched with the troops were hired civilians. Then the regiments began to enlist and to train their own bands. Today, of course, the bands attached to the various

DANCE BAND OF
THE 15TH CENTURY

branches of the armed services in the United States are famous and outstanding musical organizations.

Military organizations weren't the only ones who showed great interest in bands. The schools and colleges also began to develop them. In time, many of the bands attached to schools were as good as professional bands.

Another kind of band that became popular was the concert band. The concert band is built on the same plan as the symphony orchestra. Usually, there are no string instruments in a band; the woodwinds correspond to the strings in the orchestra.

Each group, or family, of instruments in a band contains a complete choir. For instance, there are soprano, alto, and bass clarinets, saxophones, and so forth. These give the band a rich effect. Today, more and more music is being written for concert bands, and millions of people enjoy hearing them in parks, in concert halls, and in parades.

317

Before children even learn to talk, and without having seen anyone else dance, they often express themselves naturally through rhythmic movements. Animals also dance! There are birds which actually have

WHY DO WE DANCE?

group dances, with circling, bowing, advancing, and retreating in unison!

Primitive man first danced by himself instinctively. He found that repeated rhythmic movements produced a good feeling, that they acted on his mind and emotions. This made the dance seem to have magical power, so that when he wanted to experience those feelings again, all he had to do was dance. This led to the development of group dancing. Today, there are primitive people who still dance for purposes of "magical" power. There are war dances and hunting dances, marriage and funeral dances, and planting and harvesting dances.

These primitive magic dances led to the use of dancing in religious ceremonies. Dancing was used in the temples of ancient Egypt, and the Hebrews danced during their religious rites. In the Bible, it is said that King David danced before the Ark of the Covenant to express his religious feelings.

The Greeks developed dancing so that it was not only a part of all religious ceremonies, but was a source of entertainment and became the basis of all theatre and drama. The word "orchestra" was first used to indicate the dancing area in the Greek theatre. The Greeks also used dancing as a means of physical training for their soldiers.

The Romans imitated the Greeks, but their dances became wild and corrupt. The Christians at first used dancing as a means of worship, but because the Romans had degraded dancing, the Christians later tried to ban dancing from church services. In the Orient, too, the dance has been used for religious expression from earliest times.

One of the most important forms of dance that developed over the centuries was the folk dance. This is a dance created by people in a certain region which becomes traditional and is passed down from generation to generation. Our modern dancing stems from folk dancing as well as from ballroom dancing which originated in the courts of Europe.

Man has always loved to be entertained. From the very beginning of civilization there have been jugglers, acrobats, animal trainers and clowns to entertain people. In ancient Greece there were chariot races, in China there were contortionists, and in Egypt there were trainers of wild animals.

HOW DID THE CIRCUS BEGIN?

But it was the Romans who first had the idea of combining such acts and other events into a circus. Actually, the word "circus" comes from the Latin pertaining to races rather than to a type of show. So the circus started with races, and the structures built by the Romans for these races were called circuses. The Circus Maximus was the first and largest of these. It was started in the third century B.C. and was enlarged until it could seat more than 150,000 people!

When the Romans came to these circuses, it was much like arriving at a modern circus or fair grounds. There were vendors of pastry, wine (like our soft drink sellers), and various other merchandise. Admission was free, because the government used these circuses as a way of keeping the masses content.

Meanwhile, in Rome there were all sorts of other entertainment going on which eventually became part of what we call the circus. Some theatres had jugglers, acrobats, ropewalkers and animal trainers. Some of them even had boxing bears! And at the race courses, they had people performing such tricks as riding two horses at once, riders jumping from one running horse to another, and riders jumping their teams over chariots, all of which we have in the modern circus.

During the Middle Ages there was no organized circus as such, but troupes of performers would wander about doing various acts. The first circus, as we know it today, was organized by an Englishman, Philip Astley, in 1768. He set up a building in London with a number of seats and a ring. He did trick riding on horses and had acrobats, clowns, and ropewalkers. After him, a great many other people had the same idea, and the circus became a popular entertainment all over the world.

EGYPTIAN

12TH CENTURY
ENGLISH

13TH CENTURY
FRENCH

There are many kinds of puppets, as you know. There are hand puppets, rod puppets, shadow figures, and marionettes. They are little figures operated by strings and wires from above, by rods, or by hands from below.

WHEN DID PUPPET SHOWS START?

Puppets are as old as the theater itself. The first puppets were probably made in India or Egypt. Puppet theaters thousands of years old have been found in both of these countries. Marionettes, which are puppets animated by strings from above, got their name in Italy. During the early Christmas celebrations, small, jointed nativity figures including the Christ Child and the Virgin Mary were made to move by strings. This kind of puppet became known as a marionette, or little Mary.

In China, Japan, and Java puppet showmen have made figures to represent the heroes, gods, and animals of their legends and stories. In Java, Thailand, and Greece they developed shadow-plays. They were made by moving cut-out figures against a vertical sheet lit from behind. Did you know that special operas for puppets have been written by great composers like Mozart, Haydn, and Gluck?

One of the best-loved of all children's stories tells of the adventures of Pinocchio, a puppet who came to life. You will find many of the same puppet characters famous in different lands. Punch, the famous English puppet, is known in Italy as Punchinello and in France as Polichinelle.

Puppets can also be any size needed. There are some marionettes that are only 15 centimetres tall, and some have been made 9 or 12 metres tall! Also, it is possible to make puppet animals and they can be just as good actors as people!

Puppets can also be any size needed. There are some marionettes that are only 15 centimetres, and some have been made 9 or 12 metres tall! Also, it is possible to make puppet animals and they can be just as good actors as people!

Probably the greatest honor that could come to an athlete is to win the gold medal at the Olympic Games. But did you know that the idea of having Olympic Games is more than 2,500 years old?

WHEN DID THE OLYMPIC GAMES START?

According to Greek legend, the Olympic Games were started by Hercules, son of Zeus. The first records we have are of games held in 776 B.C. on the plain of Olympia. They were held every four years for more than 1,000 years, until the Romans abolished them in 394 A.D.

The ancient Greeks considered the games so important that they measured time by the interval between them. The four years were called an Olympiad. The games were an example of the Greek ideal that the body, as well as the mind and spirit, should be developed. Nothing was allowed to interfere with holding the games; if a war happened to be going on, the war was stopped!

Fifteen hundred years later a Frenchman named Baron Pierre de Coubertin had the idea of reviving the Olympic Games. In 1894, following his suggestion, an International Congress of fifteen nations was held in Paris. This Congress unanimously agreed to revive the games and to hold them every four years. Two years later, in the rebuilt stadium at Athens, Greece, the first of the modern Olympic Games was held.

The games today include many sports that didn't even exist in ancient times, such as basketball, water polo, soccer, cycling, shooting, and field hockey.

The modern Olympics are governed by an International Olympic Committee, and each nation has its own National Olympic Committee which is responsible for its country's participation in the Olympics.

From September to November, every Saturday afternoon is American football time in the United States. In thousands of stadiums all over the country, millions of people gather to watch schools and colleges play.

HOW DID AMERICAN FOOTBALL BEGIN?

In fact, American football is the country's leading college sport.

Yet the game is little more than 100 years old. The first game of American football in the United States was played on November 6, 1869 at New Brunswick, New Jersey, between teams representing Princeton and Rutgers Universities. The game spread first among the older eastern universities, such as Yale, Harvard, and Columbia, and was later adopted by the whole nation.

Amazingly enough, a game of "football" existed as far back as the times of the Spartans and Romans. They played a type of football to condition their soldiers for warfare! When the Romans invaded England, they brought the game with them. It developed gradually, and by the eleventh century a type of kicking game was quite popular among the British. In fact, it became so popular that King Richard II abolished the sport because the players were taking too much time from archery practice!

The game of American football, as it is now known, was actually invented by accident one day in 1823. Up to that time the game that the English played was a kicking game, something like the modern game of soccer. One of the players on this particular day was William Webb Ellis, a student at Rugby.

In the middle of the game, instead of kicking the ball back as the rules required, he caught the ball and ran up the field with it! This breaking of the rules brought a great deal of criticism upon Ellis, and his captain had to apologize to the opposing captain. But that illegal maneuver marked the birth of modern American football!

The old-style game has since developed into soccer. The "Ellis version" of the game became the British game of rugby. The rugby version of the game in the United States is called American football.

TENNIS IN 1500

Some games are invented spontaneously, and some games develop over long periods of time. Tennis has an ancient history. The Greeks and Romans had ball games which later became a French game called *jeu*

WHAT IS THE ORIGIN OF TENNIS?

de paume; this was probably the ancestor of modern tennis.

The word "tennis" probably comes from the French word "Tennez!" which means, "Take it! Play!" Some experts believe the game had its beginnings in Egypt, in Persia and among the Arabs, before Charlemagne.

By the year 1300, the game was known also as "La boude," and during the fourteenth century it was played throughout France. In fact, the nobility of France was very devoted to the game, and Louis X died from a chill he caught while playing what was then a form of tennis.

Tennis has been called a royal game because of the great interest shown by the kings of France and England. Henry II was considered the best tennis player in France, and later on Louis XIV kept a regular staff to look after his tennis courts. The word "tennis" as the name of the game is first found in a book published in 1400. Henry VIII built a tennis court in 1529 at Hampton Court that is still in use today.

Tennis was introduced to the United States in the 1870's, by way of Bermuda. The game was played regularly at the Racquet Court Club in New York in 1876. Then Boston built its first court in 1876, Newport, Rhode Island, in 1880, and Chicago in 1893.

"Lawn tennis" was developed from tennis by an Englishman, Major Wingfield, in 1874. But today, especially in the United States, the name lawn tennis has been contracted to the word tennis.

You may think that skiing is a modern sport, but it is actually one of the oldest forms of travel known to man! The word itself comes from the Icelandic word scidh, which means snowshoe or piece of wood.

HOW DID SKIING BEGIN?

Some historians claim that skiing goes back to the Stone Age, and they have found ancient carvings which show people on skis. Long before Christianity appeared, the ancient Lapps were known in Scandinavia as Skrid-Finnen, or "sliders." They even had a goddess of ski, and their winter god was shown on a pair of skis with curved toes!

The first skis of which there is any record were long curved frames, often made of the bones of animals, and held to the foot by thongs.

Skiing began as a sport in Norway, in the province of Telemark. In fact, the town of Morgedal in this Norwegian province, is known as the "cradle of skiing." Because this region would be snowbound for long periods at a time, it was necessary to use skis to get about. In winter when the natives went hunting or trapping in the mountains, or to neighboring villages to market or to visit, they had to depend on skis.

And if you think skiing meets are a modern development, it may surprise you to know that in Norway they were having skiing competitions for prizes way back in 1767! The father of modern skiing was a man called Sondre Norheim, who was a native of Morgedal, Norway. He was a pioneer not only in the slalom and jumping, but also in making skis. He came to the United States at the age of 59 and, until his death in 1897, he did much to further skiing in that country.

The year 1868 is an important one in the history of skiing. That year a big skiing competition was held in the city of Christiania. Sondre

Norheim was invited to compete. He skimmed down the slope, without a stick, feet close together. As he took off from the jump, he soared through the air like a bird and landed with a slight give at the knees. A moment later he came to a standstill with a turn. The crowd was amazed at this performance, and a new age was launched in the sport of skiing.

In the United States by the way, skis were the accepted way to travel in winter in the mining camps as far back as 100 years ago!

DUTCH SETTLERS

It seems that the idea of rolling a round object in order to knock over a group of standing objects, occurred to man as one of the first ways to play a game. In the grave of an Egyptian child, more than 7,000 years old, implements have been found which were used in playing a game very similar to modern tenpins!

HOW OLD IS THE GAME OF BOWLING?

There is even evidence that during the Stone Age there was some sort of bowling game in which large pebbles and rocks were rolled at pointed stones which served as pins.

As far as written records are concerned, they indicate that bowling may have originated in the monasteries of Europe about 700 years ago as part of a religious ritual. The peasants of those days usually carried a club, even when visiting a church. It is said that the priests, in order to dramatize a point, told the people that the clubs could stand for the devil, or evil. The club was stood in a corner, and the peasant rolled a large stone or ball at it. If he hit the ball he was praised, if he failed he was told to lead a better life.

The priests became intrigued with the idea of hitting the club, which was called a "kegle." (This explains why bowlers are called "keglers.") They tried it themselves, and a game was born. Later on the nobility and landed gentry took it up. By the middle ages, bowling was a universal and very popular game in Germany.

As the game spread to England, the people became equally excited about the new game. By the time of Henry VIII, the game was so established that in 1530 the king ordered bowling alleys added to his residence!

The early Dutch settlers brought the game of ninepins to America and played on Bowling Green in New York.

HOW OLD IS THE GAME OF BILLIARDS?

Billiards, or pool, seems to be a game that leads a kind of double life. For many years in the big cities a pool hall was a place where decent people would never be found. Yet billiards has been a popular game with the aristocracy of the world. Some of the finest homes and clubs have billiard tables in them.

The game is so old that no one can say when it began. There are some authorities who claim it was played in ancient Egypt. The Greeks knew the game as long ago as 400 B.C. In the second century after Christ, a king of Ireland, Catkire More, left behind him "fifty-five billiard balls of brass, with the pools and cues of the same material." And St. Augustine mentions billiards in his "Confessions," written in the fifth century.

For some reason, billiards was mentioned by many famous writers during the sixteenth and seventeenth centuries. For example, in Shakespeare's "Anthony and Cleopatra," Cleopatra says, "Let us to billiards."

Did you know that when Mary, Queen of Scots, was kept in prison in 1576, one of her complaints was that her billiard table had been taken away! The first description of billiards in English is to be found in a book called "Compleat Gamester," by Charles Cotton, published in 1674.

According to some pictures of the game as it was played in those days, there were all kinds of obstacles on the table, such as hoops, and pegs, and "forts." The player had to go around or through these obstacles without knocking them down.

About the year 1800, the game became much as we know billiards today. In 1807 a book was published in England — the first English book written about the game — in which billiards is described very much like the modern game.

HOW DID THE GAME OF BRIDGE ORIGINATE?

Like so many other things having to do with cards, the game of bridge has an ancient history. It belongs to the "whist family" of games.

In the whist type of game there are always four players; two against two as partners. A full 52-card pack is dealt out evenly so that each player holds 13 cards. The object of play is to win tricks, each trick consisting of one card played by each player.

It is generally believed that whist originated in England. There has been a whole line of "whist-family" games, starting with Triumph, Trump, Ruff and Honours (or Slam), Whisk (or Whist) and Swabbers, Whist, Bridge, Auction Bridge—and finally, Contract Bridge. The earliest of these games were mentioned in English books more than 400 years ago!

Whist itself was originally a game of the lower classes. In the early eighteenth century it was taken up by the gentlemen in London's coffee-houses. In 1742 Edmond Hoyle published his "Short Treatise on Whist," and after this it became. very popular, spreading throughout Europe and America.

How whist became the game of bridge is not very certain. According to some people, bridge originated in Russia. They say the very name "bridge" comes from the Russian word *biritch,* meaning Russian Whist. Some people claim bridge originated in Denmark.

Another theory is that it originated in Turkey, and is connected with a pastime called *khedive,* which was enjoyed in Turkey and Egypt. It seems that Turkey was one of the first countries in which the game of bridge became very popular. The name "bridge" may come from the Turkish word "Bir-uch," meaning "one-three."

From about 1907 until 1930, Auction Bridge was so popular that at least 15,000,000 people played it all over the world. Today, Contract Bridge, which took its place, is even more popular!

All kinds of claims have been made about the invention of playing cards. Some people think they originated with the Egyptians, others give the credit to the Arabs, or Hindus, or Chinese.

HOW DID PLAYING CARDS GET THEIR NAMES?

We do know that playing cards were first used for foretelling the future and were linked with religious symbols. Ancient Hindu cards, for example, had ten suits representing the ten incarnations of Vishnu, the Hindu god.

Playing cards were probably introduced into Europe during the thirteenth century. We can trace the playing cards we have today to certain cards that existed in Italy. They were called "tarots," or picture cards, and there were 22 of them. They were used for fortunetelling or simple games.

These 22 picture cards were then combined with 56 number cards to make a deck of 78 cards. One of the tarot cards was called "il matto," the fool, from which we get our joker. There were four suits in this deck, representing the chalice, the sword, money, and the baton. There were also four "court" cards, the king, queen, knight, and knave.

From these 56 cards of the Italian deck came the 52-card French deck. The French kept the king, queen, knave, and ten numeral cards in each of the four suits, which they gave new names — spade, heart, diamond, and club. The English adopted this deck, which is the deck we now use.

The earliest European cards were hand-painted, and too expensive for general use. With the invention of printing, it became possible for most people to own playing cards.

Early cards were either square, extremely oblong, or even round, but today they are the usual size of 89 millimetres by 63.5 or 57. Many efforts have been made to put the pictures of national heros or current events on cards, but these usually end up as novelties. The figures on American and English cards wear costumes from the time of Henry VII and Henry VIII.

EARLY FRENCH CARDS

JOKER

FRANCIS BACON

Man has always looked for some way to explain life and what happened in the world about him. In primitive times, this was done by creating myths in which nature was controlled by spirits.

WHAT IS SCIENCE?

The first people who tried to think about the forces of nature not as the acts of spirits but simply as forces were the ancient Greeks. But they tried to discover truth by observation and reasoning alone, without making experiments. So they made many errors and accepted many theories that explained most of the facts, but not all.

In the thirteenth century, Roger Bacon began to use experiments rather than reasoning alone to test his theories, and almost 400 years later Sir Francis Bacon's book *Novum Organum* (The New Method) laid down the principles of the modern scientific method.

What makes a body of knowledge a science is the use of scientific method. Unlike earlier methods of thinking, it insists on careful measurements and careful experiments. Not all fields of knowledge can use the same working methods. A chemist can experiment with substances and forces in his laboratory. An astronomer cannot experiment with the heavenly bodies. But they both use the scientific method.

The first thing a scientist does when tackling a problem is to set down what is known and try to determine new facts. A scientist may form a working theory, or hypothesis, that explains certain results. He then measures, tests, or experiments to learn whether the hypothesis works out. If it does, it becomes a tested theory. Or he may wait until his work is almost finished before he forms a theory. But a theory is not considered proved until it seems clear that no other theory can explain the known facts as well.

Science never considers anything as proved for all time. A theory or law is considered true as long as it explains all the known facts. But science knows that new facts can be discovered which may require a change in the theory.

Mathematics is the science that deals with number, quantity, and form. Without a knowledge of mathematics, our whole modern way of life would be impossible!

WHO INVENTED MATHEMATICS?

For example, we would have no good houses, because men who build houses must know how to measure and count and figure. Our clothing would be very crude, because figuring is necessary to cut cloth correctly. There would be no railroads, steamships, or airplanes, nor any great industries, nor any commerce as we know it.

And, of course, there would be no radio, television, movies, telephones, or thousands of other things that are part of our civilization. The use of mathematics to measure how many, how much, or how long, is a vital part of the creation of the world we live in.

Life was much more simple for our primitive ancestors, but even they had to use the idea of numbers. Earliest man wanted to keep a record of the things he possessed. — How many tools did he have, how many weapons, how many animals? As soon as he wanted to express such ideas as one, two, many, and so on, he began to use mathematics.

In fact, counting was the beginning of mathematics. And the art of counting took a long, long time to develop. At first, it was done by scratching tally marks on a wall or painting them on papyrus, a form of paper. Early man could tell how many by looking at the tally marks, even if he didn't have the words for it.

Gradually, the ancient Egyptians and then the Greeks and Romans developed better number systems.

But counting, of course, is only one part of mathematics. The idea of form and how to measure it is very important to man, too. Primitive man used the idea of form in his everyday life, even though he didn't know how to measure form exactly. For instance, in making his primitive dwellings, he used rectangles and circles.

This was a simple, practical application of mathematics. But mathematics also is used in drawing logical conclusions from given facts, even if you're not dealing with material objects. For example, in geometry, we put everything down on paper and figure out the answers to problems. Then we put our conclusions to use in everyday life.

WHAT IS THE METRIC SYSTEM?

In deciding upon a unit of measurement, it is possible to pick anything. For example, the average height of a man could possibly have been a unit of measurement. In fact, some of the units used today in English-speaking countries are based on such things as the distance from a man's elbow to the tip of his middle finger, or the weight of a grain of wheat.

Because there have been so many differences in weights and measures used in different countries, an international system has been urged. If one system were to be adopted by all countries of the world, it would probably be the metric system.

This is a system worked out by a committee of scientists appointed in France in 1789. Great Britain and some other countries are now beginning to use the metric system in their measures. The system is now used in scientific work in most countries.

The metric system is based on a measure of length called the "metre." This is approximately one ten-millionth of the distance on the earth's surface from pole to equator. It is about 39.37 inches.

The metric system of measurement is based on 10. So it is that each unit of length is 10 times as large as the next smaller unit. There are square and cubic units for measuring area and volume which correspond to the units of length.

The unit of weight is the gram, which is the weight of a cubic centimetre of pure water. The litre is a measure used as the quart is used, but it is a little larger. The hectare, which is 10,000 square metres, is used as the acre is used, but is 2.471 acres. The metric system is more convenient to use than the imperial system because its plan is the same as that of the number system.

Here are some equivalents for the metric and imperial systems: one foot equals 0.305 metres, one inch equals 2.54 centimetres; one mile equals 1.609 kilometres; one quart (liquid) equals 0.946 litres.

Perhaps you didn't realize that the zero had to be invented! Actually one of man's greatest inventions, it was a concept that has had a tremendous influence on the history of mankind because it made the development of higher mathematics possible.

WHO INVENTED THE ZERO?

Up until about the sixteenth century, the number system used in Europe was the Roman system, invented about two thousand years ago. The Roman system was not a simple one. It is built on a base of 10. Thus the mark "X" means 10. The letter "C" means 100. The letter "M" stands for 1,000. The mark for 1 is "I," for 5 "V," for 50 "L," and for 500 "D." 4 is shown by "IV," or 1 less than 5. To indicate 1,648, you write: "MDCXLVIII." In the Roman system, to read the number, sometimes you count, sometimes you subtract, sometimes you add.

Long before the birth of Christ, the Hindus in India had invented a far better number system. It was brought to Europe about the year 900 by Arab traders and is called the Hindu-Arabic system.

In the Hindu-Arabic system, all numbers are written with the nine digits — 1, 2, 3, 4, 5, 6, 7, 8, 9 — and the zero, 0. In a number written with this system each figure has a value according to the place in which it is written.

We know the number 10 means 1 ten, because the "1" is written in the 10's place and the zero shows there are no units to be written in the unit place. The number 40 means four 10's and no units, or 40 units. The zero shows that the 4 is written in the 10's place.

The Romans had no zero in their system. To write 205, they wrote "CCV." They had no plan using place values. In the Hindu-Arabic system we write 205 by putting 2 in the 100's place to show 200, 0 in the 10's place to show that there are no 10's, and the 5 in the 1's place to show that there are 5 units.

With the invention of the zero, we would still need some way to tell the value of each figure when writing a number. The invention of the zero made it possible to drop the words or marks used to show place value or values, and to use the position of a figure in a number to show its value.

Any time we deal with the shape, size, and position of objects in space, we are involved in geometry. When prehistoric people did a certain kind of weaving and decoration, they were using geometry without knowing it.

WHAT IS GEOMETRY?

The ancient Egyptians needed geometry for remeasuring pieces of their land which had been washed away by the Nile floods. And since their religion required them to build tombs for their dead, such as the pyramids, they needed geometry for construction purposes. In fact, the word "geometry" comes from the Greek words for "earth" and "measure," and is probably a translation from an Egyptian word.

At first all geometry was intuitive. This means that facts were accepted as being true without trying to prove or demonstrate why they are true. But in 600 B.C. a Greek teacher by the name of Thales developed the idea that there must be ways to demonstrate that the facts in geometry were true. In geometry, a truth is called a theorem. Thales discovered the proofs of the theorems which people had accepted without proof until that time. This was the beginning of demonstrative geometry.

Elementary geometry is divided into two parts: plane geometry and solid geometry. In plane geometry, the only things that are considered are objects that exist on a flat surface, or plane. The objects have only two dimensions, length and width.

Solid geometry is the geometry of three dimensions. It deals with objects that have length, breadth, and thickness. Such objects are cones, spheres, cylinders, and so on.

In 280 B.C., a Greek scholar named Euclid lived in Alexandria, Egypt. He wrote the first textbook in geometry. This book, called *Elements,* was the textbook used by the whole world for nearly 2,000 years whenever they wanted to study geometry!

Today we still call elementary geometry Euclidian, but modern textbooks leave out some of Euclid's material as not essential. Everywhere you turn in modern life, you see the principles of geometry being applied. It might be in creating designs and decorations, in architecture, in interior decorating, even in landscape gardening. And, of course, many instruments in common use, such as the compass, the sextant, and the transit used by surveyors are directly related to geometry.

HIPPOCRATES

In many doctors' offices, you will see a framed document on the wall called the Hippocratic Oath. This is an oath taken by doctors when they graduate from medical school. What is this oath and who was Hippocrates?

WHO WAS HIPPOCRATES?

Before the age of scientific medicine, which we have today, man had a form of medicine that depended on magicians and witch doctors. Then, in ancient Egypt and India, a more sensible form of medicine developed. The ancient Egyptians, for example, were good observers. They had medical schools, and practiced surgery. But the treatment of disease was still a part of the Egyptian religion, with prayers, charms, and sacrifices as a part of the treatment.

Scientific medicine had its beginning in Greece when a group of men who were not priests became physicians. The most famous of these, Hippocrates, who lived about 400 B.C., is called "the father of medicine."

His approach to medicine was scientific. He put aside all superstition, magic, and charms. He and his pupils made careful records of their cases. Some of their observations are considered to be true even today: Weariness without cause indicates disease. When sleep puts an end to delirium, it is a good sign. If pain is felt in any part of the body, and no cause can be found, there is mental disorder.

Hippocrates also had strong ideas about what a doctor should be and how he should behave. This is incorporated in his Hippocratic Oath, which among many others contains such ideas as the following:

"I will follow that system of regimen which according to my ability and judgment I consider for the benefit of my patients, and abstain from whatever is deleterious and mischievous. I will give no deadly medicine to anyone if asked, nor suggest any such counsel . . . Whatever, in connection with my professional practice or not in connection with it, I see or hear in the life of men which ought not to be spoken of abroad, I will not divulge, as reckoning that all such should be kept secret."

The problem of caring for the weak and sick members of society has existed from the very earliest times. But the idea of hospitals is a new one in the history of man.

HOW DID HOSPITALS BEGIN?

The Greeks, for instance, had no public institutions for the sick. Some of their doctors maintained surgeries where they could carry on their work, but they were very small, and only one patient could be treated at a time. The Romans, in time of war, established infirmaries, which were used to treat sick and injured soldiers. Later on, infirmaries were founded in the larger cities and were supported out of public funds.

In a way, the Roman influence was responsible for the establishment of hospitals. As Christianity grew, the care of the sick became the duty of the Church. During the Middle Ages monasteries and convents provided most of the hospitals. Monks and nuns were the nurses.

The custom of making pilgrimages to religious shrines also helped advance the idea of hospitals. These pilgrimages were often long, and the travelers had to stop overnight at small inns along the road. These inns were called *hospitalia,* or guest houses, from the Latin word *hospes,* meaning "a guest." The inns connected with the monasteries devoted themselves to caring for travelers who were ill or lame or weary. In this way the name "hospital" became connected with caring for the afflicted!

Since living conditions during the Middle Ages were not very comfortable or hygienic, the hospitals of those days were far from being clean or orderly. In fact, many a hospital would put two or more patients in the same bed!

During the seventeenth century, there was a general improvement in living conditions. People began to feel that it was the duty of the state to care for its ailing citizens. But it wasn't until the eighteenth century that public hospitals became general in the larger towns of England. Soon, the idea of public hospitals began to spread, and they appeared all over Europe.

In North America, the first hospital was built by Cortes in Mexico City in 1524. Among the British colonies. the first hospital was established by the East India Company on Manhattan Island in 1663.

HOSPITAL IN THE MIDDLE AGES—1400

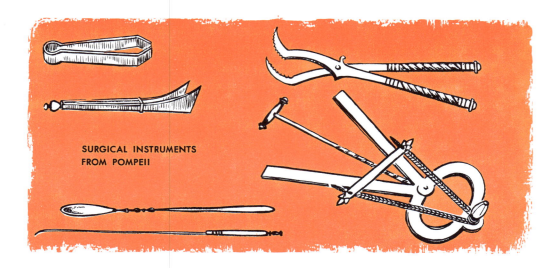

SURGICAL INSTRUMENTS
FROM POMPEII

With our modern hospitals and with surgeons who are able to perform almost any kind of operation on the body, we might imagine that surgery is a product of modern times. Actually, surgery has been carried on since very ancient times.

WHEN WAS
SURGERY FIRST USED?

Ancient peoples all over the world used flints as surgical instruments. One of the most difficult and dangerous operations of all, opening the skull, was performed in ancient times with flints! And this goes back to prehistoric times.

Flints were also used to open abscesses and to let blood. Other "instruments" for this purpose were the teeth of fish and even sharp thorns. Cataracts were removed from the eye with thorns.

As early learning in the use of tools increased, saws for use in amputation were made from flints and from bones. These things are known to be true because many mummies that have been found show the results of such operations.

When people learned how to make tools of bronze and of iron, scissors, iron needles, and other more complicated instruments came into use. With these better instruments men tried more difficult operations. There are records that prove that most of the operations done today, including major ones, were done in ancient times.

Among the relics of Pompeii are some very complicated surgical instruments. Operations were performed for thousands of years without the anesthesia that would make the patient unconscious of pain. There also was no knowledge of how to prevent infection. Operations were done long before anything was known about the causes of disease. Yet they must have been successful on the whole, or they would never have been continued.

The two things which made modern surgery possible were the discovery of anesthesia and of the cause and prevention of infection.

While it still takes plenty of courage to go through with an operation today, just imagine what it would be if there were no anesthetics and you had to suffer every bit of pain! The fact is, before the use of modern anesthetics, every operation brought agony to the patient and frequently death from pain and shock.

WHEN WAS ETHER FIRST USED FOR OPERATIONS?

Since ancient times, various herbs, gases, oils, and drugs were used in attempts to control pain, but none were completely successful. There is a good deal of controversy about who discovered anesthesia, and the credit is divided.

In 1799 Sir Humphry Davy announced that nitrous oxide (laughing gas) produced unconsciousness. Nineteen years later, another English scientist, Michael Faraday, suggested that ether be used to stop pain.

In 1842 Crawford W. Long, an American doctor, removed a cyst from a patient unconscious from breathing ether, but failed to report his experience. Horace Wells, a dentist in Hartford, Connecticut, used laughing gas successfully while extracting a tooth. In 1846 a Boston dentist, W. T. G. Morton, with Charles Jackson, gave a public demonstration of ether anesthesia at Massachusetts General Hospital, while Dr. J. C. Warren performed an operation. Since this was the first public demonstration of the use of ether, it was probably the most important step in advancing its use.

Today many new types of anesthetics have been developed, but there are two chief classes: general and local. Most general anesthetics are gases which, when inhaled, produce unconsciousness. Examples of this are nitrous oxide, chloroform, ether, and ethylene. Some may be drugs that are injected into the blood stream, such as pentothal.

Local anesthetics work by injecting a narcotic drug either at the site of the operation or as a nerve block to nerves that supply the area.

When one person has power or authority—such as a policeman, teacher, or government official—he can make other people obey certain commands he gives. But he can't make them think or feel any way he wishes. The

WHO DISCOVERED HYPNOSIS?

amazing thing about hypnosis is that a person who is hypnotized can actually be made to feel and think as the hypnotist wishes.

For example, a person who is hypnotized can be made to shiver as if he feels cold, or perspire as if he feels hot; his face can be made to turn white as with fright, or red as with embarrassment. He can even be made to hate his favorite food, or enjoy one which he always disliked. However, a person can rarely be hypnotized if he doesn't wish to be; and he can't be made to do something illegal or immoral, if he wouldn't do such things normally.

FRANZ MESMER

This strange ability to influence the behavior and feelings of people is not a new discovery. In fact. it is as ancient as sorcery, magic, and medicine. The power of hypnosis has been known to certain people since earliest times, even among very primitive peoples. It was practiced by them as a kind of medicine in the earliest days of civilization.

Today, of course, hypnosis has been studied scientifically, and this scientific history of hypnosis goes back to the latter part of the eighteenth century. There was a doctor in Vienna, Franz A. Mesmer, who began to use hypnosis on patients who were mentally disturbed. It even came to be called "mesmerism." But Dr. Mesmer didn't quite understand what hypnosis was. He thought it was some kind of force, which he called "animal magnetism." He believed this force flowed from the hypnotist to his subject.

Because of this strange theory, Dr. Mesmer and his "mesmerism" was considered a fraud by many other doctors. Then, about a hundred years later, an English doctor, James Braid, studied this subject more scientifically. He coined the words "hypnotism" and "hypnosis," and from his time on it became a subject to be studied by scientists.

WHEN DID DENTISTRY BEGIN?

When you have a toothache, or any problem with your teeth, you want something done about it quickly! Well, ancient man felt very much the same about it. So dentistry developed practically at the beginning of man's civilization. There have been dentists for as long as there have been doctors!

In fact, documents have been found from an ancient civilization which gave 52 rules for the care of the teeth, including how to bleach discolored teeth and how to prevent bad breath.

Of course, in ancient times, there was not too much knowledge concerning the teeth and how to treat them. In ancient Greece, about 2,500 years ago, there were "dentists" who extracted teeth! But they usually pulled out only loose teeth, and until about A.D. 1400, only loose teeth were extracted. As better instruments were developed, other teeth were extracted, too.

In ancient times, they didn't know what to do about toothache. In Greece, when children were teething, they were given drugs to dull the pain. As recently as 200 years ago dentists used to put a red-hot knife into the gums to help a toothache!

Cavities in teeth were first filled about the time of the Middle Ages. The fillings were made of waxes and gums. Later on, metals, especially lead and gold, were used. They were in the form of leaf, so they could be manipulated by the dentist to fit the cavity.

The modern toothbrush, by the way, was not invented until 1498. At that time, a Chinese "dentist" developed such a brush for the royal family to use.

A little over 100 years ago, all a person had to do to become a dentist was to serve as an apprentice to a practicing dentist. But in 1840, the first college for the education of dentists was established: the

Baltimore College of Dental Surgery. This was the begining of dentistry as a profession. Today, a person who wants to be a dentist must spend three to four years in college as a pre-dental student, and then attend a dental school for four years!

Today we feel very proud about our cleanliness. Doesn't nearly every home have a bathtub or a shower? Well, did you know that at one time there were more homes with radios in the United States than with bathtubs?

WHEN DID PEOPLE START USING BATHTUBS?

In spite of all our pride concerning cleanliness, we have never made as big a fuss about bathing and baths as have certain peoples of ancient times! Why right in the heart of Rome, taking up about a square mile, there were the baths of Caracalla that were probably the most luxurious baths man has ever known. There were swimming pools, warm baths, steam baths, and hot-air baths—even libraries, restaurants, and theaters to amuse the people who came to take the baths!

The wealthy classes of Rome took their baths in costly tubs or pools, and they didn't bathe in just plain water. They filled the tubs with the finest wines and perfumes, and even milk!

BATH IN PRIVATE HOME IN ANCIENT ROME

But long before the Romans, in fact before history was written, man was bathing for pleasure and for health. Swimming in rivers, of course, was always the commonest way to take a bath. But the people of ancient Crete had already advanced to the point where they had baths with running water. In ancient times the Jews took ceremonial baths on special occasions.

By the third century B.C., almost every large Greek city had at least one public bath. By this time, too, the wealthy classes had private baths and pools in their homes.

During the Dark Ages people must have looked rather dark and dirty. They just weren't much concerned about keeping clean. When the Crusaders invaded Palestine they were surprised to find that it was part of the Mohammedan religion to bathe at certain times of the day, before praying.

They tried to introduce regular bathing into Europe when they came back, but they didn't have much success. In fact, it wasn't until about 100 years ago that people began to understand the importance of bathing regularly!

Since the reason for using cosmetics has always been to make women look more attractive, we must remember that different ideas of "beauty" created different kinds of "cosmetics" all over the world.

WHO INVENTED COSMETICS?

For example, a savage African woman who cuts her skin and rubs black paint into the cuts is making herself beautiful according to the standards of her people. And when an Eskimo lady rubs grease and fat into her skin, she is using "cosmetics," by Eskimo standards!

The first ancient people whose standards of beauty were similar to those we have today, were the Egyptians. They admired healthy, shining hair. They thought a lady's lips should be well-shaped, and that her brows and lashes should be well-defined. They insisted on a good complexion and a slim figure.

As a result of this, the Egyptian lady had cosmetics and beauty secrets not very different from those used by women today. She had eyebrow paint of black and green. She used rouge several times a day. She painted her cheeks, her lips, and her eyelids. She even tipped her lashes with a black pomade to make them look longer.

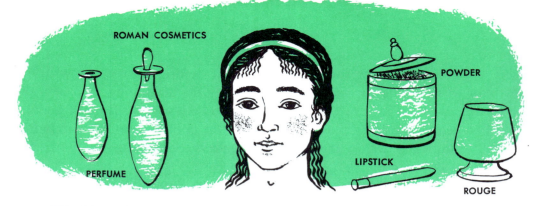

ROMAN COSMETICS

PERFUME

POWDER

LIPSTICK

ROUGE

The Egyptians were great users of perfumes. Some of them would use as many as fifteen different kinds of perfume at one time. And it was customary for Egyptian women to walk about with tiny glass bottles of perfume hidden in their dresses!

The next people to make use of cosmetics were the ancient Greeks. They not only used many kinds of perfume and painted their lips, but they used special ointments to make their hair blonde.

In fact, when the Romans conquered the Greeks, they brought back with them the Greek "beauty doctors." Thus they acquired the secrets of dyeing the hair, special face washes and skin foods for complexions, dyes for the fingernails, and so on. The fashion for waving the hair became so popular among the Romans that even young men had their hair waved!

Did you know that ancient Roman ladies made masks out of beauty clays to get smooth, clear skin, just as today's women do when they go to expensive beauty salons?

When you see a man with a beard, doesn't he somehow look dignified, or even important? In the history of man, this has been the usual attitude towards beards. It was a sign of manhood.

WHEN DID MEN BEGIN SHAVING THEIR BEARDS?

That's why you will find that in ancient times, when an important person was shown, he was usually shown with a beard. The Greek god, Zeus, was shown with a beard; drawings representing God showed a beard; Abraham, King Arthur, Charlemagne were always pictured with beards!

In our western civilization, there is no general rule about beards. Sometimes they were considered stylish and right for men to have, sometimes no man would want to be seen with a beard!

Long before the conquest of England by the Normans, the beard

HENRY VIII

SIR FRANCIS DRAKE

was considered unfashionable and not worn by men. Then the style changed and beards became popular again! The kings of England, who set the fashions that men followed, varied in their taste for beards. For example, Henry II had no beard, Richard II had a small beard, Henry III had a long beard.

By the middle of the thirteenth century, most men were wearing full and curled beards, and it was common in the fourteenth century. Then beards disappeared again during the fifteenth century, and slowly began to come back into style with the sixteenth century. It was Henry VIII who made the beard fashionable again.

During the time of Queen Elizabeth, lawyers, soldiers, courtiers, and merchants all had beards. But when Anne became queen of England, nobody who was anybody wore either a beard or moustache, or whiskers! In fact, when George III was imprisoned and his beard was allowed to grow, many of his followers felt this was the most insulting thing of all!

So you see that shaving the beard off for a man has not been a question of having a razor. These have existed for thousands of years. To wear a beard or not has been simply a question of style!

The dressing and decoration of hair by human beings is as old as civilization itself. Even in the very earliest times women had combs. In fact, the most primitive people somehow managed to make combs of one kind or another, of wood, bone, and metal.

WHO STARTED SHORT HAIRCUTS FOR MEN?

But what about hair styles? It is a curious thing to notice how important the style of hair worn by men and women has been down through the ages. Savage tribes in all parts of the world have developed peculiar hair styles which have great significance for them. The Chinese originally wore their hair in a knot at the top of the head. But when the Manchu conquered their country, they were forced to wear the pigtail as a sign of slavery. Eventually this style became popular among the Chinese and they kept it.

As civilization advanced, hair styles became more and more varied. In time, no two people wore their hair the same way. In certain countries the hair hung down loosely; in other places it was the custom to brush it up high on the head.

It is only in fairly recent times that the custom developed for women to wear their hair long and men to wear it short. Up until the Middle Ages men wore their hair quite long and treated it with the same care as women did. They curled it and wore ribbons in it. During the Renaissance they wore wigs to make their hair look longer.

Henry VIII of England finally decided to do something about this extreme style and ordered all men to wear short hair. But to make up for it, he allowed them to wear long beards and to curl their moustaches. When James I came to the throne however, men returned to the custom of wearing their hair long.

In France, Louis XIV had 40 wigmakers working for him personally. Naturally, all the gentlemen of France competed with each other for the longest, curliest wigs! Later on, people divided themselves into two camps: those who believed in short beards and long hair, and those who believed in long beards and short hair.

The style kept changing back and forth until the nineteenth century, and short hair for men has remained in fashion through most of the twentieth century, although long hair was popular for a time in the 1960s and 1970s.

LOUIS XIV

ANCIENT EGYPTIAN COMBS

ROMAN COMB

MEDIEVAL ENGLISH COMB

The first time a woman noticed that she could make herself more attractive by arranging her hair in some special way was probably the first time a "comb" was used. A comb is simply any implement with "teeth"

WHEN WERE COMBS FIRST USED?

which go through hair, thereby arranging it.

There are people who live in New Guinea called Papuans. They have very crisp hair which grows in tight ringlets. Some people believe that in order to arrange these ringlets into a big mop at the top of the head, the Papuans must have invented the comb.

But combs are one of the oldest implements of man. Some that are made of bone, wood, and horn have been found in Swiss lake dwellings where primitive man lived.

The Egyptians had combs made of ivory. In the Metropolitan Museum of Art in New York City can be seen Egyptian combs made of ebony and ivory that are thousands of years old. The surprising thing is that they look exactly like some combs made today and could be used by any woman today.

Among the more primitive peoples, combs were made of whatever materials were most handy. For example, a comb might be made of bamboo in certain parts of Asia, whereas in the Polynesian Islands there were combs made of the midrib of a coconut palm and bound with fibre. In parts of New Guinea combs were made from buffalo horn.

The small pocket comb is not a modern invention; there are combs in museums that were found in Roman ruins which are handy little pocket combs made of ivory.

Combs also provided the opportunity, during the Middle Ages, for artists to decorate them very elaborately. There are combs with pictures of saints on them, combs with colored glass and gold, and combs with Latin inscriptions.

Knowing how to make and use fire was man's first step on the road to civilization. We know that our cave-man ancestors who lived hundreds of thousands of years ago used fire, because we find charcoal and charred bits of bone in their caves. We even find stones still standing that were used as fireplaces.

HOW DID THE CAVE MEN DISCOVER FIRE?

How did men learn the trick of making a fire? The best we can do is guess. Primitive men probably knew how to use fire before they knew how to kindle it. Lightning may have struck a rotten tree and made it smolder. From this the cave man managed to start a fire, and then he kept it going, possibly for years. We know that all primitive and ancient peoples had the custom of keeping a perpetual fire going, because at first it was easier to watch over the fire than to start a new one.

When the cave men trampled among loose stones in the dark, they must have noticed sparks when one stone struck another. This may have happened for thousands of years before man became intelligent enough to strike stones together purposely. The "secret of the striking stones" was something that the priests among ancient peoples kept to themselves.

Many primitive peoples living today start fires in much the same way our ancestors did. In Alaska, certain tribes of Indians still strike stones together. In parts of China and India, a piece of broken pottery is struck against a bamboo stick, which has a very hard surface. Eskimos strike a piece of quartz against a piece of iron. And, of course, our North American Indians used to rub two sticks together.

There are many reasons why the use of fire marked a big step forward in civilization for our cave-man ancestors. Cooking made his food more tasty. Smoking and preserving food enabled him to keep his supplies longer. The points of tools and weapons could be hardened over a flame. Campfires and torches kept wild animals away. And, of course, fire protected him from the cold, so he could live comfortably in colder regions.

Today cooking is quite an art. There are great chefs, famous restaurants, thousands and thousands of cookbooks, and millions of people who pride themselves on being able to cook well.

HOW DID COOKING BEGIN?

Yet there was a time when man didn't even cook his food. The early cave man ate his food raw. Even after fire was discovered, the only kind of cooking that took place was to throw the carcass of an animal on the burning embers.

It was only gradually that man learned to bake in pits with heated stones, and to boil meats and vegetables by dropping red-hot stones into a vessel of water. Primitive peoples used to roast animals whole on a spit over an open fire. In time, people discovered how to bake fish, birds, or small animals in clay. This sealed in the juices and made the food tender. When we come to the ancient Egyptians, we find that they had carried cooking to the point where public bakeries were turning out bread for the people!

Greek civilization advanced cooking to a stage of great luxury. In ancient Athens, they even imported food from distant lands. And the Romans had magnificent banquets in their day!

Then, during the Middle Ages, the art of cooking declined and the only place where fine cooking was found was in the monasteries. When good cooking was revived again, Italy, Spain, and France led the way. These countries prided themselves on having a more refined taste than England and Germany, where the people ate chiefly meat.

A curious thing about cooking is that many primitive peoples knew almost every form of cooking that we practice now. They just did it more crudely. For instance, we cook by broiling, roasting, frying, baking, stewing or boiling, steaming, parching, and drying. The American Indians actually knew all these ways of cooking, except frying!

ROMAN KITCHEN

You may think that the chief reason for cooking food is to make it taste better. Actually, the changes cooking produces in food help us to digest it better. Cooking food also guards our health, because the heat destroys parasites and bacteria which might cause us harm.

No matter how good mother's cooking is, we like to go out to a restaurant sometimes (if we can afford it). It's not just because there's different food to eat, but we also enjoy the "going out."

HOW DID RESTAURANTS START?

Long before there were restaurants, there were taverns where people gathered to talk, have something to drink, and perhaps something to eat.

In London, there was another kind of place that was also the forerunner of the restaurant. This was the cookshop. The chief business of these cookshops was the sale of cooked meats which customers carried away with them. But sometimes a cookshop would also serve meals on the premises and was somewhat like a restaurant. There were cookshops in London as long ago as the twelfth century!

The first place where a meal was provided every day at a fixed hour was the tavern in England. They often became "dining clubs," and these existed in the fifteenth century. By the middle of the sixteenth century, many townspeople of all classes had the habit of dining out in the taverns. Most of the taverns offered a good dinner for a shilling or less, with wine and ale as extras. Many of the taverns became meeting places of the leading people of the day. Shakespeare used to be a regular customer of the Mermaid Tavern in London.

About 1650 coffeehouses also sprang up in England. They served coffee, tea, and chocolate, which were all new drinks at that time. Sometimes they served meals, too.

In 1765 a man named Boulanger opened a place in Paris which served meals and light refreshments, and he called his place a "restaurant." This is the first time this word was used. It was a great success and many other places like it soon opened. In a short time, all over France, there were similar eating places called "restaurants." But the word "restaurant" was not used in England until the end of the nineteenth century.

In the United States, the first restaurant of which there are records was the Blue Anchor Tavern in Philadelphia, opened in 1683.

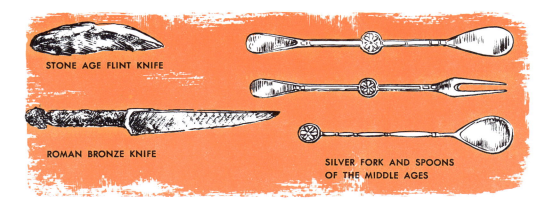

STONE AGE FLINT KNIFE

ROMAN BRONZE KNIFE

SILVER FORK AND SPOONS
OF THE MIDDLE AGES

The way man eats is considered one of the signs of his civilization. And since very earliest times man has created various utensils to make his eating habits more civilized.

HOW DID EATING UTENSILS ORIGINATE?

Some kind of spoon-like implement, for example, probably existed back in the Stone Age. We know that thousands of years ago spoons of wood, stone, and ivory were used by the Egyptians. The Greeks and Romans used spoons of bronze and silver, and some of them were the products of master craftsmen and very beautiful. During the Middle Ages spoons were made of bone, wood, and tin, while the wealthy had elaborate spoons of beaten silver.

Both knives and forks have been in existence since very early times. Some believe that the first fork was a small pronged stick, while others believe it originated with the arrow. The first actual forks were long, two-pronged affairs used only in cooking or to hold meat while it was being carved.

The fork was introduced to the table for eating purposes after the Christian Era. But as late as 300 years ago, knives and forks at the table were still curiosities! In England they were rare. In France everyone ate with his fingers until the seventeenth century.

The knife developed from fragments of flint or other stone, chipped to give it a cutting edge. It was one of the first implements to be devised by man. The use of the knife at the table also dates from about 300 years ago.

The earliest primitive men probably used naturally-made dishes. For example, a broad leaf was used as a plate, a gourd was used as a bowl, a halved coconut was used as we use a cup.

351

When man began to make pottery he began to make dishes, cups and plates. Quite often these were very beautiful, and many of them have been preserved to this day. The ancient Greeks, Romans, and Egyptians had all kinds of jugs and vessels that were works of art.

WHEN DID MAN BEGIN TO USE SALT?

Different people seem to have different needs for salt. On the whole, most people all over the world today use salt in their food. But what about the people in primitive times who weren't able to find any salt near them? They simply got along without it!

The fact is, salt was unknown in many parts of America and India until it was introduced by Europeans. There are still parts of central Africa where salt is such a luxury that only the rich can afford it.

Salt is not very necessary for people who live mainly on milk and meat, especially if they eat the meat raw or roasted so that the natural salts are not lost. But people who live chiefly on a cereal or vegetable diet, or who boil their meat, have a great desire for salt.

Man began to use salt every day with his food when he stopped being a nomad, wandering about and hunting for his food. Once he settled down to an agricultural life, salt became a habit with him.

But salt has always been more than just something to put in food. It has always had a symbolic meaning. For example, the phrase "bread and salt" is common all over the world as a way of saying food for life. In ancient times, when sacrifices were offered to the gods, salt was used as part of the offering and so had a special religious meaning.

Because salt is used to preserve foods, it became a symbol for something that lasted a long time. In Biblical times, when people wanted to make a covenant or agreement, they made it over a meal with salt, and so we have a phrase in the Bible, "a covenant of salt."

As more and more people wanted to have salt available at all times, it became an important factor in commerce. One of the oldest roads in Italy is called the Via Salaria, or the salt road, because salt was brought in along this road.

Our word "salary" comes from the word salt, because in Roman times a "salarium," or allowance of money for salt, was given to the officers and men of the Roman army!

When people are lost somewhere, as in the jungle or on a lonely island, they will try to eat almost anything when they get hungry. In some such way primitive man, in his search for food, must have tried to eat the eggs of the birds. Exactly when this happened, or where, we cannot know, of course.

WHEN DID MAN BEGIN EATING EGGS?

But we know that the chicken hen has been furnishing man with eggs for food since prehistoric times. In fact, the chicken, which probably originated in the jungles of India, spread throughout the world long before recorded history.

Chickens were known in China at least 3,500 years ago! When the Romans began pushing north they found chickens already established in England, Gaul, and among the Germans. They probably didn't reach the Western Hemisphere until the second voyage of Columbus in 1493.

Today, the single animal which is the most widely distributed food producer in the world, is the chicken. In some parts of the world, however, the duck and duck eggs are preferred. Did you know that the duck can even beat the chicken in producing eggs? There are instances where ducks produced 360 eggs a year.

If you counted all the hens in the world and the number of eggs they produced each year, it would come to about 2 eggs per week for each human being on earth!

An egg can be separated into three parts, the white, the yolk, and the shell. The white accounts for about 58 per cent of the weight of the whole egg. It consists of about 87 per cent water and 12 per cent protein. The yolk accounts for about 32 per cent of the weight of the egg. It is about 49 per cent water, 32 per cent fat, and 17 per cent protein. The shell is about 10 per cent of the weight of the egg.

Eggs are considered a good food because they supply amino acids, minerals, and vitamins.

ANCIENT EGYPTIANS BAKING BREAD

KNEADING DOUGH

POTTING DOUGH TO RISE

PUTTING LOAVES IN OVEN

Wherever you go in the world, from the most primitive savage tribes to the most elegant restaurants in the big cities, you will find that people eat bread in one form or another. Bread is simply the flour or meal of cereals after it has been mixed into a dough and baked.

WHO WERE THE FIRST BAKERS OF BREAD?

The Egyptians were probably the first to make bread, about 3000 B.C. While the Hebrews were also making bread in ancient times, it was the Egyptians who discovered yeast. By using yeast, they were able to make the dough rise, and so had "loaves" of bread, while the Hebrews baked their bread in thin sheets.

Most of the bread we eat is made from wheat. This is because wheat is the only grain which contains a substance known as "gluten." This gluten enables the loaf to rise better as it is baked, and so produces the light kind of bread we like. Rye flour, for example, does not possess this quality, so it usually has to be blended with wheat.

We also eat biscuits, corn bread, muffins and so on. These are mixtures of wheat flour with corn meal, rice, rye, or oat flour. Corn bread, hoe cake, corn pone, and spoon bread are made mostly from corn meal.

In other parts of the world what the people consider "bread" is made from a great variety of products. In Mexico, tortillas are made from corn. In Scotland, they eat Scotch bannocks—a kind of flat griddle cake made from barley meal or oatmeal.

The Swedish people eat a flat, crisp, hard bread which is made from rye flour. The Jews, for thousands of years, have observed the time of the Passover by eating a bread known as "matzoth," which is made by forming a mixture of flour and water into thin, flat, crackerlike wafers. It is "unleavened," which means it contains nothing to make the bread rise.

In some countries peas are ground into flour for bread, in others rice is used, and even acorns are used for bread flour in the Far East!

The name of everything we come in contact with has an origin, and sometimes it's quite surprising to discover how certain names began.

Take a name like gooseberry, for example. It has nothing to do with geese! It was originally gorseberry.

HOW DID FRUITS AND VEGETABLES GET THEIR NAMES?

In Saxon, *gorst* from which "gorse" is derived, meant "rough." And this berry has this name because it grows on a rough or thorny shrub! Raspberry comes from the German verb *raspen,* which means to rub together or rub as with a file. The marks on this berry were thought to resemble a file.

Strawberry is really a corruption of "strayberry," which was so named because of the way runners from this plant stray in all directions! Cranberry was once called "craneberry," because the slender stalks resemble the long legs and neck of the crane. Currants were so called because they first came from Corinth. Cherries got their name from the city of Cerasus.

The term grape is our English equivalent of the Italian *grappo,* and the Dutch and French *grappe,* all of which mean a "bunch."

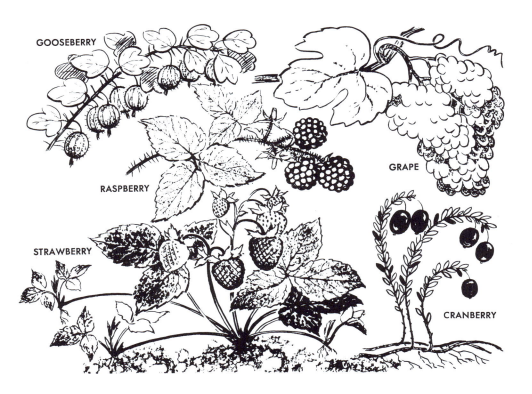

GOOSEBERRY

RASPBERRY

GRAPE

STRAWBERRY

CRANBERRY

Raisin is a French word which comes from the Latin *racenus,* a dried grape.

The greengage plum gets its name from Lord Gage, who introduced it into England, and from its greenish color when ripe. Apricot comes from the Latin *praecoquus,* which means early ripe. Melon is Greek for apple.

Tomato is the West Indian name for love-apple. The pineapple gets its name naturally from its resemblance to the pine cone. A strange name like pomegranate comes from the Latin *pomum,* a fruit, and *granatus* meaning many seeds.

Chestnuts are so named because they originally came from a city called Castana. Walnut came from the Saxon word *wahl-nut,* meaning foreign nut, since it originally came from Persia. Spinach was *Hispanach,* the Arabic word for a Spanish plant!

The coconut is the nut of a palm tree and is known and useful to millions of people. Now here's a strange thing about this tree. Nobody knows where it originated! At the dawn of history this tree was already growing in every tropical land and seems to have always been part of the landscape. Scientists believe that the nuts were carried in ancient times by the ocean tides and by man from one tropical country to another. In this way, they spread everywhere so long ago that we can't trace them back to any one place!

WHERE DID THE COCONUT ORIGINATE?

The little markings you see on the coconut are where the nut was attached to the tree. The coconut is an oblong fruit, averaging from 30 to 45 centimetres in length, and 15 to 20 centimetres in diameter.

When being prepared for commercial purposes, coconuts are split in three parts and allowed to dry. The white meat is then scooped out and dried further. It is called copra, and has a heavy, sickening odor. But from this comes the valuable coconut oil which has been used as a food for thousands of years. Today, it is also used in making soap, butter substitutes, cosmetics, and many other commercial products. Of course, we all know coconut meat as it is used in baking and candy-making.

Did you know that practically every single part of the coconut palm tree is put to use in some way by tropical peoples? Its stem and leaves furnish them with shelter. From the unopened flowers, East Indian and South Sea natives draw out a juice which they call toddy. They drink this in its natural state, or ferment it to make an intoxicating liquor.

The heart of the flower is cooked as a vegetable. The milk of the coconut makes a thirst-quenching drink. From the mass of fibers around the nut, coarse yarn is made. The husks of the nut make a valuable fertilizer. From the trunk of the tree, furniture is made. The long leaves furnish fibers from which hats are made. So you see, the coconut palm is one of the most useful trees growing anywhere!

The banana is one of the oldest known fruits in history. The earliest men of whom there is any record already knew and enjoyed this fruit!

WHERE DID BANANAS ORIGINATE?

It is believed that the banana first grew in southern Asia and that through many centuries it spread through the East and to the West. The Mohammedans called the banana tree a paradise tree, and the Hindus believed the banana tree was sacred to their goddess Kali.

Early in the sixteenth century, a priest named Father Tomas de Berlanga brought some roots of the banana plant with him to the New World. He hoped to win the friendship of the Indians with this mellow, golden fruit, and thus to convert them. From those few roots which he brought over developed all the thousands of acres of banana plantations which now exist in the tropical regions of the Americas!

The Indians, incidentally, put the banana fruit to many uses. They roasted it when green, and ate it for bread. They boiled it as a vegetable, included it in stews, dried it like figs, and even made a strong fermented drink of it!

The banana does not really grow on a tree, but on a plant. It is probably the largest plant in existence without a woody stem. The stalk, which grows from 3.5 to 9 metres and looks like a tree trunk, is really a firm mass of leaf sheaves. Most cultivated varieties of bananas have lost the power of producing seeds.

At the top of the plant is a huge tuft of drooping leaves, bright green in color, making it look somewhat like a palm tree. One large flower bud grows from the central stalk and, in due time, gives place to the fruit. As the bunch of fruit grows heavier, the stalk bends downward, so that the bananas hang with their points up. Only one bunch of bananas grows on each plant, but a bunch often weighs 45 kilograms or more!

Bananas are always cut while green, even when they are not to be shipped anywhere. The reason is that if they are allowed to ripen on the plant, they burst and spoil before they can be picked. Bananas are shipped in special vessels built for carrying bananas. They have to be ventilated by currents of cool air so that the fruit doesn't ripen on the voyage.

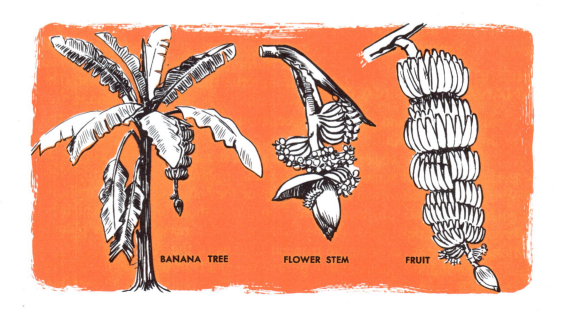

BANANA TREE   FLOWER STEM   FRUIT

On millions of breakfast tables every morning the grapefruit appears as a favorite dish. You would imagine that we would know all about a fruit as common as this. Yet the origin of the grapefruit is somewhat of a mystery!

WHERE DID THE GRAPEFRUIT ORIGINATE?

There is a fruit known as the pummelo, or shaddock, which is a bit smaller than the grapefruit. Some scientists believe that the grapefruit originated from the pummelo as a mutation, which means a variation of the original species. As far back as 1814, a scientist observed a variety of the pummelo which he described as "known by the name of 'grapefruit' on account of its resemblance in flavor to the grape."

Even today, no one is quite certain where the grapefruit originated, but the best theory is that it originated in Jamaica.

The grapefruit tree grows to about the same size as an orange tree and may reach a height of 4 to 6 metres. The fruit itself averages twice the size of an orange. Through a process of cultivation, some grapefruit have been developed which have a pink or red pulp instead of the usual light yellow. There are now actually twenty-three varieties with light yellow pulp and four varieties with pink or reddish pulp being grown in the United States.

Grapefruit was being eaten as a fruit in the West Indies long before any of it was grown on the mainland. About eighty years ago, the culture of the grapefruit began in Florida. Today it is being grown in many states and many other countries, too.

Grapefruit trees thrive best on sandy, but fertile, soils. It takes about four to six years after a tree has been planted for it to yield fruit. But once a tree begins to bear, it produces remarkably large crops of from 590 to 680 kilograms of fruit per tree!

People like to enjoy grapefruit all through the year, but the fresh fruit is available only from late fall to early spring. As a result, grapefruit canning has become an important industry. We most often see canned grapefruit in the forms of juice and segments. Grapefruit is a healthy fruit to eat; it is richer as a source of Vitamin C than most of the fruits and vegetables we normally eat. Only the orange and lemon have more Vitamin C than the grapefruit.

When you think of the potato, you think of Ireland. There's a good reason for that. The potato played a very important part in Irish history. More than a hundred years ago the people of Ireland depended upon

WHERE DID POTATOES ORIGINATE?

the potato crop for most of their food. Then, in 1846, the potato blight destroyed that whole year's crop. More than 600,000 people died of famine!

But the familiar Irish potato did not originate in Ireland. It is a native of the highlands of Ecuador and Peru. Even today it can be found there growing wild. When the Spaniards came to Peru they found the potato and brought it back with them to Spain early in the sixteenth century. From Spain it spread all over Europe and became very popular with the people.

Some people believe that the Spaniards first brought the potato to North America. But there is evidence that it was first brought to New Hampshire from Ireland in 1719.

The potato belongs to the nightshade family, which also includes the tomato and tobacco. The potato itself is a thickened underground stem. The "eyes" of the potato are really undeveloped buds.

But the potato of today is very different from its South American ancestor. The change was brought about by different methods of cultivation. A potato grower is constantly working to get certain qualities. He wants high yields per hectare, resistance to disease, keeping qualities, vigorous plants, and good color and flavor. So he selects for seed only those plants which show these qualities.

The potato is not commonly grown from seed, but from the pieces which have the buds, or eyes. These buds grow into new plants. The plant, which bears white or purplish flowers, grows to a height of from 30 to 90 centimetres. When the plants have withered, it's a sign that the potatoes may be harvested.

The chief uses of potatoes are as a food, for the manufacture of potato starch, and for the distilling of alcohol.

EYE OF POTATO

Many of us who have never lived on a farm have no idea of the skill and science that go into raising crops today. We might imagine for example, that the farmer simply scatters seeds in the ground and trusts to luck and nature for good results.

WHAT IS HYBRID CORN?

The corn crop is quite scientifically controlled today. This control began about fifty years ago when plant scientists discovered a new method of producing different kinds of corn. It was discovered that when the pollen in the tassels of the corn plant was applied by hand to the protected silks on the ear of the same plant, the kernels which were formed produced widely different kinds of corn plants.

Some of the new plants were poor, but others had very desirable qualities. By repeating this process and saving only the best plants for seed, "inbred lines" of corn were established. What was the advantage of these new lines? They might be more resistant to disease and insect pests. They may be able to stand up better in heavy wind storms.

Then it was discovered that when such inbred lines were cross pollinated, the kernels that were formed produced "hybrid" plants of even more desirable qualities. For one thing, the hybrid corn gave a very high yield; it was more productive. It was able to resist disease better and it had even stronger stalks than the corn from which it was bred. In other words, the hybrid corn, which was a combination of the best "inbred" corn, was a very superior type of corn.

Today hybrid corn is being raised all through the corn belts of the United States. Many seed companies and farmers produce hybrid seed for sale. Plant breeders make many new hybrid combinations each year to try to produce even better hybrids than are now grown.

In fact, corn is the leading farm crop in the United States, with about 2,500,000,000 bushels being grown every year. Of course, only a small part of this is hybrid corn. But even the inferior type of corn is used in hundreds of ways in many important industries. Products made from corn range from soap to paper. Scientists are finding new uses for corn every year, and the time may come when corn may be less important as a food than as a basis for wonderful products of every kind.

In a certain part of Peru, a group of prehistoric graves were found. As the scientists dug about in these graves, they found peanuts that were thousands of years old! Not only that, but there was pottery that was decorated with peanut designs.

WHERE DID THE PEANUT ORIGINATE?

So it is believed that the original home of the peanut was South America and from there it was transplanted to Africa, and eventually to the United States. Today the peanut is also raised in Latin America and Asia. In the United States alone, more than 450,000,000 kilograms of peanuts are raised a year. The yield of over 400,000 hectares of peanuts is fed directly to hogs.

The peanut is one of the most useful vegetables known to man. Peanut oil is used in vegetable shortenings, oleomargarine, soaps, and salad oils. It may also be made into glycerine for munitions. Peanut meal (left after crushing the peanut to remove the oil) is used for feeding hogs and cattle. Millions of kilograms of peanuts are made into peanut butter, sold as salted, roasted nuts, or put in candy bars.

The hulls of peanuts are used as filler in linoleum, dynamite, and paper board. Other products made from peanuts are face powders, rubber substitute, dyes, and printing inks.

The peanut belongs to the same family as the pea or bean. The peanut plant is a bush, and the blossoms closely resemble those of the pea. After the petals fade, a part of the pod elongates very greatly and its tip becomes buried in the soil. There this tip enlarges and the seeds mature. The ripened nuts, therefore, must be dug out of the soil.

Peanuts are planted late in the spring, and are dug by machinery before the frost comes. After the vines are dried the peanuts are picked by machine. A hectare can yield 35 to 50 hectolitres of peanuts.

TOWER OF BABEL

All over the world today, wherever big cities have grown up, there are very tall buildings that might be called skyscrapers. There is no special reason for calling a building a skyscraper. It's simply a name we have given to very tall buildings.

WHAT WAS THE FIRST SKYSCRAPER?

In fact, the Bible tells of an attempt to put up a building so tall that it could never be covered by the waters of any flood. This, of course, was the Tower of Babel. During the Middle Ages, the people who lived in the cities of northern Europe began to build great cathedrals. Master builders learned how to fashion stones into pointed arches and flying buttresses to raise ceilings. Tall spires were added to give greater height and majesty to these churches.

For hundreds of years afterwards, these cathedrals stood as the tallest structures in the world. It was simply because no one had discovered materials and methods of construction which could be used to build taller buildings.

In the nineteenth century, as cities grew more crowded, the value of land there rose. In order to make room for more offices on a small plot of land, it was necessary to erect taller buildings. When the hydraulic elevator was invented, it became possible to take passengers and freight as high as 20 stories. But the problem was that to put up a stone building of such height, the walls on the ground floor would have

363

EIFFEL TOWER

to be more than 2 metres thick to hold the weight of the building. So another material was required to make skyscrapers possible.

About this time, three structures were put up that used iron or steel to support great weight with safety. They were the Crystal Palace in London, the Eiffel Tower in Paris, and the Brooklyn Bridge in New York. Architects began to experiment with buildings that had steel frames.

The first skyscraper in the United States was the Home Insurance Building in Chicago, designed in 1883.

A grocer deals in food, a hardware store in household items, and a banker in money. The main business of banks is to lend money and to handle money which has been deposited with them. Of course, banks today provide many more services than just these, but it all has to do with the handling of money.

WHAT WAS THE FIRST BANK?

Ever since man had a kind of money, it has been necessary for someone to hold it for him safely, or to lend him some when he needed it. For example, in ancient Babylon, even before coins had been invented, there were men who made a business of borrowing, lending, and holding money for other people. They might be called bankers, though they were considered moneylenders. Some of that business was in the hands of the priests in the temples, and there were laws that regulated this business.

In ancient Greece, there were moneylenders, too. In Roman times, there were already large banks in existence and they carried on business with firms in widely separated parts of the Roman Empire. There were Roman laws that regulated some of the banking methods. So we might say that the first bank came into existence with the first moneylender, and that banks as such go back at least to ancient Roman times.

In medieval times the business of lending money was no longer thought of as lawful. In many places, laws were passed forbidding it. Those who did continue to lend money often had their places of business on benches in the market place. The Italian word for bench is *banco*, and this is where we get the word "bank."

In England, the business of holding and lending money was chiefly in the hands of goldsmiths. These trusted craftsmen received people's money and valuables for safekeeping and in return gave goldsmiths' receipts. These receipts passed from hand to hand, much as bank notes did later, for people were willing to take them in payment for goods and for debts.

In 1694 a group of businessmen agreed to lend a large sum of money to the English Government in return for permission to establish the Bank of England, which today is one of the greatest financial institutions in the world.

Many millions of people—possibly half the population of the United States—have a personal interest in what happens on the stock exchange. Some are directly concerned because they are part owners of companies

HOW DID THE STOCK EXCHANGE START?

through stock; others are holders of government and other listed securities; and yet another group are holders of insurance policies and savings bank accounts, since banks and insurance companies invest much of their assets in listed securities.

A stock exchange is a market for the purchase and sale of securities, such as shares, stocks, and bonds. Such markets have existed for centuries. They had their beginnings in the regular meetings, usually in a coffeehouse or restaurant, of a few men who acted as intermediaries between buyers and sellers. They did this for a commission.

In London for example, the stockbrokers used to meet at Jonathan's coffeehouse in Change Alley. In 1773 they moved to a room in Sweeting's Alley to which they gave the name stock exchange.

In the United States, to pay for the cost of the Revolutionary War and to finance other activities, stocks and bonds had to be sold to the public. But the people didn't want to invest in securities unless they could easily resell them. So a market place for securities was needed.

The brokers of that day decided to meet every day under the branches of an old buttonwood tree on Wall Street. These men were the 24 original members of the New York Stock Exchange. Their trading floor was a small plot of ground protected by the branches of a tree—but that was the first stock exchange in the United States.

In other parts of the world, stock exchanges sprang up even earlier. The origin of the Paris Bourse, which means market, has been traced back to the money-changers market in the year 1138. In Amsterdam, the first exchange was founded in 1611.

We are always hearing about how what happens on Wall Street somehow affects the lives of people all over the world. What is actually meant by "Wall Street," and how can it influence the lives of millions of people?

WHAT IS "WALL STREET?"

Wall Street is literally a street in the lower part of New York City. On it or near it are concentrated   the chief financial institutions of the United States.

Wall Street owes its name to Peter Stuyvesant who, in 1652, as Governor of the little Dutch settlement of New Amsterdam, ordered a wall built there to protect the town from attacks by the English. After the Revolutionary War the government offices of the city, of the State of New York, and the United States were located there. President George Washington was inaugurated there in 1789, and the first United States Congress met there.

Today, "Wall Street" indicates the whole financial district, which actually extends several blocks north and south of the street, and also includes an area west of Broadway. In this section are found the headquarters of banks, insurance companies, railway companies, and big industrial corporations. It is also the home of the New York Stock Exchange, which is probably the single most important institution in all of Wall Street.

The securities of about 1,500 different companies producing many kinds of goods and services are traded on the New York Stock Exchange. Within a few minutes after each sale of a stock is made, it is reported to brokerage firms all over the country. These offices receive the information by telegraph on the famous "ticker tape."

WHEN DID INSURANCE BEGIN?

Insurance is protection against financial loss. In order to protect his future, a person may join a group in which each member pays a certain sum of money regularly with the guarantee that the group will pay any loss suffered by any member. This is known as a mutual company. Or, he may pay an organized commercial company which carries a large amount of capital to take the responsibility of any loss that he suffers.

There are many, many kinds of insurance in effect today and we won't attempt to describe them all. A partial list includes life, fire, health, accident, automobile, title, liability, burglary, and even crop, rain, and earthquake insurance.

Since one of the earliest business activities that involved a great deal of risk was shipping, marine insurance was probably the first kind of insurance. There are records of ancient law that indicate the existence of marine insurance as early as 300 B.C. in Rome. Some historians believe that Claudius, the Roman emperor, originated the insurance of ships in A.D. 43. It is probable that in the twelfth century the Lombard merchants of Italy introduced marine insurance to German merchants, and by the thirteenth century, this form of insurance was widely used in Europe.

In 1583 in London, a group of men insured the life of William Gibbons, a sea captain, who was probably the first man ever insured. Lloyd's of London, the most famous insurance association in the world, was begun in 1689 in a coffee house kept by Edward Lloyd in Tower Street, when patrons interested in shipping clubbed together under a mutual plan. In 1734 Lloyd's men began issuing Lloyd's List, which gives information about ships and crews. It is issued today by the shipping industry all over the world.

The first life insurance company in the world, as far as records show, was the Amicable Society for a Perpetual Assurance, founded in London in 1705. The first life insurance company in the United States was the Presbyterian Ministers' Fund of Philadelphia, founded in 1759.

The first fire insurance company in the country was the Friendly Society for the Mutual Insurance of Houses against Fire, founded in 1735 in Charleston, South Carolina.

If you were stranded on a desert island and you wanted to get something from one place to another, what would you do? You would carry it! In primitive times human muscles were the only means of transporting anything. Man was his own "beast of burden."

WHAT WAS THE FIRST MEANS OF TRANSPORTATION?

In time man tamed certain animals and taught them to carry riders or other loads. The ox, the donkey, the water buffalo, the horse, and the camel were used by early man in various parts of the world for transportation.

This satisfied man for thousands of years, but then he wanted to find some way by which animals could transport more goods. So he developed crude sledges and drags to hitch to his animals.

Flat-bottomed sledges and sleds with runners were fine on snow, but not much good on regular ground. So man developed the rolling

drag. This consisted of sections of logs used as rollers under a drag or platform. When the platform was pulled, the logs under it rolled. This made the work easier than pulling the platform along the bare ground. As the platform moved along, it passed completely over the logs at the back. Then these were picked up and put under the front end of the platform.

After a long time, someone thought of cutting a slice from the end of a log and making a hole in its center. This was a wheel, one of man's greatest discoveries. When two wheels were joined by an axle and the axle was fastened to a platform, man had made a crude cart.

Solid wooden wheels were heavy and clumsy, and they wore down quickly. In the course of thousands of years, man improved the wheel. By building wheels with separate hubs and spokes and rims, he made them lighter and more efficient. He made rims and tires of copper or iron so that the wheels would last longer. At last he learned to use rubber tires, and improvements in these are being developed by scientists experimenting with synthetics.

Animal tracks through forests and jungles were probably the beginning of man's roads. They were easier and safer to use than to force new ways through dense undergrowth. The earliest roads made by men for

WHAT WAS THE FIRST HIGHWAY?

their own use were probably footpaths leading from their shelters to the nearest streams and hunting grounds.

When men began trading with one another, roads became more important. The great overland trade routes across Europe and Asia came into use for the transportation of such things as amber, silk, and precious stones. These were merely tracks and trails well worn by constant use.

Probably the earliest stone-paved road was built in Egypt about 3000 B.C. when the Great Pyramid was built. In order to move the huge stone blocks making up the pyramid, a smooth road of polished stone, about 18 metres wide and 805 metres long, was built.

Short lengths of paved roads were built on the island of Crete about 1500 B.C. The Carthaginians are believed to have built a system of stone-paved roads as early as 500 B.C.

The Romans were the great road-builders of ancient times. Roman wagons and carts had fixed axles and could not make turns. For this reason, the Roman roads were built in straight lines wherever possible. Over a period of about 600 years, the Romans built more than 70,000 miles of surfaced roads which extended over their whole empire. The first and most famous of these paved roads, the Appian Way, was begun in 312 B.C.

In America, some of the Indian nations had reached a high degree of civilization. Over a thousand years ago the Incas of Peru constructed a paved road about 4,000 miles long, from Ecuador to Central Chile. In Yucatan roads built by the Mayas were straight, solidly constructed of stone, and covered with a cement mortar which gave them a smooth, white surface.

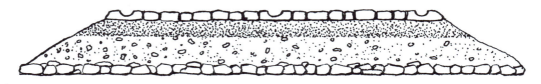

CROSS SECTION OF ROMAN ROAD

KING CANUTE
1017—1066 A.D.

We tend to think of Britain as being part of Europe since the beginning of history, but actually this isn't so. It wasn't until the first century B.C., when the Romans invaded Britain, that anyone in Europe knew anything at all about Britain. Its history before that is something we know very little about.

WHO WAS THE FIRST RULER OF ENGLAND?

At the time of the first invasion, the inhabitants were called Britons. They spoke various Celtic dialects, practiced some agriculture, raised cattle and horses, and used iron for their tools and weapons. Most of them lived in thatch-roofed huts in small villages. It was the Romans who built cities there and connected them with roads.

When the Romans left, early in the fifth century, the inhabitants were left weak and divided. Hordes of Angles, Saxons, and Jutes came from Denmark and the country around the Rhine. After the Angles settled there, the country came to be called England.

Seven large kingdoms developed from the hundreds of small tribes that had settled in England. The original Britons were forced back into the highlands of Wales and Scotland.

The seven kingdoms together were called the heptarchy, and in the ninth century, they were united under Egbert, who was the first king of all England. By this time, the English had become Christians and were united in faith with most of the continent of Europe.

Under King Alfred the Great, they were again obliged to fight for their homes against pagan Danish invaders. It was not until the eleventh century that the country finally became united under the Danish king, Canute.

Later on, an Anglo-Saxon king, Edward the Confessor, came to the throne, and under him, the country enjoyed 24 years of peace. But after his death, disputes broke out again as to who was to succeed him. Finally, William, Duke of Normandy, invaded England in 1066 and was later proclaimed king.

This Norman conquest of England changed English life so much that it is considered the beginning of an entirely new period of English history.

The story of mankind has been divided by historians into three great sections—ancient times, the Middle Ages, and modern times. The Middle Ages span the time between the fall of Rome and the beginning

WHAT WERE THE MIDDLE AGES?

of modern times in the fifteenth century. Of course, when you consider such a great period of time, it's difficult to give exact dates for the beginning and for the end. One age merges gradually into the next. But the date most commonly used as the beginning of the Middle Ages is A.D. 476, when the last of the Roman emperors was dethroned. Its end is usually marked at 1453, when Constantinople, the capital of the Eastern Empire, fell to the Turks.

What was life like during the Middle Ages? What important things happened during this time? This was the epoch during which Christianity triumphed over pagan Europe. In the Middle Ages, the feudal system grew and then decayed in Europe, and the foundations for modern nations were laid.

Although this was the age of chivalry, there was also much cruelty. Lords expressed noble and romantic beliefs in flowery language, but they treated their serfs and slaves with inhumanity.

This was a time when people had unquestioning faith. In no other

time did religion play so important a part. The Church and State were not only bound closely together, but often the Church was the State. Towards the end of the Middle Ages, the popes began to lose their power in matters that did not deal with religion.

Modern commerce began in the Middle Ages with the search for new sea routes to India and China.

Science did not make great progress during the Middle Ages, and most of the literature of the time dealt with chivalry and battle. Architecture in the Middle Ages was expressed most fully in the magnificent Gothic cathedrals and their stained-glass windows.

Do you know what the word *renaissance* means? It is the French word for "rebirth." The Renaissance was a period of rebirth that took place in Europe between the fourteenth and sixteenth centuries.

WHAT WAS THE RENAISSANCE?
During the Middle Ages which preceded it, a great many things in life had been neglected. During the Renaissance, learning was revived. Commerce, art, music, literature, and science flourished. The Renaissance changed the whole way of life in Europe.

Before the Renaissance, most people lived on large estates, called manors. There were few towns or cities. All social life centered in the manor, in the nobleman's castle, or in the bishop's palace. Europe was divided into countless small states, each ruled by a prince or a nobleman.

During the Renaissance, this way of living changed completely. Towns and cities grew rapidly as commerce, industry, and trade developed. Wealthy merchants became important. Instead of numerous small states, larger units of government grew up and became nations. People began to use coined money.

People also began to question their old beliefs. They became more interested in the affairs of this world and less concerned about life in the next. This was when the revolt against the practices and ideas of the Roman Catholic Church took place, which resulted in the Reformation and the establishment of the Protestant religion.

The Renaissance didn't begin suddenly, though sometimes the date for its beginning is given as 1453 when Constantinople fell into the hands of the Turks, or 1440, when printing was invented. The forces that brought it about had been at work for many years before.

The Renaissance reached its height first in Italy before spreading to the other countries of Europe. In Italy there was gathered a great group of brilliant artists, among them Leonardo da Vinci, Michelangelo, Raphael, Titian, Botticelli, Cellini, and others whose work we still admire today.

HOW DID DEMOCRACY ORIGINATE?

Let us see what we mean by democracy. The word "democracy" comes from the Greek language and means "rule of the people." As we use the word today, we usually mean a government where the people help to direct the work of the government.

Political democracy has appeared in two general forms. A government in which all the people meet together to decide the policy and to elect the officials to carry it out is known as direct democracy. When the people elect representatives to carry out their wishes, the government is known as a representative democracy. Because direct democracy is not possible on a large scale with many people involved, almost all forms of democracy practiced today are the representative kind.

No nation can be considered democratic unless it gives protection to various human liberties. Among these liberties are freedom of speech, movement, association, press, religion, and equality before the law.

Political democracy began early in history. In the Greek city-states, especially Athens, there existed direct democracy. In Athens, however, the ruling class of citizens was only a small part of the population. Most of the people were slaves, and these, together with women and foreigners, had no right to vote or hold office. So while a form of direct democracy did exist in ancient Athens, we would today find fault with many of its aspects.

Modern democracy owes a great deal to the Middle Ages. One idea of the time was the contract theory. It was believed that a contract existed between rulers and their subjects by which each was required to perform certain duties. If the ruler failed to perform his duties, then the people had the right to take back the powers they had given him.

Modern representation also began in feudal times because of the needs of kings. The feudal monarchs called representative meetings in order to request grants of money. They felt people wouldn't object to new taxes if their representatives agreed to them beforehand. But this helped establish the idea of representation.

Today Europe is divided into many countries. But from about the ninth to the fifteenth centuries, it was like a single country. It was divided into great estates, and the people who lived on them didn't think of

WHAT WAS THE FEUDAL SYSTEM?

themselves as Frenchmen, Germans, or Englishmen. Instead, each man owed loyalty to his landlord, and the landlord owed it to a still greater landlord, and the greatest of all owed it to the king.

The local lords who ruled over vast estates did not wish to have the trouble and expense of administering the whole of their estates. But since they needed supporters and fighting men, they granted pieces of land to men of noble birth who swore an oath of allegiance to them. These men were the knights. The land owned by a knight was called a manor. Some knights didn't own land but were supported by a lord at his castle.

Under the lord of the manor were the serfs and the villeins. The serfs had to stay on the manor. When land was bought and sold, the serfs were included. They worked the lord's land, but he didn't feed or clothe them. Instead, he gave them bits of land which they worked as their own. These lands could not be taken away from them, and their children could inherit them by paying a fee to the lord. The villeins were serfs who pay a fixed sum to the lord for their land instead of paying taxes on what their land produced, as the serfs did.

The manor was self-supporting, which means the people didn't have to import anything from other manors in order to live. The lord provided flour mills, wine presses, and sheepfolds which the serfs used, but paid for.

If the lord was a good one, the serfs could live fairly comfortable lives. They worked long and hard, but they were protected by the lord, and their needs were taken care of. In fact, when the feudal system began to break up, it wasn't so much a result of the serfs rebelling as it was that the lords began to object to the powers of the king. Parliaments were started, nations were born, and serfs soon became free.

HAMMURABI

The concept of justice, or law, comes into being as soon as any kind of social relationship is created. For example, Robinson Crusoe, living alone, had no need for laws. There was no one with whose rights he

HOW DID OUR LAWS ORIGINATE?

could interfere by exercising his own freedom of action. But as soon as his man Friday appeared, there was a chance of conflict between his rights and those of his servant. Law then became necessary.

The purpose of law is to set down and to make clear the social relationships among individuals and between the individual and society. It tries to give to each person as much liberty of action as fits in with the liberty of others.

Laws usually develop from the customs of a people. The earliest known system of laws was formed about 1700 B.C. by Hammurabi, King of Babylon. He set down a code, or complete list of laws, that defined personal and property rights, contracts, and so on.

Customs grew into laws because the force of government was put behind them. Later, laws grew from decisions that were made by courts and from books in which lawyers wrote down what had been learned. Still later, laws were set down in statute books, or codes, by kings and legislators.

The Romans were a great law making people and the law books of Emperor Justinian, who lived from 527 to 565, summed up 1,000 years of their working-out of laws. During the Middle Ages, people's actions were largely governed by the church, which developed a body of laws called canon law.

In the twelfth century, the Roman law began to be studied in Italy and gradually spread to the rest of Europe. Thus, a body of laws, based on the Roman law, developed into what is called civil law, as contrasted with the canon law. At the same time, the courts of England were making many decisions about law, and from these grew up a body of laws called the common law.

In 1804, Napoleon put into a book all the civil laws of his time. This Napoleonic Code is the foundation of the law on the continent of Europe and in Central and South America. The common law system, which developed in England, is the basis of the law in the United States, Canada (except Quebec), Australia, and New Zealand.

The supreme law of the United States is written out in the Constitution. It is the one set of laws that everyone — no matter what city or state he lives in — must obey.

WHAT IS THE BILL OF RIGHTS?

When the Constitutional Convention met in 1787 to draw up the Constitution, most of the delegates took for granted that there were various rights people had that didn't have to be written into the Constitution. But Virginia and many other states felt that it would be wiser to protect those individual rights by having them written down, and so they insisted that a Bill of Rights be added to the Constitution.

Ten amendments, known as the Bill of Rights, were added to the Constitution. The Bill of Rights guarantees that:

1. People have the right to say and write what they wish, to meet together peaceably and to complain to the government. Congress cannot set up an official religion or keep people from worshiping as they wish.

2. The states have the right to arm and drill their own citizens in a state militia.

3. In peacetime, people cannot be forced to take soldiers into their homes.

4. An official cannot search a person or his home or seize his property without a warrant. A warrant (a paper signed by a judge) can be issued only if it is necessary to catch a criminal or to prevent a crime.

5. No person can be put on trial unless a grand jury has decided that there is enough evidence for a trial. No person can be tried twice for the same crime. No person can be forced to give testimony against himself. No person can be executed, imprisoned, or fined except after a fair trial. Private property cannot be seized for public use unless the owner is paid a fair price.

6. A person accused of a crime must be tried quickly; the trial must be public; he has a right to have a jury hear his case; he must be told of what he is accused.

7. In a lawsuit for more than $20, a person can demand a jury trial.

8. An accused person has the right to put up bail.

9. The rights listed here are not the only rights that people have.

10. The powers not given to the federal government nor forbidden by it to the States, belong to the states or to the people.

WHAT IS THE MAGNA CARTA?

Today people everywhere are deeply concerned with their rights, their freedom, and laws that protect them against tyranny and oppression. The Magna Carta, or the Great Charter, was the first step toward constitutional liberty for English-speaking people everywhere in the world. It was signed by King John of England in 1215, and it laid the foundations for a new kind of government.

At the time of King John, there was much oppression, the courts were corrupt, and justice was not practiced. So the barons who ruled under the King decided to try to get back some of their old rights and privileges, which they believed were more fair to themselves and the people. On June 15, 1215, they and some churchmen of England gathered an army together and forced King John to sign the Magna Carta.

The original Magna Carta contained 63 articles, most of which were concerned with the rights of nobles. But some of them were reforms that led to ideas that were for the good of all men, because in it the nobles promised certain rights to the freemen under their control.

There are three articles in the Magna Carta that are important for people living today because of their influence on the development of freedom and justice under law. One article declares that no freeman shall be deprived of his life or property without a verdict of his peers

(equals) or by the law of the land. You can see how this principle helps protect you against injustice or tyranny.

Another article in the Magna Carta states that justice shall not be sold, denied, nor delayed. This principle protects people who are tried in a court of law because it is intended to prevent judges from being bribed, or trials from being put off for a long time while the prisoner sits in jail.

A third article provides that federal taxes cannot be levied without the consent of the council of barons. In our own time, this principle means that we cannot be taxed unless the representatives we elect to government approve the taxes.

WHY DO WE HAVE TO PAY TAXES?

Taxation has been resorted to in all developed communities to pay for public services provided by the ruler or other form of government. In the Roman Empire tax gathering was farmed out to contractors known as Publicani, who paid the State an agreed sum and then collected what they could. In England the earliest example of the central government's attempt to impose a national tax was the Danegeld in the 10th century. Under the Plantagenets, the monarch depended for his income partly on the revenue from the Crown lands and partly from fees collected from his principal tenants in place of the obligation to perform military service on their king's behalf. Later, when these sources of income proved insufficient the king gradually exercised the right to levy other taxes, notably import duties on certain goods entering the kingdom, and export duties on goods leaving it.

But as parliament grew stronger as an institution, the principle was accepted that the monarch could not levy additional taxation without the approval of parliament. This had a very important influence on the development of political institutions in Britain. Charles I unsuccessfully attempted to levy Ship Money without the consent of the House of Commons and paid dearly for his indiscretion. When William III and Mary came to the throne in 1688 it was laid down once and for all that no taxes were to be levied without parliamentary consent.

Taxation falls into two main classes; *direct* and *indirect*. The principal forms of direct taxation (i.e. those assessed directly on individuals or corporations) are income tax (including surtax) in its various forms, death duties and estate duties. Indirect taxes (i.e. those borne by all who use the article, commodity or service taxed) include purchase tax, customs and excise duties, and stamp duties. Customs duties are payable on import and are calculated either on value or quantity, according to the nature of the article. Excise duties are levied on home-produced goods (e.g. beer and whisky), or goods processed or refined within the country (e.g. motor spirit).

There is an expression that "death and taxes are always with us." In one way or another, people have been paying taxes since very ancient times. But there is a big difference between the taxes of ancient times and the taxes we pay today.

WHEN WERE TAXES FIRST STARTED?

In ancient times people paid a tax on things they consumed, and they had to pay a tax, or duty, on imported articles. These taxes were levied by the rulers on the people, and were usually as high as they could possibly bear. It was the duty of the underprivileged classes—slaves, vassals, peasants, colonists, and conquered peoples—to support the ruling class.

With the exception of certain taxes in ancient Egypt and Rome, there were never any direct taxes on income or wealth. The average person simply had to pay a tax for practically everything he did or used.

Only in recent times has a new idea of taxation arisen, that taxes are paid with the consent of the people, and that their representatives decide and impose the taxes in order to support the government. It is a sign of people governing themselves when they decide on what taxes to pay and pay them willingly (though of course no one is very happy about paying taxes).

Some of the most important events in history took place as a result of the people's protest against paying oppressive taxes imposed on them by their rulers. The Magna Carta, and the French and American Revolutions were related in part to the desire to establish a fair and representative system of taxation.

In England, an income tax was established for the first time in 1798. In the United States, the federal government obtained most of its revenue from taxes on customs, liquor, tobacco, and the sale of land until about the time of World War I. At this time and later, the government adopted an estate tax, developed a tax on the income of corporations and individuals, and established many other taxes.

In the United States, each state also has its own taxes such as those on gasoline, retail sales, motor vehicles, and income taxes.

In these times of world tension, we hear a great deal about the United Nations. What is it? Why was it established? What is it supposed to do? We can give only a brief description of the United Nations here, but here

WHAT IS THE UNITED NATIONS?

are some things you should know about it.

The United Nations is an organization of governments. It was set up to prevent war and to build a better world for all by dealing with problems which can best be solved through international action. The UN constitution, known as the Charter, was signed at San Francisco on June 26, 1945, by representatives of 50 nations.

According to the Charter, the UN has four chief purposes. The first is to maintain peace by settling disputes peacefully or by taking steps to stop aggression, that is, armed attack. The second is to develop friendly relations among nations based on the equal rights of peoples and their own choices of government. The third is to achieve international cooperation in solving economic, social, cultural, and humanitarian problems. And the fourth is to serve as a center where the actions of nations can be combined in trying to attain these aims.

The UN is divided into six main working groups. The first is the

General Assembly. Made up of all the members, each with one vote, it is the policy-making body of the UN.

The second is the Security Council, which is responsible for the maintenance of peace. China, France, Great Britain, the Soviet Union, and the United States have permanent seats and special voting privileges. The other six members are elected by the General Assembly for terms of two years.

The third is the Economic and Social Council with eighteen members. Its job is to promote the welfare of peoplés and to further human rights and fundamental freedoms.

The fourth is the Trusteeship Council which supervises the welfare of dependent peoples under the UN and helps them towards self-government.

The fifth is the International Court of Justice which settles legal disputes.

The sixth is the Secretariat, the administrative and office staff of the UN. Its chief officer is secretary-general of the United Nations.

Man has been around on this earth for a long, long time. Yet in all his long history, the biggest change in his daily life has taken place in only the last 200 years! This change in the way man lives and works is

WHAT WAS THE INDUSTRIAL REVOLUTION?

based mainly on the development of the machine. We call this exciting period the Industrial Revolution.

As far back as history goes, man has been making tools. But only after the year 1750 were real machines invented. A machine is like a tool, except that it does nearly all the work and supplies nearly all the power. This change, from tools to machines, was so important and so great, that it began to affect every phase of our lives. In tracing how one development led to another, you will see how this was so.

Before man could make much use of machines he had to harness new sources of power. Before the Industrial Revolution man used only his own muscles, the muscles of animals, wind power and water power. To operate the new machines he had invented, man developed a new source of power–steam. This made it possible to build factories, and they were built where the essential raw materials were available and close to markets.

As machines were used more and more, a need arose for more iron and steel. And for this, new methods of mining coal were necessary. Then, as machines were able to turn out more and more goods, it was necessary to improve transportation to get them to the markets. This led to the improvement of roads, the building of canals, the development of the railroads, and also the development of large ships to get some of these products to faraway markets.

As men began to do business with markets all over the world, better communication became important. So the telegraph and telephone were developed. But there was a still greater change to come. As factories developed and large and expensive machines began to be used, people could no longer work at home. So men began to leave their homes and go to work in factories and mills. In time this led to the "division of labor," which meant that in a factory a worker did only one job all day long instead of turning out the entire product as he used to do at home.

And finally, the Industrial Revolution made it possible to produce plentiful and cheap goods which everybody could afford.

In trying to build machines that do work for him, man has usually freed, or changed, or channelled the forces that exist in nature. When we boil water we change it into a gas, which we call steam. This gas tries to

HOW DOES A STEAM ENGINE WORK?

expand, that is, push aside or ahead whatever is in its way. A steam engine uses this force in steam to do work.

When you look at a tea kettle that has water boiling in it, you can see the steam spreading as it leaves the spout. If you put a cork in the spout and hold down the lid it will blow the cork out. A steam engine is much like a kettle with a lid that rises and falls but does not come off. As the lid goes up and down, it can be made to do work. In an engine, we call this lid a piston.

Many people tried to make steam engines, but they couldn't solve certain problems. In some cases the steam had to be at high pressure in order to do its work and this would cause the boilers to burst. In other cases, the water had to be heated over and over again, which wasted a lot of coal.

Finally James Watt invented a steam engine in which the power of the expanding steam was applied directly to the piston during the stroke that did the work. In his engine the piston was raised up three feet in a cylinder by the pressure of the steam. Then the weight of the piston and piston rod lowered it again to the starting point. This is called a single-acting engine. Since steam would be let into the cylinder during the entire stroke of the piston, it wasted a lot of steam. In modern steam engines, only a small quantity of steam enters the cylinder. The expansion of the steam does most of the work.

Later on, Watt added a third part to the engine—the condenser. This was a hollow chamber connected to the cylinder by pipes and valves. The steam would go into it and be condensed into water again before there was more used steam to be taken away.

The third great improvement developed by Watt was when he found a way to make the steam push the piston both ways. Instead of using the weight of air to press the piston down, the steam did the work. In this way, the piston did the work as it moved up and as it moved down. This is called a double-acting engine. The piston in a steam engine can be connected to a pump, a lever, or a crank and made to drive machinery.

HOW DOES A WINDMILL WORK?

No one knows where or by whom the windmill was invented. A boat can sail at right angles to the wind by slanting its sail slightly. In the same way, the "fan" or "sail" of a windmill can be driven around in a circle even when placed at right angles to the wind. The windmill is like a huge propeller, with the source of power that turns it coming from the wind instead of a machine.

The first windmills were used in Holland about 800 years ago to drain the flat fields of water. At one time windmills were common in all the flat countries near Holland. The chief use of a mill as we know it is to grind grain. In most countries mills are placed near running streams, a mill dam is built, and the water turns the mill.

But in the flat countries the streams are too sluggish to be used in this way. So windmills are built to grind the grain. In Germany there are mills in which the whole tower can be turned to face the wind as it changes. But in Holland only the roof of the windmill is revolved.

This is done by a small windmill, which is located on the other side of the roof from the big windmill and at right angles to it. When it begins to work, it turns a mechanism which sets the roof moving on little wheels and soon the big windmill is facing the wind.

The fans of a windmill are usually made of wood over which canvas has been stretched. Ropes are attached to the fans so that they can be adjusted if the wind is too strong. The fans are often 12 metres long!

Windmills of an improved type are still used in the United States and Australia. Windmills in the United States are made almost entirely of galvanized sheet steel. Each has a rudder which swings the wheel around on a pivot to catch the wind from every direction. Windmills are especially common in parts of California and in some dry regions of the West. They serve as a cheap source of power for pumping water from wells to irrigate fields, or to water cattle in pastures.

Refrigeration is the process of making and keeping things cold. The way to make things cold is to remove heat from them. So refrigeration is any process that removes heat to make cold.

WHO INVENTED THE REFRIGERATOR?

In ancient times, of course, snow and ice were the natural way to refrigerate things. Wines were cooled in this way. But even in ancient times another way to produce cold was known.

This was the process of dissolving certain salts in water. Materials like saltpeter and ammonium nitrate, remove heat from the water in which they dissolve. Thus they lower the temperature of water. Salt lowers the freezing point of water. When salt is put on ice, the ice changes to water. For this change to take place, energy or heat is needed. This is supplied by the water and so its temperature falls.

So the earliest methods of refrigeration used natural ice or snow, or used salts dissolved in water. But there is another process that creates refrigeration. This is called evaporation, the change of a liquid to a

MICHAEL FARADAY

vapor. When you put a little water or alcohol on your hand, you feel the coolness as the liquid takes heat from the hand and evaporates.

It was this principle of evaporation that led to the creation of our modern refrigerators. In 1823 Michael Faraday learned how to change ammonia vapor to a liquid by compressing or squeezing it and then removing heat from it. When the pressure is removed and this liquid is allowed to evaporate again, it takes up heat and produces cold.

Why did this make our modern refrigeration possible? Because we now had a way to change something first from a vapor to a liquid—giving up its heat. Then we could change it back from a liquid to a vapor—taking up heat. By controlling this process and having it take place continuously, we have our modern refrigerators.

The first refrigerating machine to use this principle was built by a Swiss inventor named Carl Linde in 1874 to cool beer. In 1877 Linde used ammonia as the liquid in such a machine and modern refrigeration was on its way.

The word microscope is a combination of two Greek words, *mikros*, or "small," and *skopos*, or "watcher." So microscope is a "watcher of the small!" It is an instrument used to see tiny things which are invisible to the naked eye.

WHO INVENTED THE MICROSCOPE?

Normally, an object appears larger the closer it is brought to the human eye. But when it is nearer than 25 centimetres, it is not clear. It is said to be out of focus. Now if a simple convex lens is placed between the eye and the object, the object can be brought nearer than 25 centimetres and still be in focus.

Today we describe this simply as using a magnifying glass. But ordinary magnifying glasses are really simple microscopes, and they have been used as such since remote times. So when we speak of the invention of the microscope, we really mean the "compound microscope." In fact, today when we say "microscope," that's the only kind we mean.

What is a compound microscope? In this kind of microscope, magnification takes place in two stages. There is a lens called the "objective" which produces a primary magnified image. Then there is another lens called the "eyepiece," or "ocular," which magnifies that first image. In actual practice, there are several lenses used for both the objective and ocular, but the principle is that of two-stage magnification.

The compound microscope was invented some time between 1590 and 1610. While no one is quite sure who actually did it, the credit is usually given to Galileo. A Dutch scientist called Leeuwenhoek is sometimes called "the father of the microscope," but that's because of the many discoveries he made with the microscope.

Leeuwenhoek showed that weevils, fleas, and other minute creatures come from eggs and are not "spontaneously generated." He was the first to see such microscopic forms of life as the protozoa and bacteria.

Today the microscope is important to man in almost every form of science and industry.

The sun was man's first clock. Long ago men guessed at the time of day by watching the sun as it moved across the sky. It was easy to recognize sunrise and sunset, but harder to know when it was noon, the time when the sun is highest above the horizon. In between these times, it was difficult to tell time by the position of the sun.

HOW DOES A SUNDIAL TELL TIME?

Then men noticed that the shadow changed in length and moved during the day. They found they could tell time more accurately by watching shadows than by looking at the sun. From this it was an easy step to inventing the sundial, which is really a shadow clock. Instead of trying to guess the position of the sun and thus the time of day, the shadow gave a more accurate idea of the sun's position.

The first sundials were probably poles stuck into the ground. Stones placed around a pole marked the positions of the shadow as it moved during the day. Thus men could measure the passing of time. Later, huge stone columns were used. Cleopatra's Needle, now on the Thames Embankment in London, was once part of a sundial. Smaller sundials were used too. One small Egyptian sundial, about 3,500 years old, is shaped like an L. It lays flat on its longer leg, on which marks show six periods of time.

About 300 B.C. a Chaldean astronomer invented a new kind of sundial, shaped like a bowl. A shadow thrown by a pointer moved along and marked 12 hours of the day. This sort of sundial was very accurate and continued to be used for many centuries.

Today sundials are built in gardens for their beauty rather than for their usefulness. However, on the walls and window sills of old houses one sometimes sees crude sundials. They are so arranged that a nail or the edge of the window casing will cast the shadow. In an accurate sundial, the pointer must be slanted at an angle equal to the latitude of the place where it is to be used. A vertical pointer will show the correct time only at one latitude and at one season. If the dial is flat, the hour marks must be spaced unequally on it.

ROMAN
OIL LAMP

CANDLE
LANTERN

COAL OIL
LAMP

Before man discovered fire, the only heat and light he had was provided by the sun. Since he couldn't control this, he was quite helpless in dealing with cold and darkness.

HOW WERE LAMPS FIRST MADE?

Probably more than 100,000 years ago, he discovered fire. Then he began to notice that some materials burned better than others. Perhaps he observed that fat dripping into the fire from roasting meat burned brightly. As time passed, man began to select materials which, when burned, provided better light. Splinters of certain woods were stuck into the wall and they burned slowly. Pine knots were used as torches. Animal fats were placed in shallow stone dishes and moss and other materials were used as wicks. These were the first oil lamps. Exactly when this happened we cannot know, since it was before recorded history.

The first candles were made by melting animal fats, such as lard and tallow, and pouring the liquid into a mold such as a hollow bamboo. Fibers twisted together were strung through the center so that when it cooled, the solid rod of fat had a wick in the center. Thus, the candle was created at an unknown date long before Christ was born.

Lard was used in lard-oil lamps in New England around 1820. From whale blubber, oil was extracted for whale-oil lamps. In fact, whatever kind of oil was easiest to obtain was used for lamps. Along the Mediterranean there are many olive trees. So olive oil was used for lamps there. The Japanese and Chinese obtained oil for their lamps from various nuts. Peanuts would probably be used for oil for lamps today—if mineral oil in the earth had not been discovered.

Petroleum was discovered in 1859. By heating this oil in a closed vessel, a thin colorless product known as kerosene is obtained. This became the oil most commonly used for lamps. In fact, it was first called "coal oil," because people thought petroleum was associated with coal.

Do you have an oil lamp in your house today? Many homes keep one on hand to use in an emergency if the electricity should fail!

ABACA (MANILA HEMP)

Men have always needed rope for the rigging of ships, for hauling things, and for tying bundles. So ropemaking is one of the oldest industries in existence.

HOW IS ROPE MADE?

The first ropes were knotted together from leather thongs, pieces of bark, or even roots. The ancient Egyptians made ropes from vegetable fibers, and these resemble the ropes made today.

All fiber used in making ropes is generally called "hemp," but it may come from many different plants. The best rope material is the fiber of a plant called the abaca, which grows in the Philippines. This fiber is generally known as Manila hemp. It is easier to work with and stronger than other forms of hemp. The century plant of Mexico provides a material for making rope and so does coconut fiber. Rope can be made from cotton and flax fibers, but it is too expensive for general use.

Until the 19th century ropes were made entirely by hand on rope-walks. These were long, low buildings in which the ropemaker walked backward, step by step, unwinding the fibers from about his waist. At the upper end of the walk, a boy turned a wheel to which one end of the rope yarn was attached. This wheel kept twisting the yarn while it was being spun.

Today almost all rope is made by machinery. The fibers are passed through a series of machines called breakers, which look like steel combs. They comb the fibers out thoroughly, clean out the dirt, straighten out the snarls, and turn the rough mass of fibers into a "sliver." This is a straight, continuous ribbon of loose threads, equal in thickness. These slivers are sent to the spinning machines. Here they are twisted into yarn and the yarn is wound onto spools or bobbins.

The bobbins are mounted on a revolving disk. The yarn is put through a metal tube which presses the separate pieces together and as it comes out it is twisted together into a strand. Then the same process takes three or four of these strands and twists them together to make a rope.

Each time the fibers are twisted the twist is made in the opposite direction from the last one. In this way the different twists counterbalance each other and keep the rope from untwisting.

It is a curious thing how boys of all times in all countries seem to get the same idea about games. The game of marbles for instance, which is played in every city in this country, has been played all over the world practically since the beginning of history!

HOW ARE MARBLES MADE?

Nobody knows just when marbles began, but it probably goes back to the first time somebody discovered that a round stone pebble would roll. And that goes back at least to the Stone Age. Scientists have discovered among Stone Age remains little balls which were too small to be used for anything but games.

Long before the Christian Era, children in ancient Egypt and Rome were playing with marbles. In Europe, marbles were played in the Middle Ages. In England the game of marbles developed from a game called "bowls".

Today, some form of the game of marbles is played almost everywhere in the world. The South American boy called his marbles "bolitas." In China, boys play a game of marbles that involves kicking them.

The Persian peasant boy plays with marbles he has made out of baked mud or he uses small stones. Even the Zulus play a game of marbles!

In the United States, boys play with two kinds of marbles. They are called "shooters" and "play marbles." Shooters are also called "taws" in some sections of the country. A shooter or taw cannot be larger than 19 millimetres in diameter, and may be smaller than 0.53 millimetres. It may be made of glass, baked clay, agate, or plastic. It is the player's favorite marble which he uses over and over again to shoot at other marbles.

Play marbles, or "mibs," are the marbles at which the player aims his shooter. They are made of baked clay, glass, stone, onyx, marble, alabaster, or plastic. Sometimes the play marbles are named after the material they are made of, such as glassies, clayies, and agates.

Most of the natural baked clay marbles and those of natural onyx come from Ohio. Glass marbles are usually made by melting the glass and, while it is hot, pressing it between the two halves of polished metal molds.

Today we have dolls that walk, talk, cry, sleep, eat, drink—they are made to be as much like living beings as possible. But suppose a little girl is very poor and her parents can't afford to buy her a doll? She might take a piece of wood and wrap it in a cloth and say it's her doll. And it would be a doll! For a doll is simply whatever a child wants to consider a doll.

WHO MADE THE FIRST DOLL?

That's why we can never trace the idea of dolls back to its beginning. Even before recorded history, wherever there were children, there were dolls. Indian children used a slab of wood with a knob for

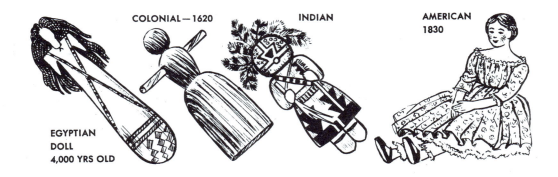

EGYPTIAN DOLL 4,000 YRS OLD

COLONIAL—1620

INDIAN

AMERICAN 1830

a head for their dolls. Persian children played with dolls made simply of folded cloth with a face painted on it. And dolls made of clay or bone have been found in the graves of children of primitive peoples in all parts of the world.

Some authorities say that dolls were at first used only in religious rites. The children might be allowed to hold the doll or image, but they were forbidden to play with it as a toy. But others believe that children of prehistoric times did play with dolls.

Among the earliest dolls known to us are those of the ancient Egyptians. They seem to have been very fond of dolls. They made them of wood with flat painted beads strung on threads. Egyptian dolls have been found that are more than 3,000 years old!

The ancient Greeks, too, had very interesting dolls. They had well-shaped heads, and the arms and legs moved by means of strings. Even today, in various parts of the world, children have dolls that are quite different from ours, and which the children prefer to ours! The little Eskimo girl has a doll made of carved whalebone. The Mexican girl has dolls made of baked clay, and may think our dolls are too pale.

Modern dolls are made of wax, cloth, yarn, papier-mâché, and other materials. The heads of the most expensive dolls are often created by very good artists. But as you probably know, a girl's favorite doll may not be the most expensive one at all!

We may think of glass as being produced by the mixture of some very special chemicals in a very special way, a sort of miracle of chemistry. But actually, glass is made by a rather simple process using quite ordinary materials.

WHAT IS USED IN MAKING GLASS?

Glass is a substance made by "fusing" (melting together) certain materials, and then cooling the mixture so that the atoms arrange themselves in an unorganized pattern. What materials? Well, about 95 per cent of the raw materials in the earth could be used in making glass! The most important materials used in making glass, however, are: sand (silica), soda, limestone, borax, boric acid, magnesium oxide, and lead oxide.

Nature herself produced the first glass. About 450,000,000 years ago molten (melted) rock in the core of the earth forced its way to the surface and broke through the earth's crust in volcanoes. When the hot

EGYPT
1500 B.C.

ROMAN
300 A.D.

lava contained silica and cooled rapidly, it formed a glass as hard as a rock. This volcanic glass is called obsidian.

Glass has been made by man since very ancient times. The Egyptians, more than 5,000 years ago, knew how to make a kind of colored glass with which they covered stone and pottery and sometimes made into beads. Perfume and ointment bottles made of glass were used in Egypt more than 3,500 years ago.

The Roman Empire (1st century B.C. to 5th century A.D.) was one of the greatest periods in the history of glass. It was at this time that man learned how to blow glass and thus form hundreds of different shapes and sizes of glass objects.

Today, of course, there are many new ways of making glass that have been developed. But this is the basic process. The raw materials for glass are brought to the glass factory and stored in huge bins. The raw materials are carefully measured and then mixed into a "batch." Then broken glass of the same formula, called "cullet," is added to the batch to speed the melting. The batch is fed automatically into the furnace. The glass then flows out of the furnace at lower temperatures.

Then the glass goes through many processes such as blowing, pressing, rolling, casting and drawing–depending on the type of glass that is being made.

Glass blowing is one of the oldest of skills. But as modern machines have been developed and perfected, and as the use of glass has increased, glass blowing by hand is becoming rarer and rarer.

HOW CAN GLASS BE BLOWN?

When glass is in a melted state, it can be "worked" in many ways. It can be blown, pressed, drawn, or rolled. For hundreds of years, the chief method of working with glass was blowing.

The glassworker gathered a ball of molten glass on the end of his

blow-pipe and blew, just the way you would blow a soap bubble. Using his skill, he shaped the glass as he blew, and drew it out to the correct thinness. He kept reheating the glass to keep it workable, and then he would finish it with special tools.

In this way, many kinds of glass objects were made. Glass could also be blown into molds and shaped in that way. Surprisingly enough, window glass used to be made by blowing a long cylinder of glass which was split and flattened to produce a sheet of glass. Of course, the size of these sheets was limited by the lung power of the glassblower!

Today, this method of blowing glass (called "freehand") is still used to produce special scientific apparatus and very expensive and beautiful glass articles. But the demand for glass containers such as bottles became so great that efforts were made to create a glass-blowing machine, and finally in 1903 the first automatic machine for blowing glass was invented.

This machine uses a vacuum to suck in a sufficient amount of glass to form each bottle. First the neck of the bottle is molded. Then compressed air is turned on, and the finished bottle is blown. After that, the bottle is automatically annealed, which means it is cooled gradually to make it tough and strong. This machine can turn out more bottles in one hour than six men doing free-hand blowing can do in a day!

Later, another machine was developed for automatically blowing light bulbs, which made possible the wide use of electric light. Most of the world's bottles, jars, tumblers, and other blown-glass containers are made by machine.

Index

W

Wall Street, 366, 367
War of Roses, 79
warrens, *see* rabbits
Washington, George, 367
wasps, 140, 141
water, *see* echo, erosion,
 evaporation, floods, geyser,
 spring
waterfall, 32
waterspout, 40
Watt, James, 384, 385

weaving, 110
webs, spider, 133
weddings, 284-286
Wegener, Alfred, 25
whale, 120, 121
wheel, 369
"whist family" games, 328
wildcats, 112
wild-ox, 117
will-o'-the-wisp, 281
windmill, 385
winds, 41-43
wolves, 94

wombats, 94
wool, 109, 110
workers, bee, 129, 130
writing
 Braille, 298
 hieroglyphics, 299, 300

Y

yarn, 110
yeast, 58, 64, 354
yellow fever, 138

Yellow River, 31
Yellowstone Falls, 32
York, House of, 79
Young, Brigham, 290

Z

zero, 333, 334
zinc, 56
zoology, 88
zymase, 64

Below is a list of words appearing in the text in American spellings:

aluminium	aluminum	flavour	flavor	mould	mold
armour	armor	grey	gray	neighbour	neighbor
behaviour	behavior	labour	labor	odour	odor
centre	center	lustre	luster	plough	plow
colour	color	manoeuvre	maneuver	theatre	theater
favourable	favorable	marvellous	marvelous	traveller	traveler
fibre	fiber				